How the Future Worked

Russia through the eyes
of a young non-person

Alexander Boot

PUBLISHING

Published by
RoperPenberthy Publishing Ltd
Springfield House
23 Oatlands Drive
Weybridge
Surrey
KT13 9LZ

ISBN 978 1 903905 82 1

Cover design by Bernard Burridge
Printed and bound in the UK by PublishPoint from
KnowledgePoint Limited, Reading

To the memory of my parents,
with love and contrition

'I have been over into the future, and it works.'
Lincoln Steffens, upon visiting Lenin's Russia in 1921

You cannot fathom Russia with the mind
All common yardsticks are deceiving.
We are a very special kind,
Our Russia's something to believe in.
F.F. Tyutchev (1803-1873),
in my own, rather poor, translation

'I cannot forecast to you the action of Russia.
It is a riddle, wrapped in a mystery, inside an enigma...'
Winston Churchill

Plus ça change, plus c'est la même chose.
Alphonse Karr (1808-1890)

CONTENTS

FOREWORD:
THIS BOOK ISN'T
WHAT IT APPEARS TO BE

IT ONLY PRETENDS TO BE the memoir of a certain Alexander Boot. In reality it's about Russia – admittedly as seen through my eyes.

Russia has existed for over 1,000 years, most of which she has spent in relative isolation from the world, stewing in her own juice. This has created a certain deficit of self-perception, with the Russians still arguing whether they are the westernmost Asian country, the easternmost European one, or both or neither or something in between. Hence the Tyutchev stanza I quoted in one of my epigraphs: 'You cannot fathom Russia with the mind'.

Churchill's famous description of Russia also points out her enigmatic nature. The great man has a point: Russia is indeed full of mysteries. Some of them, however, are relatively easy to solve, such as why Russian sports shops sold 500,000 baseball bats in 2009, but only three baseballs and just one baseball glove. Even allowing that this great sporting nation may play the game to different rules, the disparity is puzzling – but it won't stay that way for long. Thousands of other mysteries present more of an intellectual challenge.

Naturally foreign academics set out to prove that Russia is perfectly intelligible to a properly trained mind. Yet those same Russians who ridicule Tyutchev's grandiloquent pronouncement, as most do, ridicule the academics even more. They sense that any true understanding of their country does reside in a native knowledge for which there is no substitute.

Whatever this knowledge is, and however it's acquired, you won't find it in an academic tome. But some of it, not all of course, you will find in this book.

For I grew up in Russia, for my sins. As I fled it in my early twenties, now, in my sixties, I can claim the best of both worlds: the native knowledge of the place and the kind of emotional detachment that comes from being 40 years and hundreds of miles away from it. Using the latter I shall try to communicate the former.

I'll relate quite a few anecdotes, all true to life, things that happened to me and my friends when I was growing up in Moscow and elsewhere in Russia. (I've changed the names of most personages to protect their sensibilities. They'll still probably recognise themselves, but one hopes others won't.) As you follow those little stories, some amusing, some tragic, you'll learn the same things I learned as a youngster – and the same way I learned them, by living through them. But Russia has changed, you might say, and 40 years is a lot of water under the bridge. Well, it is and it isn't.

Some things have indeed changed, some haven't and never will. It's those immutable things that I'll try to convey and they are more important than the changes, which as often as not are superficial and transient. The more things change, the more they remain the same, as the French say.

PROLOGUE: BIPOLAR BEAR

WHEN I WAS LITTLE, my mother always took me for walks around the Kremlin. That was a natural destination: we lived but a few hundred yards away. Mostly she wanted to take me to Alexander Garden sprawling at the Kremlin's north wall. Children were supposed to be taken for walks in gardens, my mother had no doubts on that score.

I begged to differ. Even though the narrow strip of Alexander Garden offered neither visual nor olfactory protection from the busy traffic outside, it was nevertheless far too bucolic for a confirmed urbanist in the making. The garden, for all its charming grottoes and memorial obelisks to the Great Dead Socialists, left me cold. Seeking more interesting sights, I always dragged Mama another hundred yards towards Red Square. [As opposed to English, the words 'Mama' and 'Papa' are stressed on the first syllable in Russian, and that's how I'd like you to read them from now on.]

The Lenin Mausoleum was the first port of call there: I'd stay in front of the squat ziggurat structure keenly watching the two guards of honour standing to attention at the entrance. They were supposed to be motionless and I'd spend a minute or two hoping to see them twitch a muscle or bat an eyelid.

From time to time I'd cheat by pulling faces at them. Physiology being what it is, I never had to wait very long for a confirmation that those were indeed two young men and not wax statues. After that they'd lose claim to my attention, though I'd linger for another minute or so to admire their rifles. At that age I was fascinated with firearms, especially since leading a bayonet charge against German positions was my chosen career path at the time.

And then I'd be drawn to the onion domes of St Basil's Cathedral (or rather Temple, which is what the Russian word 'khram' really means) at the south end of the square. At my tender age I didn't know that the church wasn't really consecrated to Vasily the Blessed, and neither was it a cathedral in any true sense of the word. My mother probably didn't know those things either, for otherwise she would have mentioned them in the historical background she provided for my enlightenment.

What she did mention was that the church was built during the reign of Ivan the Terrible to commemorate the victory over the Tartars. Once it had been completed the tsar was so moved by the ineffable beauty of St Basil's that he allegedly had the architects' eyes gouged out to prevent them from replicating the masterpiece elsewhere. (For some reason, this sure-fire method of protecting copyright has never caught on in the West.)

The questionable ethics of this, probably apocryphal, accolade didn't escape even my underdeveloped moral sense. But it took me another decade or two to reassess my aesthetic rating of the church. At the time I thought it was the most beautiful thing on earth, especially since the Kremlin with its great cathedrals was still off-limits to visitors and would remain so until I was five.

The fact that St Basil's was a church meant nothing to me. In a country where aggressive atheism was a test of loyalty and therefore a precondition for survival, my parents went even beyond the call of official policy. The word God was never mentioned at home and I had no idea what churches were for. All I knew was that some of them were prettier than others and, as far as I was concerned, St Basil's was the prettiest of the lot.

Its nine domes were painted different yet equally lurid colours, and they reached for the sky like tongues of flame in a bonfire. Even their textures and heights were all different to make the overall picture sufficiently varied to hold the quicksilver attention of a three-year-old.

I responded to the gay exuberance of the structure and if it was indeed a stone bonfire I felt the urge to dance around it, in the manner of Russian peasants celebrating some quasi-Christian but in fact pagan feast. In a city of dull colours and drab streets St Basil's was a source of joy, happiness, unbridled energy. Hardly a week went by that I didn't insist on being taken there.

Then one day, when I was four or so, we went inside for the first time. On the way in I was imagining what we were going to see, using the visible exterior as the table of interior contents. Bright pictures on the walls painted turquoise, canary-yellow and scarlet-red, elaborate carved furniture in the mock-peasant style, floors of jolly stone tiles or perhaps ornate oak parquet... As I had never seen the inside of a church before I didn't know what to expect in terms of ecclesiastical paraphernalia. But my aesthetic expectations weren't unreasonable, considering the joyous, life-asserting physicality of the exterior.

We walked in and I shuddered with fear. There must have been some disappointment mixed in as well, but fear is what I remember. The interior was dark, gloomy, stark, austere. Low vaulted ceilings were pushing me down to the uneven stone floor, the dull brownish monochrome of the walls was a sore sight for the eyes, iron bars on the tiny windows were prison-like. The odd wooden bench was the only furniture to be seen, and as we walked from one macabre cell to the next there was nothing on the walls but a few unframed icons so blackened by age that one could barely discern the painted images. The atmosphere was oppressive and would have been so even without one's expectations having been raised by the exterior bursting with life. As it was, the contrast was unbearable.

After that I'd still ask to be taken to Red Square – there were few other places of similar interest within walking distance. And I'd still saunter around St Basil's a few times now and then. But I never again went in.

It took me another couple of decades to get to see the great cathedrals of Western Christianity and perhaps as long again to realise what, apart from the obvious architectural differences, set them apart from St Basil's. It wasn't so much a difference of style as one of substance.

A Western cathedral is a synthesis of the exterior thesis and interior antithesis: of the physical and metaphysical, body and soul. It's the Athanasian creed in stone, a representation of God in man and man in God. The exterior welcomes visitors with the stone statues of saints and the exorcised devils of gargoyles; the interior shows exactly what sanctified the saints and exorcised the devils. Thanks to modernity's chosen form of art criticism, some of the statues are headless, but that's par for the course.

The overall statement is whole, complete, perfectly synthesised. It took the Church half a millennium after Christ to understand and accept the great Christian synthesis of the same person being fully divine and fully human, and it's no wonder that only then was Christendom ready to erect its great cathedrals. Nor is it surprising that it was this synthesis that acted as the fermenting agent of a new civilisation the likes of which the world had never seen. Athens and Jerusalem fused into one; God and man in one; the physical and metaphysical as one.

In St Basil's there is no synthesis. The exuberant physicality of the exterior is in no way connected with the deathly gloom of the interior, neither just aesthetically nor even spiritually. The thesis and antithesis don't come together. The body and soul aren't conjoined – they stay separate, and they tear each other apart. Hyperactive exterior, depressive interior: that way, as a Shakespeare character puts it, madness lies. The church bears witness not to the unity of God and man but to the bipolar personality of Russia.

And that way also lies a possible solution to the mystery of Russia that has always baffled not only visitors but, more important, the Russians themselves, especially those capable of taking a more or less detached look at their own land. Natives and outlanders alike highlight the enigmatic, mysterious nature of Russia. Few realise that the country is so incomprehensible because it's mad, and sane people can't really get their heads around madness.

Russia, as a collective entity, has never learned the art of synthesis. Her thesis and antithesis are at daggers drawn and they hate each other enough to keep thrusting the blades into the country's flesh. Preoccupied with first principles and last things, she doesn't know first things about creating a passable life for her people.

Her frantic exuberance can be at the drop of a hat replaced by the kind of manic depression for which no psychotropic drug is known. Her self-sacrificial kindness instantly gives way to inhuman cruelty. Her suicidal docility can turn into homicidal aggression in the blink of an eye.

Against the background of a primeval physical life she can create, and in the next breath destroy, a sublime culture. She can first delight the world and, in the next historical instant, terrify it. Her rulers have nothing in common with the ruled; her classes aren't intermingled in their mores. Nowhere else can one observe a culture and civilisation that don't mesh at all; in Russia they seem to exist on different planets, not just different planes. And covering it all is the giant mythological umbrella of a Russia holy, innocent, omnipotent or otherwise superior to other nations.

In short, she shows every clinical symptom of a split personality, bipolar disorder and self-delusion – three kinds of madness for the price of one. Add to this frequent flare-ups of both paranoia and irrational aggression, and the mystery, or rather clinical picture, is complete.

But it took me years to understand all this.

THE RIGHT TO
A HAPPY CHILDHOOD

1

WALKING WAS A SKILL I HAD ACQUIRED only recently, and a neophyte's zeal animated every step I took. To Mama's displeasure, some of those steps were taken through the orange mud out of which my uncle's dacha stuck like a monument to man's triumph over the elements.

It was one of those putative summers outside Moscow when diagonal yellow rain temporarily gives way to grey drizzle only to come back an hour later at a slightly different angle and turn the soil into an impassable morass.

That is, it was impassable to Mama, Grandma, Nanny and other responsible adults who had been walking long enough to be aware both of nature's pitfalls and their own limitations. To me it was very passable indeed, thank you – especially with my feet snugly protected by unusual rubber boots. The boots fastened with belts, at the end of which were snaps decorated with tiny swastikas. Not five-pointed stars. Not hammers and sickles. Not even portraits of Lenin as a curly child. Thirty-two years after the advent of the future that worked and four years after Hitler's demise, my boots proudly displayed the ancient Hindu emblem appropriated and popularised by the Nazis.

At my tender age I was already aware of the significance of that institutional symbol, as most Russian children were. After all, anti-Nazi propaganda was blaring all over the country with a gusto undiminished by the end of the war four years ago.

The romance of the Great Patriotic War was being wedged into the hole formed by disappearing revolutionary cravings, and 'fascist' was replacing 'bourgeois' as the bogeyman of the official Soviet lore. Once in that hole, there the romance has remained to this day. So post-perestroika Russian children are still weaned on a diet of cinematic 'halt' and 'hende hoch' leavened with explanations of how Stalin saved the world.

When appearing on a round snap, 'the fascist sign', as it was called in Russia, divided it into sections in a pattern not dissimilar to an old-style football. In fact Mama took advantage of that resemblance to respond to my point-blank demand for an explanation.

Not yet sure of my ability to win a confrontation with adults, I chose to accept that the swastikas were indeed footballs, even though the resemblance wasn't so close as to deceive even a young eye. However, Nanny, who obviously wasn't in cahoots with Mama, took me out for a walk the next day and, for lack of anything better to do, made fun of my politically incorrect footwear.

Even a child of two would have realised the importance of political correctness, Soviet-style, and from then on I categorically refused to wear the offensive item. I did ask out of idle curiosity how the otherwise splendid boots had found their way onto my feet. Mama explained they were 'spoils of war' and I nodded, having suspected as much.

There was nothing unusual about such peaceful items being described in that bellicose way. For most men had been to the war and returned with varying amounts of goods plundered from German households.

Papa's best friend, for instance, was a major in the Smersh, an organisation whose multiple functions included the vetting of German civilians at the end of the war. 'Uncle Zhenia', as I called him, didn't squander such a responsible position on *bono publico* concentrating instead on his own *bono*. He managed to get out a railway carriage full of clobber and until his death Uncle Zhenia's flat looked like a museum of antique furniture, china, crystal and silver.

The capacity for plunder increased with rank. Privates and NCOs were limited to a suitcase or two, staff officers to perhaps a railway carriage, and generals to whole trainloads. Marshal Zhukov, second only to Stalin in the military pecking order, took this trend to its logical conclusion by turning his dacha into a grandiose display of venality.

The marshal was partial to egg-sized gems, so the forty-odd Old Masters he had also looted were by no means the most valuable part of his collection. At the other end, the collection even included 2,000 pairs of women's stockings, and one hopes they weren't for the marshal's own use. Stalin, who had a puritan streak there somewhere, took exception to Zhukov's acquisitiveness if not his taste. It was this more than the tyrant's jealousy, as is fashionably averred these days, that sent the marshal's career into a tailspin only reversed by Khrushchev a few years later.

My uncle Boris ended the war as a mere first lieutenant, and a sapper to boot. That branch of service had no clout at all when it came to dividing the spoils. This type of clout was not only directly proportionate to rank but also inversely proportionate to mortality. And sappers, whose life expectancy at the frontline averaged about two months, weren't a patch on Smersh officers whose lives were threatened mostly by such natural causes as alcoholism and syphilis.

Therefore Boris had to limit his self-awarded prizes to several Swiss wristwatches. That contraption held a lot of fascination for Russian soldiers, most of whom had never seen, much less owned, a wristwatch before the war. As Boris didn't mind spreading the largesse the first watch I ever owned was a steel Omega he gave me for my thirteenth birthday. Working only sporadically, the Omega was modest compared to the Swiss watches that had followed similar paths onto some of my classmates' wrists. But it was the thought that counted and I cherished the watch, wondering occasionally if there was a single timepiece left in Germany in 1945.

Papa ended the war as a private in a penalty battalion, and the pecking order of looting didn't reach quite so low. He was fortunate not to have been shot in the chest by the retreating Germans – or in the back by Uncle Zhenia's colleagues who were propping up the rear in a manner indigenous to the Red Army. The Soviets executed about 158,000 of their own soldiers during the war, to encourage the others as Voltaire once said. Those 10 full divisions were just those executed following a verdict by a military tribunal. Many more were shot even without the benefit of such a formality. That, however, was small beer compared to the non-stop cull of civilians in the Soviet rear. Some six to nine million were murdered during the four years of the war, way in excess of the average annual score of the Bolshevik regime.

Papa was a prime candidate for rough treatment and was fortunate to escape it, more or less. Thus the boots I eventually rejected and a few other cheap trinkets was the best Papa could have hoped to nick. One could only admire the prescience he had displayed in having picked just the right size about two years before I was even a twinkle in his eye.

The fact that Papa ended the war so ignominiously had a direct bearing on his life and, vicariously, on mine. For after the war he wasn't allowed to live in Moscow and I didn't see much of him for months on end. The events that had precipitated his troubles are rather extraordinary and deserve to be told as a separate story.

The Odyssey of Private Leo Boot, just as he told it thousands of times to anyone willing to listen and quite a few who weren't.

In 1940 Papa took his degree at the Mendeleyev Institute of Chemical Technology where one of his friends was Uncle Zhenia, the voracious looter to be, and another Nikolai Dudorov who 15 years later became Khrushchev's Interior Minister.

All able-bodied males were supposed to do military service. University graduates had the choice of either going to officers' school and serving for at least three years thereafter or else enlisting as NCOs for one year only. Papa opted for the shorter commitment and was sent to an artillery regiment as a chemical-warfare specialist.

Soviet artillery units were supplied with stocks of chemical rounds, which proved embarrassing when those fell into the Germans' hands during the Red Army's flight at the beginning of the war. As the Nazis wanted to counter the bad press they were getting in countries outside their control, they'd generously share with the Red Cross whatever evidence of Soviet nastiness they could uncover.

The Russians' record-breaking retreat had prevented them from destroying all such evidence and the Germans had a field day. They gleefully showed the world the bodies of thousands of GULAG prisoners the Russians had hastily shot on the run, and also the NKVD dumping ground at Katyn, where 15,000 Poles had been re-educated with small-calibre bullets in the nape of the neck.

Chemical shells were another part of the prized catch the Nazis waved under the noses of Swiss officials to show that their cause was just. Then they went on to commit their own atrocities that somewhat undermined both their claim and the world's willingness to listen.

Papa was one of the hastily retreating Russians as his

demobilisation order had arrived only hours before Hitler beat Stalin to the punch by opening hostilities on the Eastern front. The order was rescinded before Papa had time to pack. His regiment went into action on June 25, three days and 100 kilometres into the German advance.

Eventually the remnants of several mortally wounded Russian army groups, about two million men in all, gathered around Kiev. There they were told to stand to the last man, Stalin's favourite order he tended to issue without much regard for the situation. In this case the situation was bleak.

Instead of taking a dug-in, two-million-strong army head on the Germans crossed the Dnieper north and south of Kiev, with Guderian and Goth checking their Baedeker's for the shortest route to Moscow. The Russians were left behind and couldn't fight to the last man because the Germans were otherwise engaged and wouldn't come out to play. Breaking through the pincers north and south was impossible. But there was a corridor twenty miles wide to the east through which the army still could have retreated had it been allowed to do so.

Meanwhile the CO, Marshal Budyonny, the old Civil War cavalry commander, applied his trusted tactics by attacking Guderian's tanks with several squadrons of moustachioed Don Cossacks. The Cossacks wore red ribbons saying 'From the Don to Berlin!' across their shoulders and waved their sabres in a manner that would have scared the living bejeesus out of any sensible person.

The Germans, however, weren't unduly impressed because the armour of their tanks provided adequate protection against the razor-sharp blades whereas the latter couldn't ward off cannon shells and machine-gun bullets. Having quickly lost most of his beloved Cossacks, Budyonny ran out of fight, fled with his entire staff in a heavily escorted bomber and took no further part in the hostilities. After the war he was made responsible for horse breeding and could be seen only in the government box of the Moscow Hippodrome, or else at state funerals.

At one of those he delivered a eulogy that made the rounds in Moscow's sly-tongued salons. The deceased was General Oka Gorodovikov, a fellow Cossack and Budyonny's comrade from the Civil War whose handlebar moustache rivalled Budyonny's own. Verbal skills weren't the old warrior's most salient strength, but the words he chose to eulogise his friend were memorable:

'Oka was an interesting man,' said Budyonny, courageously fighting the lump in his throat. 'An extremely interesting man. I remember back in the old days Oka would swing his sabre and splice a man in half all the way down to the saddle...' And tears finally overcame the aging hero.

At the time of his flight, tears were overcoming everyone else. Two million men were left behind German lines and had to fend for themselves, unable to fight, forbidden to retreat. A week later the escape route slammed shut as the two prongs of German armour converged east of Kiev. The senior Soviet commander present, one who had missed Budyonny's flight to Moscow, issued the order to break out through the enemy lines in small groups. The NKVD overseers hastily shot the general for displaying such unsanctioned timidity, then followed his order without delay. (The official announcement of Gen. Kirponos's death said that he heroically killed himself rather than fall into enemy hands. If so, the general must been a contortionist of no mean attainment: he shot himself twice in the back of his head.)

What once had been an army of fighting men became a herd of stampeding, terrified cattle. In the subsequent flight through the swamps and thickets of Eastern Ukraine most of the cattle were corralled: according to Soviet sources 600,000 were taken prisoner. Independent historians put the number at much higher than that.

Papa had an added incentive not to fall into Germans' hands: his eclectic blood mix featured the Jewish element too prominently for him to rate his chances of survival as odds-on. So he and two of his comrades waded through the swamps for a fortnight until they collapsed from hunger and exhaustion right in front of a German patrol.

As they had no papers, Papa felt free to modify his name slightly by adding the Ukranian suffix 'enko'. Actually he needn't have bothered for our name derives from a Polish ancestor (it means the same in Polish as in English, a source of comfort for all the Anglo-American Boots). But to a Russian ear Boot sounds suspicious whereas 'Bootenko' is simon-pure, and it was under that name that Papa was escorted to the nearest POW camp.

The camp was remiss in the area of creature comforts: it consisted of a barbed-wire fence and a few tents for the guards. Twenty thousand prisoners lived *al fresco* and would have had to dine that way too, except that no food was provided. When after a couple of days the emaciated prisoners began dying at a rate that even the German guards found worrying, a lorry full of dirty raw potatoes was wheeled in. This unassuming repast was instantly devoured without the benefit of prior cooking.

That the death rate slowed down after the meal is testimony to the wisdom of those who place three small potatoes at the cornerstone of the recommended daily diet. But years before this nutritional revelation struck home, the Germans realised that in a few days they would have nothing but 20,000 stiffs on their hands. The camp clearly suffered from overpopulation, a problem that was only partly solved by a visiting unit of SS *einsatzgruppen*.

The visitors lined up the prisoners and demanded that all the Jews, communists and political instructors take three steps forward. After that, those stupid enough to have done so were shot (most of them by a young pince-nez'ed officer who, according to Papa, looked like a Moscow intellectual).

Those clever enough to have stayed put were flashed out by the Ukrainian guards who were better than the Germans at identifying Jews, at least before the SS got the necessary on-the-job training. Thankfully, though he had only settled in Russia 20 years earlier, Papa spoke with a perfect Moscow accent, which few Jews did at the time. That and his blond Nordic looks enabled him to pass the examination with flying colours. But first he experienced some anxious moments when one of the Ukrainians lingered in front of him for a second before fingering someone else.

The sieving-out eased the overcrowding somewhat but it didn't solve the problem. The Germans then announced that all Ukrainian prisoners born west of the Dnieper would be allowed to leave and walk to the nearest towns where they were to register with the local German authorities. Papa, his eye ever on the main chance, claimed he was a West Ukrainian, received a *laisser-passer* and went to the bottom of the queue at the exit from the camp.

There he lived through another scare when a sergeant from his regiment passed by and recognised Papa who was too weak to cover his face fast enough. 'And what are you doing here, Jewboy?' was how the sergeant greeted his comrade-in-arms. Papa's reply was equally cordial: 'Shut up or I'll kill you.' 'Well, we'll see about that, Yid snout,' scowled the sergeant and went to look for a guard.

As Papa didn't care much for this turn of events he walked straight to the checkpoint at the gate. There, had Papa begged the guard to let him jump the queue in anything other than the fluent German he had learned from the German side of our family, he would have died in the next 10 minutes. But his imploring 'bitte, kamerade' moved the guard and he waved Papa through, much to the vociferous dismay of others in the queue.

Falling down every twenty yards but picking himself up each time, Papa staggered on to the nearest village where some kind souls offered him a loaf of bread and a piece of lard. That simple fare gave Papa enough energy to walk a hundred miles over the next week to the city of Dnepropetrovsk.

The problem of immediate survival out of the way, Papa had to consider his long-term prospects of getting more bread and lard. That consideration took him straight to the labour exchange.

There were three queues there, two long and one short. The long ones were for Russians and Ukrainians; the short one for *Volksdeutschen*, Soviet citizens of German descent. Papa, sticking to his legend, went to the queue for Ukrainians and waited his turn. To kill time he chatted up a pretty *Volksdeutsch* girl who told him she was single, named Emma and so pleased to have met a Ukrainian who could speak such lovely German (Papa never could resist the temptation of showing off his linguistic ability).

What she didn't tell him, but her eyes did, was that Papa's well-oiled charms had just claimed yet another victim, an advantage he was always likely to press home. In this case speed was of the essence for survival was at stake, not just another notch on the tool of conquest. Thus inspired, Alex Bootenko, aka Leo Boot, lay the charm on so thick that Emma, who hadn't been laid since the start of the war, and whose brain was sharpened by celibacy, soon came up with the winning scheme.

'Get in the queue with me,' she invited, 'and we'll claim you're my husband, Alex …er … Schultz.' Papa, whose own intelligence didn't need sharpening, crossed over and underwent a second name change in a week. An hour later he moved in with Emma and her mother who was so happy to have a man in the house and so taken with Papa that she welcomed him as her own son.

It was as mother to son that she reminded him that all Russian Germans were required to go through an ethnic-purity test at the local Gestapo office within a month of moving into the city. Papa's spirits sank as he feared that the test would include an examination of a certain demonstrably un-Aryan part of his anatomy. But he brightened up when Frau Zommer went on to explain that the physical part of the examination involved cranial measurements only. The cultural part was elementary and, since he already spoke good German, would cause no difficulties. In any case she'd give him a crash course in the intervening month.

The next four weeks were among the happiest in Papa's life, which is a poignant comment on his previous and subsequent life in Russia. Frau Zommer was as good as her word, teaching Papa all kinds of Teutonic trivia, with the meaning of the *Schweinfest* and the lyrics of *O, Tannenbaum* figuring prominently. Food was plentiful, and Emma turned out to be so good in the sack that Papa had uncharacteristic problems coping with her ardour. In short, he had everything a man needed for happiness, especially a man who couldn't afford to be too choosy.

But then came the moment of truth, the Gestapo appointment. For all of Emma's reassurance that he now possessed everything it took to be a real German, Papa walked to the converted school with trepidation. Yet things worked like a charm.

He entered the examination room, clicked his heels together, shot his right arm up and screamed 'Heil Hitler!!!' with such piercing enthusiasm that the three Gestapo officers at the examiners' table winced with contempt at such a lack of subtlety. In Papa's book, however, a lot of contempt was better than a little suspicion and he continued to sound like an SA stormtrooper on speed.

The Germans warmed to him after a while, measured his skull and congratulated him on having the kind of physique that wouldn't embarrass an SS officer. They then issued a certificate describing Papa as 100-percent Aryan and wished him the best of luck in the Reich. As an afterthought they mentioned that the railway station needed a foreman of the maintenance crew and gave Papa a written reference so glowing that he landed the job that very day.

When recounting that odyssey to me Papa always stopped just short of admitting that the ensuing two years had been the happiest of his life. But one could easily be forgiven for forming that impression. The station master, a Wagner-loving SS *sturmbannführer*, became Papa's patron and friend. He invited Papa to card-playing, beer-drinking, *Horst-Wessel*-singing stag parties every Saturday night, while Emma became the best wife he ever had, my mother most emphatically included.

'You see,' he explained to me years later, 'those Kraut women really know how to please a man [unlike your mother, was the unspoken refrain]. Not only did she shag me rigid every night [refrain], but in general she was prepared to wash my feet and drink the water [refrain]. And her mother was the same – minus, he-he-he, the shagging of course.'

A true idyll if you've ever seen one, but it couldn't last for ever. The end was brought about by the rapidly advancing Soviet troops.

The thought of evacuating with the Germans did cross Papa's mind, but the odds in favour of such a move didn't look good. Papa was never much on joining the losing side, and in this case the winning side included his real wife and their three-year-old daughter. So he decided to stay behind and wait for the Soviets to arrive.

But breaking the news to Emma was out of the question – and not only because Papa hated a scene more than anything else in life. Even though he knew no William Congreve, Papa was aware of the sentiment behind the phrase 'hell hath no fury'. He decided that this particular woman should not be scorned, at least not so that she could do something about it.

Papa lovingly loaded Emma, her mother and their belongings on the last westward train and joined them in the compartment. He then checked the clock, announced nonchalantly that there was some time left before the departure and asked the ladies if they'd fancy some ice cream. Emma, who had a sweet tooth, begged him to hurry as there were only ten minutes left.

Papa assured her with his usual gallantry that he'd fly through the sky to satisfy her every whim, jumped out onto the platform, jogged to the station and hid in the lavatory. From there he could see the train but not be seen by anyone on it. When the train chugged off, her desperate shriek, only silenced by the train's ear-busting whistle, told Papa that Emma hadn't realised until the last moment that she had been had. Next problem.

Which was formidable. For historically the Russians have a dim view of their soldiers falling into enemy hands. When, for example, the sixteenth-century Polish king Stephan Báthory released 2,300 Russian POWs, they were immediately slaughtered on return, which was by no means a unique such incident in Russian history. Papa may not have known that story, but he had definitely heard the rumour about the fate of the 10,000 Soviet POWs returned home by the Finns after the disastrous winter campaign of 1940. Apparently they were greeted as heroes, then taken to the Archangel area and shot to the last man. The rumour turned out to be true years later, but even at that time it sounded eminently believable.

In the big war too, the Red Army didn't countenance captivity as an acceptable alternative to suicide for a soldier. 'There are no Soviet POWs,' Stalin explained. 'There are only traitors.' Thus former POWs were often liberated only to go straight into another concentration camp where the guards spoke Russian but, on the down side, the weather was worse. But even such a fate could have been deemed too good for a soldier who not only had been taken prisoner but had collaborated with the Germans, albeit in the modest capacity of repair foreman.

When the Soviets moved in, Papa had to undergo a series of interrogations at the Smersh, compared to which his test at the Gestapo had been child's play. The only reason Papa was allowed to survive the first interrogation was that the NKVD officer across the desk admitted he had never heard a story quite like that before. Papa thus escaped a quick bullet at the nearest wall and was allowed to go through complete vetting, which included confrontations with several Russians who had known him as Herr Schultz.

His luck was good: they all gave him glowing references, assuring the NKVDist that Herr Schultz had helped the resistance movement. That wasn't exactly true as Papa not only hadn't helped but was blissfully unaware of the existence of any such movement. He did, however, shield from the Germans' wrath two of his underlings who had been caught stealing sacks of salt from a freight train. The Germans explained they didn't do business the Russian way and reached for their Lugers, with only Papa's intercession saving the wretches. No wonder they gave him a clean bill of health, especially since that elevated them from the role of thieves to that of resistance fighters.

Asked for a weightier character reference, Papa named Dudorov whose star was rising in Moscow. The reference was so good that after a brief six-month screening Papa was allowed to redeem his sins in a penalty battalion. He entered Germany on the armour of a T-34 tank, miraculously survived and, with Dudorov again pulling a few relevant strings, was demobilised a few months before the war ended.

But even his friend's pull wasn't sufficient to keep Papa in Moscow and he was 'administratively' (that is, without trial) sentenced to 'minus 50 times 10'. That meant he wasn't allowed to live in the top 50 cities for 10 years. Still, Papa thanked his lucky stars for having received only a slight wound during the war and a mere slap on the wrists after it. He was fortunate not to have lost a limb, for the Soviets detested the ungainly sight of those abbreviated creatures jangling their medals in city centres. One night they were all rounded up and shipped off to an Arctic island, never to be seen again.

As Papa had all his limbs intact, he got a short furlough in Moscow before being sent to a far-away glassworks, and he spent that time courting my mother. He was free to do so as his pre-war wife had been so impressed with the 'missing, believed dead' notice she had received in 1941 that she had promptly married someone else. Papa discovered this when he showed up unannounced on his old doorstep only to find another man wearing his pre-war jammies. His odyssey was over.

2

My mother was at that time 26, ready to get married and smitten with the dashing veteran, even though she wasn't impressed with his manners. Having grown up in a dog-eat-dog street environment, Papa's manners could only have been learned at the school of hard knocks. So until her death 43 years later Mama had to listen to the symphony of champing sounds Papa produced every time he chewed something.

His idea of how to woo a girl also ran across the grain of Mama's upbringing. For example, she remembered until her dying days the magnificent bouquet she had received from Papa who had complemented two real buds with half a dozen paper roses. It's testimony to Mama's love for Papa that she recovered from this affront and went on to marry him in 1946. I was born a year later, my genes reflecting the irreconcilable conflict between Papa's *bon vivant* opportunism and Mama's relentless gentility.

Since Papa wasn't allowed to live in Moscow, and we couldn't join him permanently for fear of losing our Moscow residence permit, I had only spent perhaps two years in Papa's company before he was allowed to resettle in Moscow in 1957. That time was broken up between stints in godforsaken Byelorussian and Ukrainian holes where he worked, and his occasional visits to Moscow, never lasting more than a few days at a time.

As a result, Papa didn't have much influence on my upbringing. He hadn't even attempted to play a role in it until I was 12 or so and he realised I could understand off-colour jokes. Until then I had been raised by Mama who believed only in one set of values, those of the pre-revolutionary intelligentsia, but with a modern twist. Her notions were indeed twisted.

An historian by education, Mama grew up in an actor's family, but where her father was histrionic, she was hysterical. As all Kudashevs, she had a Manichean concept of right and wrong, and was prepared to enforce her views in every reasonable – and often unreasonable – way. When I was born she decided to dedicate her whole life to my well-being and abandoned her post-graduate course at Moscow University. Since money was in short supply, she took up sewing, and my childhood unfolded to the accompaniment of the even rattle of her ancient Singer treadle.

The rest of the time she spent on shielding me from the corrupting egalitarian influence of the outside world. This was an amazing aspiration in someone who tended to swallow communist propaganda hook, line and sinker. Indeed Mama believed in the universal brotherhood of the abstract proletariat – but only as long as she could keep the concrete proletarians in our neighbourhood at arm's length.

Adhering to this version of Bollinger bolshevism, Mama kept me out of crèche and kindergarten, those unfailing forges of the Soviet man. Instead she took me on long daily walks in Alexander Garden. But her efforts to squeeze my youthful temperament into the straitjacket of gentility were only variably successful and occasionally led to her embarrassment.

Once, for example, I ran onto the flower bed at the foot of the monument to Great Dead Socialists and began to trample the multi-coloured tulips. As Mama couldn't follow me onto the consecrated ground, she had to reason with me from afar. Eventually I relented and we walked away briskly before the cops arrived.

On another occasion, Mama tried to pair me off in a sand box with another boy who had just learned to walk. He was still unsteady on his feet, which I proved by punching him in the chest with both fists. The boy was in fine voice though, and when he landed in the sand he screamed so desperately that it took Mama ten minutes to quiet his mother down.

Until I went to school I had had little contact with other children and found it hard to see myself as a member of a collective. This was something a Soviet child was supposed to be, and something Mama always told me I should aspire to become before anything else. This 'don't do as I do, do as I say' education failed miserably in my case, and the resulting bloody-mindedness eventually rendered my life in Russia impossible.

We'd walk down Herzen Street in the direction of the cute grottoes of Alexander Garden, or rather Mama would walk and I'd pretend to be too tired to move under my own steam. Mama would carry me until her arms grew numb, which was soon for I was a hefty child. 'Isn't it time you walked on your own darling feet,' Mama would ask, only to receive the pre-emptive reply: 'When it's time I'll tell you.'

Along the way Mama would read to me the huge slogans adorning every building. It was all 'down with' this or 'glory to' that. I was too young to see the incongruity of, for instance, a slogan saying 'Glory to Soviet builders!' displayed on an abandoned ruin, but I didn't remain too young for long. Mama would also point out portraits of our leaders displayed in their 20-foot-high splendour everywhere. That I could identify them at age two confirmed her belief that I was a genius, even though I occasionally confused Voroshilov and Bulganin (both sported professorial goatees) or Molotov and Shvernik (both had neatly trimmed grey moustaches).

Mama regaled me with stories about the revolutionary exploits of Comrades Lenin, Stalin, Beria and Voroshilov, and I was developing a bored, familiar kind of affection for all of them. At the same time she'd tell me stories about such less sanguinary personages as Bach, Tchaikovsky, Tolstoy, Chekhov and Shakespeare. The way she spoke about them suggested they were, in their own way, almost as worthy of respect as the comrades.

The loudspeaker, always blaring in the room we shared with my grandparents, maintained the same duality, easily switching from a TASS message on the heinous American imperialists to some Brahms. Mama wasn't musical but she knew that the educational ideal she had in mind for me included music as a necessary constituent.

That's why she'd often read up on the pieces played and tell me about them. Thus from an early age I was able to identify various compositions and occasionally even the performers. David Oistrakh, for example, was unmistakeable, and I once demanded an explanation of why his Saint-Saens sounded better than any other violinist's.

The secret, Mama explained in a way that misled me until I was ten or so, lay in his instrument. Thanks to the generosity of our Soviet government he was allowed to play this rare Italian violin made in the eighteenth century by Antonio Stradivari. Lesser lights had to make do with ordinary fiddles from which they were unable to extract the same mellifluous sound. The only other violinist who was allowed to use Oistrakh's instrument was his son Igor, Mama continued. But she didn't explain why in Igor's hands the same violin sounded so different, leaving me to figure it out for myself.

The programmes were slanted towards Russian music, the guidelines being (as I discovered 20 years later) 50 percent Soviet composers, 25 percent Russian pre-revolutionary, 25 percent everyone else. Since every concert hall followed roughly the same guidelines, many

Russians have a warped view of the relative significance of various composers. Today one can hear even Russian musicians talk about the unsurpassed genius of Tchaikovsky or refer to the fleet-fingered Rachmaninov as the Russian Bach.

The Russians may have perfected that kind of parochialism but they didn't invent it. Witness, say, the English going overboard in praising Elgar, who is little known outside the UK. The Russian conductor Gennadiy Rozhestvensky, who introduced Elgar to Russia in the 1970s, once played an amusing prank on a female professor of the piano at Moscow Conservatory. That formidable lady demanded to know who was that Elgar and what his nationality was. 'I'm not sure,' replied the mischievous conductor, 'but I think he must be Spanish. You know, El Greco, El Gar. It's that kind of name.'

The post-war years saw a twilight-zone drive towards establishing Russian 'priority' in matters cultural, scientific and technological. Not only was Tchaikovsky proclaimed the most sublime musical genius ever, but Pushkin was billed as by far the most brilliant poet, unknown to the toiling masses in the degenerate West only because of the imperialists' sharp practices. And Mayakovsky stood on a pedestal as the modern keeper of Pushkin's flame.

Polzunov invented the steam engine, Kotelnikov the parachute, Mozhaisky the aeroplane, Popov the radio, Petrov the electric bulb, Lodygin the electric arc, Tsiolkovsky the rocket, the Cherepanovs the locomotive. And anyone disseminating information that contradicted those indisputable historical facts had to be re-enlightened at the educational facilities under the auspices of The State Administration for Camps (GULAG for short).

That fate almost befell my uncle, Papa's elder brother, who was a world-renowned authority on cement and a member of the USSR Academy of Sciences. In one of his lectures he made a reference to Portland cement, as he was ignorant of the fact that this material had russified its name in the previous couple of days. That was a lame excuse, as far as the Party cell was concerned. For the next week Uncle Cement was expecting arrest at any moment, but he was saved by the intercession of Kaganovich. In his former job as Construction Minister, this Politburo member had been familiar with Uncle Cement's work and so was willing to overlook his unfortunate, if unwitting, lapse into the employ of the CIA.

Mama never had such lapses. She believed the Party was infallible and attempted to instruct me in the same vein. Unfortunately, she forgot that one's success, or indeed survival, in Russia hinged not on what one did, not on what one believed, and not even on what one professed, but on what one was.

All people were divided into two sharply, if subliminally, defined categories: 'one of us' (*nash*) and 'not one of us' (*ne-nash*). The former belonged in Russia and were prepared to do anything at all – lie, dissemble, inform on friends – to make sure they continued to belong. The latter didn't belong, and wouldn't no matter how hard they tried: there was that elusive something about them that simply didn't fit. Every Russian knew which category he fell into and also knew that everybody else knew.

While many intellectuals were *ne-nash*, far from all *ne-nash* were intellectuals, and the overlap between the two groups couldn't possibly exceed 50 percent or so. Thus my uncle the Academician was a *nash*, and my illiterate Byelorussian nanny, who talked to me about God, wasn't.

Communism played a certain role in this polarity, but not in any straightforward way. Most people who honestly believed in that quaint idea were in the 1930s shot 'like mad dogs', in the prosecutor Vyshinsky's appropriate phrase. However, the jargon remained, acting as a sort of password one uses to gain entry and then forgets. The difference between the *nash* and *ne-nash* in this respect was 1) the readiness to use it and 2) the ability to keep a straight face when doing so. The *nash* had both. The *ne-nash* sometimes had 1) but never 2). I had neither.

Much like Americans who know class distinctions exist in their country but hate to talk about them, Russians will seldom discuss the *nash/ne-nash* watershed. But they are all aware of it and won't be misled by any paradoxes that could throw an outsider off track.

For example, Papa who grew up in a religious family, as a child sold shoes for a living, never belonged to the Party, was twice a 'traitor to the motherland' (himself, POW; son, political émigré) and was always indifferent to every progressive ideal – was a *nash*. That's why he lived a turbulent but, by Russian standards, agreeable life.

On the other hand Mama, who grew up with communist parents, as a child screamed atheist ditties outside churches and synagogues

('Down, down with priests, the rabbis and the lot// We'll prove by means of science that there is no God!'), who believed in the cause of the Party, who, for fear of spiritual contamination refused to take holidays abroad even when they were on offer (a rare privilege in those days) – was a *ne-nash*. That's why she died a broken, bitter woman, having had her entire life torn to shreds on the rack called Russia.

For all the stories of Grandpa Lenin or Uncle Stalin she fed me, she couldn't help spicing up my educational diet with a drop of Tolstoy here or a dollop of Bach there, all shaken with a dash of moral absolutism. And faster than you could say 'dichotomy' she produced a dedicated, intuitive *ne-nash* who was proud of his *ne-nash*ness and despised the *nash* mentality with a passion that's still burning bright decades later. In her very failure Mama succeeded.

On the days she had to go shopping she'd protect me from the push, shove and swear of endless Moscow queues by dropping me off at the Tretiakov Gallery, one of the two major art collections in our city. The other was the Pushkin Museum, but I wasn't allowed to go there until my teens. For the Pushkin exhibited Western paintings, many of them featuring female nudes. Mama could talk about the aesthetic aspects of the female form till the critics came home, but sexual prudery was seated deeper in her brain than artistic appreciation. She wasn't about to let her four-year-old angel cast his virginal eye on the unbuttoned degeneracy perpetrated by the likes of Titian and Rubens.

Russian painters, in which the Tretiakov specialises, were a different matter – what with all the figures being fully draped and some even locked in the rigid poses of revolutionary oratory. Though mildly upset by my lingering longer in front of Kramskoy's Christ in the Desert or Ivanov's Christ's Appearance to the People than before The Arrest of a Propagandist or Lenin Addressing a Crowd from an Armoured Car, Mama decided I could be safely left to my own devices. Thus the collection founded by a pre-revolutionary merchant began to act as my babysitter.

Later those duties were shared by the Moscow Conservatory, opposite our house. Mama would drop me off at a matinee recital and go about her business, which as often as not was queuing up for food. Before long I insisted on being taken to evening concerts as well. Mama seldom joined me because her appreciation of music was purely theoretical, and Papa, whenever he was in town, never did. Years later

I did take them to a decent concert, and Mama kept looking at me throughout with tears of pride in her eyes. Papa slept.

My childhood was thus more or less solitary and, though by nature a gregarious type, I had hardly had any contact with other children until I went to school at age seven. It's not that Mama didn't believe in my socialising with my coevals. On the contrary, she often talked to me about the importance of belonging to a collective, a euphemism for becoming a *nash*. She simply didn't condone my dealing with any children below what she saw as our station, insisting on her right to vet potential playmates and reject the more objectionable ones. 'Don't play with that boy, he won't teach you anything good,' she used to tell me.

I didn't necessarily see a quick five-a-side as an experience replete with didactic potential. But as long as Mama controlled my movements there was precious little I could do about it. She insisted that I conform to the ethics and aesthetics of the intelligentsia, and no deviations were allowed.

People like Mama realised they had a mission in life and, though their own claim to membership in the intelligentsia was somewhat tenuous, did all they could to make sure their children would qualify. This was the *ancien régime* version of the process one sees in America where poor people, especially immigrants, devote their whole lives to providing their children with an opportunity to get rich.

In their case, this explains why second-generation Americans are usually better off than their parents. In Russia this explains why cultural attainment is more widespread among my contemporaries than among our parents. And why many of the dazzling lights of Moscow's literary salons had parents who read, as opposed to extolled the virtues of, only the Russian answer to pulp fiction.

Cultivating a child's exclusivity in the rancid environment of a Moscow communal flat was a tall order. Most of us who were brought up that way have turned out to be odd, often combining the attitudes of a bookish don with those of a razor-toting lout. In practical terms, Mama's heroic efforts made my life a misery, as it's difficult for a little boy to look down upon his malodorous habitat when he has to live his life smack in the middle of it. And Mama's vetting of potential playmates reduced my social options to prematurely myopic children who couldn't play sports, never swore and were nerds long before the term was invented.

Mama's sewing failed to augment Papa's income appreciably, and we had no money at all. Mama had to make all the clothes I wore, and if you look through our family photo albums you'll see many pictures of me clad in plus-fours, sailor blouses, bows and berets. What you won't see is the anguish I felt in having to wear clothes that made me stick out like a sore thumb among other children. They all wore standard-issue Soviet garb that came in two or three basic styles. Somehow that made them feel they could claim sartorial, and by inference moral, ascendancy over me.

While I was under Mama's protection they taunted me from afar; when I grew older, taunting gave way to assault. But even before that I had begged Mama to buy me normal clothes. 'Please, Ma, I want to be standard,' I'd sob. But Mama had neither the money nor the inclination to satisfy that request, and I had to live with monkey suits until I went to school and started to wear the regulation paramilitary uniform.

Toys presented another problem. We simply couldn't afford any, and I had to learn how to make my own out of loose sticks of wood. Tree bark was particularly good for carving little boats, using matches for the masts and paper for the sails. In April, when the snow melted and vigorous rivulets would run along the kerbs, I'd drop those boats into the water and watch them sail away to some magic destination far away from the drabness of Moscow.

Actually, with the wind getting warmer and the first buds popping out, one could overlook the drabness and heave the customary sigh of relief all Russians breathe at the end of winter. One could be moved by the vulnerability of the sweet eighteenth-century mansions, with their cracked masonry and asymmetrical windows. One could be touched by the dainty fifteenth-century churches and forget they had all been converted into warehouses. One could unbutton one's overcoat, inhale the spring and watch the tree-bark boats speed towards the waterfalls of the drains.

Those few real toys I did have Mama made me give away to less fortunate children, which she called sharing. Since I wasn't allowed to keep any for myself, sharing wasn't an accurate word. But Mama, along with most survivors in her generation, believed in the sinfulness of private property on the one hand and in the desirability of imbuing me with selfless attitudes on the other. In that she succeeded only to a certain extent.

The whole process wasn't dissimilar, in some convoluted way, to the childhood experience of my English wife. At roughly the same age she used to be taken by her upper-middle-class grandmother to the local alms house where Penelope would give the residents gifts of tea, clothes and coal – and learn how to communicate with the less fortunate. What in her case was a genuine article, was in mine a caricature. For the bottom quickly falls out of upper-middle-class values when one has to share a loo with twenty neighbours and spend one's life enveloped by the smell of piss so thick one has to wade through it.

I especially regretted having to give away the only valuable toy I ever had, a tank that moved in all directions, drove around or over obstacles and shot its cannon with realistic electric discharges. Since it had a black cross rather than a red star painted on its side, the tank had clearly followed its normally sized cousins into Russian captivity. It must have been brought out of Germany by one of my relations as part of the spoils of war.

At my first birthday party that I remember, one of the socially acceptable children gave me a present of an old German camera (which too must have by-passed the normal distribution channels on its way to Moscow). It was a medium-format Leica that, as far as I could tell, had every feature intact. Except that it didn't work, and couldn't be repaired as the necessary spare parts weren't available. It could, however, function as a toy, and little Lyovushka and I spent a few merry hours playing with his camera and my tank.

When the evening was drawing to a close, Mama took me aside and asked if I had enjoyed the party and the gift. When I admitted I had, she said, 'Well then, the least you can do is give your tank to Lyovushka.' My protests didn't make a dent in the armour of Mama's expropriatory resolve. Suffocated by suppressed tears, I silently handed over my tank to the little shit, who couldn't believe his good fortune.

My life always changed dramatically whenever we spent a few months with Papa in little factory settlements near Konstantinovka, near Briansk, near Gomel, but never actually in those places. At that time, whenever I was asked back in Moscow where my father lived, I always said he lived in 'Near', the collective secondary locale of my childhood. Our living conditions were better in those places than in Moscow, as Papa in his capacity of Chief Engineer was entitled to his own flat.

When we lived in the provinces, Mama felt she could loosen the reins a bit and let me roam on my own. Unfortunately, she didn't realise that, while Moscow children only despised me as an oddity, those in far-away places would hate me as 1) a Jew, 2) a Muscovite, 3) an 'intel', and near Gomel, which is in Byelorussia, 4) a Russian. I accepted the last three with proud equanimity, but the first one baffled me.

'Jew' was nothing to me but a constituent of many elaborate curses. I thought the word was desemanticised and didn't associate it with anything I was. So when called a 'bloody Jew' I'd respond by calling those freckled village urchins 'bloody Jews' right back. I thought it was just an ordinary everyday expression like 'your mother's a whore', 'up yours', 'go climb a dick' and other similar phrases I had already learned from my actor grandfather and his friends.

Mama, raised in the spirit of revolutionary internationalism, had chosen not to elucidate the issue for a long time, keeping that particular skeleton in the cupboard where she felt it belonged. But finally she sighed and explained that we deserved that particular soubriquet almost as much as the other three.

The urchins didn't stop at verbal abuse. Every morning our door near Gomel was decorated with a swastika drawn with laudable symmetry in fresh manure. When that happened, Mama would sob for fifteen minutes or so. Having been taught to be protective towards women, I tried to console her by stroking her hair and promising to kill those bastards next time, an empty promise if you've ever heard one.

The settlement was called Kostyukovka, a word etymologically related to the Russian for 'bone'. It was dominated by the Stalin Glassworks where Papa and just about everybody else worked. Chemical waste from the plant flowed into a stinking ditch that encircled Kostyukovka the way Guderian's tanks had encircled Kiev 10 years previously – and one suspects with the same lethal outcome for those who had to breathe in those chemicals all their lives.

Behind the plant sprawled a collective farm that grew wonderful apples, mostly Antonov and Pippins. Though the apples belonged to the state, the farmers didn't mind selling them to us for a pittance, a bucketful costing about as much as a kilo back in Moscow.

As there wasn't a single *ne-nash* in Kostyukovka, Papa was in his element, which is more than I can say for Mama and me. He spent his days at work and his evenings at his colleagues' places, playing chess and preference, the Russian version of whist. When we came along, Mama chatted with the colleagues' wives who entertained her with stories of Papa's amorous conquests accomplished while we had been in Moscow.

Much to the annoyance of his friends, I often peeked over Papa's shoulder, asking for a brief explanation whenever the rules of the games they played weren't self-evident. In six months or so I could hold my own in chess against any of them, not that this was saying much, and could have probably done the same in preference had I been allowed to gamble. These modest achievements, coupled with my precocious literacy, reinforced Mama's belief that I could rival Leonardo in the universality of my genius. And she didn't mind sharing this article of faith with the world at large.

Papa was also proud of me and made me deliver public performances when we had parties in the flat. Those were infrequent because Mama hated to socialise with the people aware of Papa's profligacy, which meant more or less everybody. On the rare occasions that we did have guests, Papa would make me beat adult chess players and then climb on top of a chair and recite poems by Pushkin, Lermontov and Mayakovsky. On request, I also gave reading demonstrations, going through passages from the books the guests had brought with them because they suspected I knew all our own reading matter by heart.

While in Kostyukovka I discovered sunsets. Mama would take me out for long strolls, and as we walked up the main road in the direction opposite to Gomel we could watch the fieriest of balls dropping below the most unobstructed of horizons. As this was a sight a Muscovite born and bred had no chance of seeing in his own city, it would hold my quicksilver attention for a while.

Mama generally tried to encourage my interest in nature, which was then and regrettably still remains tepid at best. But I remember walking towards the biggest sun I had ever seen and bombarding Mama with questions.

'Why is the sun so orange today?' 'Because it's going to be very hot tomorrow.' 'How far is the moon?' 'Three hundred thousand kilometres.' 'Would I be closer to it if I climbed on top of this tree stump?' 'Not really.' 'But of course I would be. Not by much, naturally, but still closer.' 'It's not enough to count, silly-billy.' 'Why does everybody hate me?' 'Surely not everybody. I don't hate you, Papa doesn't hate you, Boris doesn't hate you.' 'I understand that. Why do other boys hate me, is what I mean.' 'Because you are better than they are.' 'But if that's true, they should respect me, not hate me.' 'People don't like it when someone's better than they are.' 'Mama, I don't want to be better than anybody if that means all boys are going to hate me for the rest of my life.'

Mama was trying her hardest to protect me against egalitarian onslaught, to a point where I hadn't learned how to dress and undress myself until I went to school at age seven. That was annoying as at that age other, streetwise, boys could not only dress themselves but already knew how to undress neighbourhood girls.

Papa never interfered, except occasionally trying to add a touch of common sense to my upbringing. Once he observed the first fight of my life when I attacked a slightly older boy for taunting me. I threw a wild punch, the boy ducked expertly and my fist landed high on his forehead. The ensuing pain incapacitated my right hand, and the boy easily beat me up.

'Never punch with the fist, except in the stomach,' advised Papa in the midst of Mama's sobbing as she wiped the blood off my lip. 'You'll hurt yourself more than the other bloke. Punch upwards with the heel of your palm. He'll drop like an apple off a tree.'

'Lyova!' screamed Mama. 'What are you teaching him, Lyova?!? Why don't you devote more time to your son's upbringing instead of whoring around? Why don't you teach him something useful, not how to become the same hooligan scum you were at his age?'

'Well, the lad needs to know how to take care of himself.' 'What the lad needs is a real father, not someone who whores around.' Mama wouldn't allow the train of her thought to be derailed.

I didn't know what 'whoring around' meant but wished scenes of that nature were less frequent in our family. Mama and Papa never saw eye to eye, and hardly a day went by without Mama screaming her head off and Papa trying in vain to reason with her. But I never thought he was a bad father and reserved my toughest questions for those rare occasions when it was just the two of us men.

'Is there a God, Papa?' 'Do. Not. Be. Stupid. Of course there bloody well isn't.' I wouldn't let him get off scot-free, especially since I was having daily conversations on that subject with my local nanny. I tried to look down on that old illiterate woman but never quite managed to do so. She emanated the kind of light one sometimes sees in Russian peasant women but hardly ever in their men.

'If there is no God, then who created man?' 'Man originated from the ape. It's called evolution, and there was this Englishman, Darwin by name, who proved it conclusively in his book *The Origin of Species*. You'll read it when you grow up.' 'And where did the ape come from?' 'What?' 'The ape. The one man originated from. Where did that come from?' 'From another ape, you know, a lower order of ape.' 'And where did that one come from?'

I'd thus lead Papa all the way down to the amoeba and make him resort to the rhetorical fallacy of telling me I'd find out all those things for myself when I grew up. He had nothing to be ashamed about though, for unbeknown to me I was using the line of thought Aquinas had developed as proof of God's existence. It took philosophers 600 years to refute that logic, and even then not at all convincingly.

But Papa had read neither *Summa Theologiae* nor *The Critique of Pure Reason* and was disarmed in the face of the rudimentary childish reasoning I had borrowed from my nanny. She hadn't read those books either, or for that matter anything else, but possessed the purity of faith I've always envied and never attained.

While Mama was a materialist because that's what one was supposed to be if one wanted to avoid premature death in a militantly godless state, Papa was a visceral materialist. He had refused to acknowledge the existence of spiritual realities until he turned 70 and started thinking about eternity or, more precisely, about the existence of an afterlife that would enable him to chase women even after death.

In that, Papa followed a common, almost Cartesian, path to faith. But he never went all the way, having been thwarted by his inability to find out where exactly all those souls go and how they copulate if all their mateable bits are dematerialised. Of course, had he read Swedenborg, he could have found his answer, such as it is, but Papa had never heard of the Scandinavian quack. In short, he was a *nash*, but a good, kindly sort who always respected my extra-material interests – even though deep down he could never understand why people would ever read books with no dialogue or pictures.

Reading such books in Russia performed the function that in the West was divided among TV, penny arcades, rock'n'roll, funnies, a race down the main drag, clothes, houses, accents – in short, a combination of enlightenment, entertainment and status seeking. Also, in a society where success was unattainable in any material terms, at least for most people, books acted as rungs on the social-climbing ladder. One's social standing was often measured by what one had read or could at least pretend to have read. Time was measured in books, not in days. Days were made up of pages, not hours.

However, real books were seldom available as they were always published, if at all, in minuscule circulations that by-passed bookshop counters. Instead they meandered straight into the black-market book fair. Costing 50 to 100 times their publishers' prices, they were thus beyond the reach of precisely the kind of people who were most likely to be interested in them. As a result, books were often bought collectively and passed around a gradually widening circle until they fell apart.

These were augmented by contraband: foreign-published *Tamizdat* or mimeographed *Samizdat* books (respectively, 'There-Publishing', meaning published in the West, and 'Self-Publishing' – both puns on *Gosizdat*, The State Publishing House). Many young Muscovites hardly ever read anything else. The rumour had it that one enterprising woman even mimeographed a copy of *War and Peace*, for otherwise her son would never have gone anywhere near it.

Good books were the forbidden fruit that is, as we know, sweet. They were universally sought and voraciously devoured, which was the up side. But there was a down side as well. Because a limited number of titles circulated among a practically unlimited number of people, we all read more or less the same few books as they became available. Most of us suffered from such lopsided reading, eyeing enviously Western intellectuals who could read what they wanted, not what they could find.

Moreover, as our demand by far exceeded the meagre supply, most people couldn't get their hands even on those few books that were making the rounds. Such a failure spelled social death unless one could hide it behind a convincing smokescreen. If Plato was the order of the day, everyone – but everyone – had to be able to discuss those shadows on the cave walls. If it was Camus, then one had to be able to refer to his work when talking about existential alienation. Since, as I've mentioned, most people were unable to read the books in question, they often found themselves on shaky ground.

One such instance was typical. When I was in my early twenties, many of my friends were musicians (a situation that still hasn't changed, actually). One of them, Valeriy, was an avid reader, and an even more avid show-off. For that reason he always had a volume of Plato prominently displayed on his coffee table to act as a reminder that in matters of the mind Valeriy was a force to be reckoned with.

Once another musician dropped by (he later became an international celebrity) and espied the coveted tome. 'Have you read it?' asked Valeriy as a prelude to boasting that he himself had. 'I have,' smirked the future star dismissively. 'It's all crap. And anyway, Plato ripped everything off Montaigne.'

Such chronological lapses notwithstanding, there's no gainsaying the social, not just intellectual, value of reading in the Moscow of my youth. Naturally, the moment the situation changed, and other, more palpable prizes became available, real books were no longer needed. Few young people in Russia read them any longer.

In my day, however, a *ne-nash* had to read voraciously if he didn't want to be stuck in the social no-man's land. Thus one could routinely overhear on buses, say, conversations on the relative merits of Fichte and Schelling, or Plato and Aristotle. On balance, having lived in different countries, I prefer the Western way, where there are no social prizes to be won for reading Pascal or Dostoevsky, quite the opposite. Thus the only people who do so are either professional 'intels' or else disinterested souls driven by a genuine inner need.

When I was little, however, I took seriously all the non-stop diatribes in the Soviet press against the money-grabbing materialism of the West, as opposed to the Russians' quest for knowledge and concomitant power.

'To learn, to learn and once again to learn,' Gorky had said shortly before he was poisoned like a rat by the NKVD. So, for lack of anything more exciting to do, learn I did.

And then it was time to go to school.

THE RIGHT TO AFFORDABLE HOUSING

1

NEXT TIME YOU HEAR AN EXPERT from one of the better universities, or, worse still, a journalist, claim he understands the Russians, ask him this question: 'Have you ever lived in a Soviet communal flat?' And if he answers 'no', call him a liar, throw him out of your house and refuse ever to talk to him again. Unless, of course, he recants, which he probably won't.

The communal flat is the microcosm, it's the distillation of the Russian spirit, the stage for tragedies and comedies compared to which Shakespeare's plays are soap operas and everyone else's are commercials. The communal flat is the forge of character, the smithy of taste, the educator of souls, the judge and the jury. More important, the communal flat was my childhood.

Nabokov's memory spoke to him in continuous narrative, a carefully woven fabric of a Bach fugue arranged for the romantically minded by Busoni. Much as I admire both Nabokov and Bach, my own memory speaks in the modernist staccato bursts of discordant sounds, in images more worthy of Kandinsky than Metsu. The memory is thus divorced from the rest of me, but it would be wrong to let the rest of me interfere. After all, one's memory is a sieve that retains what's needed and lets the rest run down the drain. What settles between the holes is the stuff of which understanding is made.

Thus the communal flat of my childhood comes back to me in a potpourri of sounds, a kaleidoscope of images, a bouquet of smells. Oh, the smells of my native land! Both Pushkin and Lermontov described them in glowing terms, making it clear even to a neophyte that they never darkened the threshold of a communal flat.

A Bordeaux wine taster would perhaps be able to analyse the bouquet better, but for the time being you'll have to make do with my nasal memory. It comes back with sweat, bodies that go unwashed for weeks, underwear that goes unlaundered for months, outer clothes that have never seen the inside of a cleaner's, sauerkraut, stale urine, dried sperm, condensed vomit, cheap cigarettes, alcohol vapours and decaying teeth. That was the communal olfactory background against which individuals could smell their own lives.

In our flat there were 22 of them. They were divided into six families, each occupying one room and sharing the kitchen, lavatory, bathroom, corridor and telephone. These days class-conscious Englishmen, who can't help noticing that I don't move my lips when reading and sometimes use words of more than two syllables, remark accusingly that I must have been upper-middle class back in Russia.

That's God's own truth. For not only did my mother try to protect me from egalitarian influences, but the flat, indeed the whole building in which I grew up, was decidedly upmarket. Most tenants there had degrees from decent universities, held responsible jobs and sneered at the equivalent of the lower-middle class.

Those people could only dream of such luxury. Their lives were circumscribed by the so-called 'corridor system', in which dozens of rooms (each housing a family), one kitchen, one bathroom and one lavatory hid on either side of a smelly winding corridor perhaps 300 to 500 feet long. Our poor relations lived in one of those. I liked to visit them because in their corridor one could ride a tricycle around numerous bends at most satisfying speeds.

The lower classes looked even upon the corridor system with the same expressions one sometimes notices on the face of a rubbish collector driving his lorry through an exclusive neighbourhood. They lived in communal barracks at the outskirts of Moscow, not what you'd describe as fashionable suburbs. Their lavatories were outside and consisted of a hole in a wooden frame erected over a pit and enclosed in an unheated wooden shack.

In winter, when outside temperatures plunged to minus 40C, certain activities you take for granted became life-threatening. Predictably, just like during the American westward expansion, human ingenuity defeated the elements. Our heroic compatriots would do their business onto newspaper sheets spread over the floor of their rooms. They'd then carefully fold the paper, discreetly put it under the bed and dump it into the outhouse on their way to work in the morning.

They worked in places like the Red Proletarian Factory or Car Depot

No. 6 and went there by public transport, where their odours intermingled. Someone with a reasonably sensitive nose needed a gas mask to enter a Metro train on a hot day, but entering was the easy part.

The real trial came when the train suddenly jerked to a stop, and all the short-sleeved passengers grabbed the overhead rail not to fall down. In doing so, they'd raise their arms, thus adding a certain armour-piercing quality to the already pungent smell of their bodies and clothes. Typically, they had no bathrooms at all and several times a year washed in communal baths, whether they needed to or not. This was seen more as a social occasion than a hygienic imperative.

Communal apartments of one type or another were by no means a rarity in Russia. In my time, about 90 percent of the urban population lived in them. Now, 40 years later, 15 percent still do, according to the official data. Unofficially, the number is much higher for, say, a one-bedroom flat housing three generations of the same family doesn't fall into that category. It would be classified as a 'separate flat', whereas most Russians, when hearing an unqualified 'flat' mentioned, would still assume that it's a communal variety.

Now, history may indeed repeat itself first as a tragedy and then as a farce. However, the first event in the flat that I recall coherently comes back to me as a detective story, and that's how I'm going to tell it.

Grandpa walked into the room and beckoned us to the door. Sensing that something important was afoot, Mama, Papa, Grandma and I followed him to the kitchen without arguing. As our room was next to the front door, to get to our destination we had to walk the entire length of the corridor, unlit for considerations of fiscal prudence. Bumping into the handles sticking aggressively out of the doors of the other five rooms, we passed the bathroom, then the lavatory, executed a neat 90-degree turn and found ourselves in the kitchen. By contrast it appeared to be brightly lit.

The view was familiar: two gas cookers with eight rings between them, one assigned to each family, two up for grabs (the nightly battles for those two were worthy of Dostoyevsky's pen at its most dramatic); six rickety tables for preparing food and washing dishes afterwards; two clothes lines hung with faecally stained underwear quite past laundering. Some of our 17 neighbours completed the scene. In the tradition of the Russian characters so aptly described by the classics and enacted on the stage of the Moscow Art Theatre, their mouths were smiling but their eyes weren't.

Grandpa, incidentally, was himself an actor at that famous theatre. By the time I was born his personal repertoire had crystallised to one role only, that of Stalin, whom he impersonated in The *Chekists* and other Moscow hits. In the past he used to play other roles as well, such as Schiller's Karl Moor (after whom a famous London journalist is named), and according to Mama, if no one else, his performances had been brilliant.

Like most actors, he was histrionic off-stage as well, a tendency that showed in the semi-circular sweep with which he pointed at our own kitchen table. There, between two dirty plates and a half-finished cup of tea with a cigarette butt in it, lay a lock of hair plucked out of Grandpa's thick mane. He was waiting for us to guess who the perpetrator was.

With his keen eye for dramatics, Grandpa had staged the scene to be silent and motionless, much like the celebrated finale of Gogol's *Inspector General*. The stage was set for a whodunit.

Who? Who had ripped that hair out of his head? To be more specific, which member of which of the other five families had graduated from verbal to physical assault? This time? Make no mistake about it, higher education or no, they were all to varying degrees capable of violence towards their neighbours, and certainly towards Grandpa.

Because, truth to tell, Grandpa wasn't exactly God's gift to mankind. A fake moustache was the only makeup he needed to play Stalin, and this physical resemblance must have reflected at least some commonality of character. Indeed Grandpa, to the best of his waning ability, tried to rule our family as relentlessly as his look-alike was ruling the country. At that time Stalin had about a year left to live, and Grandpa, a much younger man, was to outlive him by only three years. He spent that time in unemployment and artistic oblivion, as the demand for his speciality had gone down.

The room in which we all lived was registered in Grandpa's name, and hardly a day went by without him using that fact as leverage against my parents. At 22 by 18 feet, it was the largest room in the whole flat, and the neighbours resented that.

After my uncle and his wife had moved out, only the five of us lived there. That fortunately still kept us below the nine-metres-per-head limit. Beyond that limit families could be 'densified' – that is, made to share their quarters with any number of strangers it would have taken to bring their average area down to the prescribed level.

Muslin curtains hanging from rods placed some two feet below the ceiling sub-divided the room into three sections. My parents and I had the two smaller areas, my grandparents the largest one. We didn't gripe about this inequity because each of ours had a window, while theirs was lit at all times by a bulb shielded by a tasselled orange shade. Also, their area doubled as sitting room, dining room, Grandpa's study and my playroom.

We considered these conditions adequate, if not luxurious. The only trouble was that I was mildly tubercular, and Grandpa chain-smoked devilishly strong cardboard cigarettes, laying a permanent, orange-glowing smokescreen in the room. Doctors believed that was bad for me, and Mama pointed out this medical fact to her father on numerous occasions, and in rather elevated tones. But Grandpa replied reasonably that he only smoked in his own section. And even if he didn't the little shit would survive anyway.

This created a rift between Mama and Grandpa, and they weren't on speaking terms until Grandpa's final illness. Such detachment was a difficult thing to pull off when the warring parties lived in one, albeit sub-divided, room and had to share the dining table.

I remember vividly our meals after Grandma died. Mama and I would huddle at one corner of the table, eating milk soup, carrot patties and other delicacies prepared by Mama who had been conscious of the health aspects of food long before this became fashionable. Grandpa would sit opposite us, eating herring and fried potatoes washed down with an inevitable '100 grams' (the Russians have their own measurement units when it comes to vodka). Mama regarded his culinary tastes as the work of the Devil, but I rather liked his food, if not yet the beverage that accompanied it. The vivacity of the table talk rivalled that in a Trappist monastery canteen.

The ceiling leaked, and I liked to lie in my bed looking at the bluish water stains. Depending on the angle, and which eye I used, they looked like fairy-tale characters one second and Comrade Chapayev the next.

Vassiliy Ivanovich Chapayev, a legendary cavalry commander in the

Civil War, had his exploits immortalised in the film every Russian saw on average once a year. As the stains became larger, I could clearly see the hero's moustache, his fur cloak flying behind him, his fur hat rakishly aslant, his sabre ready to slice through yet another capitalist hireling. It was like watching clouds with their peculiar shapes, but better.

In my appreciation of the stained ceiling I was at odds with the rest of the family who, as grown-ups would, were more concerned with safety than aesthetics. Indeed, as the ceiling grew soggier, larger and larger pieces began to fall down, damaging the waxed parquet floor we all took turns polishing, and threatening to damage our skulls as well.

Eventually, constant appeals to the regional maintenance department, accompanied by letters to higher authorities, including Grandpa's *alter ego* in the Kremlin, had an effect. A crew of builders arrived, collected their advance and started drinking endless glasses of vodka. That was the Russians' answer to the ubiquitous cups of tea consumed by their English counterparts under similar circumstances.

Actually, the difference here is more important than the similarity. For though drinking tea delays work, it seldom renders it impossible; whereas downing several eight-ounce tumblers of rotgut inevitably has just such an effect. That's why Russians who are worldlier than we were never give builders and other handymen any vodka, or indeed any money with which vodka could be bought, until the work has been done.

In this case, the builders stayed lucid long enough to bring half the ceiling down, exposing the rafters running through the attic and the grinning faces of the local guttersnipes who used the attic as a community centre, pub and lavatory. After that the builders went on a week-long bender and didn't come back until another letter to the Kremlin. Meanwhile we slept with our clothes on – not only out of modesty but also because our ribbed radiators couldn't handle the heat exchange with the ice-cold attic.

All this drama was unfolding on the top floor of a Palladian house situated less than a mile from Red Square. The Conservatory was across one street and the Interior Ministry across another. Our building was constructed in the eighteenth century by the architect Kazakov as investment property for Count Menshikov, the grandson of Peter I's favourite. As these days it houses some kind of ministry, the building has been renovated, and its white columns look striking against the lurid background of its turquoise walls. Both were dirty-grey when I lived there, with large pieces of stucco fallen out and spidery cracks everywhere.

Before the revolution the flats used to be occupied by rich merchants and minor noblemen who wanted to be within fawning distance of the Kremlin. I think, however, that they lived no more than one family to a flat, which arrangement was still practised below us by the great actress Vera Pashennaya.

A much more successful thespian than my grandfather, she nonetheless was friendly to him and transferred those feelings on to me. In the good tradition of the Russian acting profession she'd try to teach me some of the essential vocabulary whenever she caught sight of Mama pushing my pram in the courtyard.

'What a lovely baby,' she'd intone in a rich baritone, 'is he Kudashev's grandson? What's his name? Sorry, dear, I'm no good at names. Coochy-coochy-coo, aren't you a gorgeous baby, who's a baby doll then, now say "Mama's a slag", say "Papa's a wanker…" '.

To Mama's horror I could reproduce some of those words with recognisable clarity at the precocious age of eight months. That reinforced Mama's belief that I was a genius and made her steer my pram away whenever Pashennaya's bulky frame emerged out of her limousine.

Much as I appreciated the tuition, I hated to reciprocate with the kisses she demanded because I didn't consider her pretty enough and refused to accept her, warts and all. To fend off unwelcome advances I once had to turn Pashennaya's lessons against her, telling her to 'kiss my arse' when she peeked into my pram. At that time I must have been all of two years old, which young age enabled me to escape punishment.

I wasn't so lucky when I tried, at the same age, to apply my newly acquired education at home where Grandma constantly pestered me with her 'open your darling mouth, close your darling eyes' attentions. That was irritating even though the pay-off would be a sweet or a tangerine section. Acting on a tip from my platonic friend Pashennaya, who was at the time hogging the headlines with her performance in *Too Clever By Half*, I once played the same trick on Grandma. But when she opened her mouth I spat into it, said 'you-u-u old bitch', and was then chased all over the flat by a belt-swinging Grandpa.

Grandpa's grip on the family seldom slackened. Only Papa was in a position to stand up to him when he was in town, but Grandpa's iron will easily overcame his son-in-law's physical superiority. I recall just one instance when Grandpa failed to have his way.

We used bedpans at night, especially in winter: it was too much bother to get dressed and stagger along the 20 yards of icy corridor to the loo that might be occupied anyway. One particularly cold night, when Papa was in town, he helped me onto the chamber pot. But, half asleep, he reversed the right and left boots as he put them on my feet. This didn't escape the attention of Grandpa who, ever the stickler for propriety, demanded immediate correction.

When Papa replied I wasn't walking anywhere and it was none of his business anyway, Grandpa tried to shove him aside and do the job himself. However, this one time, mutiny written all over his face, Papa pushed back. Grandpa appraised the situation and retreated, describing Papa's mother in the language I had already learned from my friend Pashennaya but had been told not to use.

The neighbours couldn't escape the pressure of Grandpa's authoritarian tendencies either. Once he didactically threw the Flustovs' kettle out of the kitchen window, explaining that there was no point in assigning the cooker rings if people ignored the assignments. Falling down from the third floor, the kettle could have caused a few headaches, but didn't because it landed on a flowerbed.

A month later Grandpa collared Col. Tranchuk, another neighbour, as the latter was veering out of the loo. Grandpa told him that if he, as a military man, couldn't improve his marksmanship to a point where half his piss didn't end up on the floor, at least he should have the good manners to wipe up after himself. Otherwise Grandpa would report him to his District Commander, General of the Army Moskalenko.

The accusation was only partly fair because the good colonel was rather neat by Russian standards and made a mess just twice a month, on paydays, when he'd drink a litre of vodka and get smashed. If you think drunken stupor is a figure of speech, you obviously never saw Col. Tranchuk on the first and sixteenth of every month, propped up against the kitchen wall at a 45-degree angle, in full regalia, eyes shut, standing to slanted attention for hours on end. (His wife, a real Gorgon, would deny him access to their room whenever he was drunk.) Still, as the rows of medals on his tunic showed, he was a man of courage, who only chose not to break the grip on his collar because of the catastrophic nature of Grandpa's threat.

It was such incidents that made the neighbours hate Grandpa even more than they loathed one another. That's why we felt duty-bound to consider all of them as potential suspects in the hideous attack that had left a wide clearing in the thicket of Grandpa's mane.

On second thoughts, one family could be ruled out. Yes, the Flustovs had borne a grudge against Grandpa since the kettle incident. But they, an enfeebled grandmother, frail mother and two adolescent sons, simply didn't have the physical wherewithal to do anything about it. But the remaining four families merited a closer look.

Take the Shapskys for example. True, Comrade Shapsky himself, an old Polish aristocrat, was past the age of violence, if not the age of romance. As I found out later, he was a photography buff who kept pestering my mother with elegantly old-fashioned advances: 'Nyutochka, I'd dearly love to photograph you in your delicious altogether, reclining in this à-la-devil-may-care fashion.' Knowing Mama, he probably didn't get anywhere.

Though violence wasn't quite his thing, he wasn't above petty larceny. Electrical engineer by trade, he took advantage of our system of paying electric bills. All the communal areas had a meter, and the tenants contributed in proportion to the number of people in their families. In addition, each room had its own meter, with each family settling its own bills.

Comrade Shapsky, displaying the hands-on ingenuity you'll seldom find in a nobleman, connected his private meter to the communal one, thus saving a fair chunk of his income every month. Besides ingenuity this feat must have required stealth. He would have had to work noiselessly in the middle of the night, tucking a wire under the wooden moulding on the wall and routing it a good 20 yards to the communal meter. Be that as it may, Comrade Shapsky had achieved his goal two years before I was born. The trick went undetected for 18 years, when the Tranchuks moved out and the Fotkins moved in.

Comrade Fotkin possessed a combination of qualities that proved to be Comrade Shapsky's undoing. First, he was an electrical engineer himself; second, he was a man of common birth and not at all averse to violence; third, he was in his prime and capable of swift action.

After barely a fortnight in the flat, he figured the scam out, kicked Shapsky's door down, grabbed the senescent aristocrat by the scruff of the neck, dragged him into the kitchen, silently pointed at the larcenous wire and smashed Comrade Shapsky's still handsome face into the wall. After that incident the electrical status quo was restored. And Comrades Shapsky and Fotkin were soon on speaking terms again, which attested to the former's all-forgiving, almost Tolstoyan nature.

Now Mrs Shapsky was something else again. Glaphira Nikolayevna was a schizophrenic who never talked to anybody and occasionally did odd things. Once she assumed the full Lotus position on top of her kitchen table and stayed there for 12 hours, swinging a slotted spatula rhythmically between her knees and never changing posture. And on another occasion she acted in a way that suggested she wasn't at all safe to have around.

There was no telephone in the adjacent flat, and a neighbour's 14-year-old daughter asked Mrs Shapsky's permission to use our communal phone in the corridor. Glaphira Nikolayevna nodded in her usual taciturn manner, then went to the kitchen and put a pot of water on the fire. As ours was the only phone for 22 people, a strict three-minute limit was observed on all calls. But since everybody else was off to work and Glaphira Nikolayevna never used the phone, the pesky teenager saw fit to overstep the limit by at least 10 minutes.

By that time Mrs Shapsky's water had come to a boil, and she expressed her indignation by carrying the pot into the corridor, sneaking up behind the girl and splashing the entire contents on her back. This retribution left permanent scars on the girl's back and Glaphira Nikolayevna's reputation. Ticking her as a possible, we moved on in our detective effort, going down the list of other suspects.

The Renners? Another possible. Comrade Renner, having been sacked from the KGB for excessive cruelty, had moved into the flat only a few months earlier by marrying Mrs Renner, the Official Resident.

Roman Renner was a wiry, bilious man with smouldering eyes who always wore a striped dressing gown and was addicted to tea. A bit of a misanthrope, he'd emerge out of his room only when he needed to boil some water. He'd then rush back, holding the red-hot kettle in front of him, and woe betide anyone who wasn't quick enough to flatten himself against the corridor wall. Many years later, when I had grown up and he had grown old, I stopped his progress with a shoulder-to-shoulder tackle, after which he at last became more considerate.

While hatred was the only emotion he evinced readily, he respected Grandpa for his spirited portrayals of Stalin, Comrade Renner's idol. In fact, peeking through his keyhole, I had once seen Grandpa's portrait in Stalin make-up on his wall. Thus pulling Grandpa's hair out probably would have constituted for Comrade Renner an act of *lèse-majesté*. This consideration may have disqualified him as a suspect but brought into sharp focus the issue of his wife.

Mrs Renner was known to us as Olga Volgina, the Gypsy singer, who practised her art by singing scales all day long in a voice that spanned the range from basso to contralto. Olga Ivanovna was short, yet so fat that she had to turn sideways when walking down the corridor. Her face looked like a glistening Calamata olive with sideburns and moustache, which in combination with massive mammaries made her what many Russians would describe as a handsome woman. No longer in the spring of her life, she had before marriage supplemented her income by subletting a corner in her smallish room to a procession of graduate students, mostly Georgians.

When I was old enough to be trusted with such facts, Mama explained to me the true nature of those arrangements. But meanwhile I had enjoyed a profitable relationship with the Georgians who admired me for speaking better Russian than they could (true) and being a genius of Renaissance proportions (false). As a token of respect, they regularly stuffed my pockets with tangerines, Turkish delight, khalva and, amazingly, fresh garlic shoots.

Now of course the Georgians were all gone, leaving in their wake bittersweet memories and at least one ruined reputation. In Mama's eyes a woman capable of debauched behaviour was capable of anything. But the only violent activity Mrs Renner had ever been involved in had featured her strictly on the receiving end. Thus she could probably be ruled out as a prime suspect, for the time being.

The Tranchuks? Now we were getting warm: they were the ones

who had perpetrated violence on Mrs Renner when she was still Miss Volgina. Comrade Tranchuk, the mingent colonel in the infantry, was an officer but, despite having graduated from the Soviet answer to Sandhurst, demonstrably not a gentleman. To keep things in balance, his wife wasn't a lady.

When two years earlier Mrs Tranchuk had found out that her husband had surrendered to Miss Volgina's sultry charms, she unleashed a thunderous offensive on him, choosing the communal kitchen as her battleground. Now, while tranquillity was by no means a normal state there, fisticuffs weren't an everyday event either. So the tenants welcomed the action as an interesting diversion and all came out to watch, while being careful not to be drawn in. They all knew the sage Russian proverb 'two square off, you piss off'.

The battle raged for several days, with the neighbours acting as observers and occasional referees. Throughout the internecine hostilities Comrade Volgina demurely stayed in her room, subsisting on tinned foods and using the bedpan that she emptied into the communal lavatory late at night.

Attack won the day. Not only did Col. Tranchuk realise the error of his ways, but he also showed willing by joining forces with his wife in a frontal assault on Comrade Volgina when olfactory discomfort had finally forced her out into the open.

As close-knit families tend to do, the couple worked well as a team. They drove Comrade Volgina into a corner, where she couldn't throw her weight around, and really worked her over, with the wife understandably landing the heavier punches. Comrade Volgina kept appealing to the neighbours present but succeeded only in eliciting humorous remarks based on her weight, loose morals and Gypsy origin.

This history of violent behaviour made the Tranchuks prime suspects, especially since Grandpa was Jewish. That was a problem in Madam Tranchuk's eyes. Though an atheist in good standing, she routinely referred to Jews as Christ killers, expressing heartfelt regrets that Hitler hadn't quite finished the job. Still, a suspicion needs *prima facie* evidence to become an accusation. In the absence of such the search had to continue.

The Doikos? The trail was getting scalding hot. Comrade Doiko was an Aeroflot navigator who only turned up in the flat for a few days every month. His dashing uniform and thick moustache appealed to me, as flying planes and shooting Germans down was one of my career aspirations at the time.

On his first day back home, Comrade Doiko would always get drunk early, go down to the courtyard and have his 10-year-old son point out those of his playmates who had offended the boy while Comrade Doiko had been up in the air. He'd then beat the little bullies with his fists. Since the offenders were rarely older than 13 or so, and Mr Doiko, at 5'10" or so, towered over everyone in the building, the fights were one-sided. But the odds usually swung the other way when the little rascals' fathers got into the act. To his credit Comrade Doiko would take his lumps like a man, even when being kicked into a snivelling defeat.

In short, one could observe a violent streak there somewhere. But on that fateful evening Comrade Doiko was out of town, flying a milk run from Moscow to Kursk. This alibi may have exculpated him personally but not the rest of his family, especially not his wife.

Margarita Doiko, Ritka for short, could probably take her husband in a fair fight. Imagine a sturdy Amazon, both breasts emphatically intact, with unevenly bleached hair and pounds of makeup constantly running down her thickly powdered masculine face, and you'll know what Mrs Doiko looked like.

What you won't know, and neither did Mr Doiko, is that in his absence she divided her time between orgies and mayhem. The first time I ever heard the word 'orgy' was when I overheard Mama talking to the cops about Mrs Doiko's noisy escapades of the night before. At that time I thought 'orgy' was all about drinking and fighting, and couldn't understand what the big deal was. Didn't everybody drink and fight?

This is the first but by no means last time that you'll see me mention orgies. I'd venture a guess that at least half of the sexual experience urban Russians accumulated by the time they got married involved more than one couple in the same room, often in the same bed. Under those conditions, it would have taken a latter-day St Anthony, or else Joseph rejecting the pharaoh's wife, to limit one's attentions to one's own date. And few people resemble the nicer historic personages. A certain amount of cross-pollination inevitably followed and, to many, any other form of sex began to appear dull, uneventful and almost perverse after a while. In fact, I knew several men who could function sexually only in the presence of their friends and their 'cadres', our slang for dates.

A friend of mine experienced that problem on his wedding night, the first night he had ever spent with a woman alone. In the morning he phoned everyone he knew with the same plea: 'Please, old chap, please? Just for a couple of nights, eh? You don't even have to bring your own cadre, the wife will organise a couple of girlfriends. Listen, I have three workbenches [beds or sofas, in our parlance] and I can't get it up for the bitch [his bride] without you lot, the old gang.'

If you think that this form of romantic collectivism bespoke innate depravity, perhaps you're right to some extent. But to a much greater extent, it reflected an inhuman residential crisis.

With young people seldom having as much as a room, never mind a flat, they could call their own, the question of 'where?' loomed much larger than 'whom'. Also, one wasn't allowed to check into a hotel in one's own city (a residence permit was stamped on the internal passport without which no one could be admitted to a hotel). That's why a youngster whose parents, or for that matter spouse, were away for a few days or even hours, was under heavy peer pressure to share the quarters with friends.

Usually those occasions came up on short notice, and dates had to be found instantly. Hence the black books all Moscow males carried and filled with names that had to do more with hope than expectation. They would then leaf through them feverishly, trying to line up a girl and as many of her friends as she could find for that very night. And hence the rather low grade of the human material one often found at such unplanned parties, as nice girls from good families were seldom available for orgies on an hour's notice.

Ritka, if her face was anything to go by, had a heavy dose of testosterone coursing through her veins, and so was hormonally committed to sharing her room with friends whenever her husband was snowed in somewhere like Murmansk. But that was the least of her problems, or rather the problems we had with her. For Ritka treated the communal kitchen, lavatory and bathroom as her own bailiwick.

Take the loo, for example. Its usage was as strictly rationed as the telephone's, with the same three minutes acting as the allowance, especially in the morning when at least a dozen tenants with full bladders queued outside, some hopping in place, all banging on the door. Ritka paid as much attention to the time allowance as Comrade Stalin did to pleas for mercy. She stayed in as long as her bowels moved her, responding to loud protests by breaking wind contemptuously.

And if you think that was bad, wait till you hear this. Each family had its own detachable seat hanging on the loo wall when not in use. Although each seat prominently displayed a DO NOT TAKE!!! sign, the Amazon invariably took somebody else's seat. Not only that, but she often abused it in the manner of many Russians who, for hygienic reasons, refuse to sit on the seat and instead stand on it and squat down, often creating ballistic mishaps. Whenever this unacceptable behaviour was tactfully brought to Ritka's attention, she'd respond either with violence or with invective that was vile even by Russian standards.

Same with the bathroom. Each of the six families was entitled to one bathing day a week, with Sunday free for all. On any other than their own bathing day the tenants were allowed to wash their hands – and that was it. To her credit, Ritka never abused the bathroom as she did the adjacent facility, since she never took a bath on somebody else's day and seldom on her own. But her reaction to trespassers was ferocious.

Whenever somebody, especially a woman, sneaked into the bathroom on Ritka's day, her inner countdown button would be pushed. The Amazon, displaying the patience of a born stalker, would wait as long as it took for her prey to undress, get under the shower and soap herself.

She'd then turn off the bathroom light (the switch was outside) and cut off the hot water by shutting a valve on the pipe that ran along the corridor, making it perpetually damp. The combined effect of near-freezing water and darkness would make the violator rush out of the bathroom, clutching a skimpy towel to her breasts, leaving lathery trails on the floor and screaming bloody murder.

That is exactly what almost happened to a dripping Mrs Flustov once, when Ritka grabbed a flat iron off the ring and threw it at her. The red-hot projectile missed, which fact was later pointed out to Mrs Flustov by the yawning cops as they were reluctantly taking down her complaint. In short, if Ritka wasn't a suspect, I don't know who was.

Please don't get the impression that we went through this analysis step by logical step, as we stood in the middle of the kitchen riveted to grandpa's pointing finger. We didn't. Rather, all this information zapped through our minds in a kaleidoscopic fashion. Papa, displaying his version of English pragmatism, was the one to break the suspense with the question 'Who?', posed in a matter-of-fact manner.

Grandpa was satisfied that he had milked the dramatic potential of the situation for all it was worth. 'The ssslut,' he hissed in a stage whisper that could be heard fifty yards away. 'That slut Ritka'.

So it was Mrs Doiko after all. Well, this time the licentious Amazon had gone too far. All right, Grandpa might have called her a whore once or twice in response to some catty remark. Russians seldom look upon an exchange of epithets as *casus belli*, and you can routinely overhear seven-year-olds describe their elders in terms that would suggest intimate familiarity with deviant sexual practices.

Violence is a different matter, as it frequently escalates to mutilation and murder – this even without firearms being available. That's why most Russians will go to any length to discourage physical assault, even if it means pre-emptive action with bricks, sections of lead pipe or whatever else may be handy. I'm not talking here about warding off life-threatening attacks but, let's say, one boy slapping another in the schoolyard. I was such a boy, so I know.

One day I was playing with some friends in the courtyard outside our block of flats, when a local bully, a boy perhaps two years my senior, took exception to the shape of my nose. So he broke it with one punch and knocked me out flat with another, expertly aimed just under the ear. When I came to, my friends were around me, helping me up. There were half a dozen of them. They had the numbers on the bully and could have interceded on my behalf – but didn't because so far I had done nothing to earn their respect.

In a Moscow courtyard one didn't earn respect by listening to *St Matthew's Passion* or reading *War and Peace*. One earned it by showing heart. In other words, by fighting – win, lose or draw. The more 'intelligentsia' one was in appearance and demeanour, the less one could survive without the respect of those urchins – because without their respect one couldn't walk the streets unless escorted by an adult. Without their respect one might as well be dead.

By age 12 I had learned all that the hard way, which is why I didn't do what came naturally – cry – but did something that required a conscious decision, a hard choice. I picked up a piece of brick off the ground and, choking on my own blood, walked up to the bully from behind. He was chatting with a couple of his friends and didn't see me come up on his blind side. His friends did but, not wanting to miss a good show, chose not to warn their mate. Without making a sound, I hit him on the back of the head with the brick, hoping to put him down and gain myself some time to walk away with dignity. But the blow wasn't hard enough and though it broke the skin on his scalp and drew a lot of blood, as scalp wounds do, it didn't slow him down.

Dignity was no longer a concern; speed was. I ran as fast as I could towards my friends, knowing the enraged bully was gaining on me, hoping I had done enough to earn my friends' respect and merit their assistance. Apparently I had because, as the bully caught up with me, Seryozha Frolov, a tenacious little bulldog, jumped on his back, hooking his arm around the bully's throat. The rest of us went into him in a heap, and we had a minute's kicking time until the bully's reinforcements arrived and we fled.

Grandpa acted in essentially the same spirit, if not the same sanguinary fashion, in response to Ritka's assault. The remaining four years of his life were devoted to retribution, which, the mature adult that he was, he sought in the governmental arena rather than in the asphalt-clad courtyard of my childhood.

For once, the tenants stood united: Grandpa must have done enough to earn their respect, and Ritka enough to earn their lasting animosity. In addition to their other sterling qualities, our neighbours were born snitches, and anyway one didn't have to be a KGB detective to collect compromising material on someone like Ritka.

What resulted from this combined effort was weekly reports on Ritka's debauchery and hooliganism. These were compiled and forwarded to the Regional Prosecutor's office, which was responsible not only for law enforcement but also for upholding the high moral standards expected from Soviet citizens. Each conflict with a tenant was likewise documented, and finally the Prosecutor had to act.

By his decree, Ritka Doiko was evicted from the flat, even though her family wasn't. But since the protracted litigation had uncovered some of the juicier details of her behaviour, Comrade Doiko felt called upon to divorce his wayward wife and stay in the flat.

Shortly after his victory, Grandpa came down with thrombophlebitis. Our family doctor, armed with all the advances of Soviet medical science, which the papers said led the world by a wide margin, applied a dozen leeches to his legs and told him to stay in bed for two days. No sooner had the doctor left than Grandpa cursed, said he wouldn't be confined to bed by those little suckers, tore the leeches off and got up abruptly. A clot broke loose, hit his heart, and Grandpa died on the spot.

We grieved, but the neighbours didn't. Except perhaps Comrade Renner who, looking for ammunition in yet another kitchen squabble, said to Mama she sure had a big mouth for someone who had murdered her father. Mama shrieked, putting the trumpets of Jericho to shame. Papa, who couldn't stand hostility of any kind, stuck his index fingers into his ears; I laughed; life went on.

2

At this point, my memory goes into the fast-forward mode, at least as far as the flat is concerned. Perhaps it's because no real drama occurred there for quite a few years after Grandpa died, and for one's memory to moor at a certain point in the past there has to be an anchor of some sort.

One such anchor dropped when I was almost sixteen. At that mature age I craved social acceptability, which in Russia is impossible for a young man to attain without getting violently drunk at least twice a week. In my case it had to be more often that that, for I had to overcome the social stigma of being 'intelligentsia', 'intel' for short, in the eyes of some of my peers, and 'the animal' in the eyes of some others.

Penelope, my English wife, claims that it was precisely this unlikely combination of qualities that attracted her but, if true, that happened 20 years later. At sixteen or so, contradictions in my personality effectively meant not fitting in anywhere, a virtual ostracism. The saving grace came from booze, for both groups, those who despised the wimpish intellectual and those who looked down upon the animal, drank like fish.

That lit up a clear path to social advancement, as all I had to do to be accepted was to drink like a still bigger fish, I'll see your snapper and raise you turbot, I'll see your swordfish and raise you Mako shark. This I achieved at some cost to my health and to the dismay of my poor mother who didn't approve of any deviation from the strict moral code to which all Kudashevs adhere like zealots. Unfortunately, their absolutist zealotry was mixed in my blood stream with the relativist laxity of the Boots. As a result I would go on relativist binges and occasionally pass out in public lavatories or on park benches in broad daylight – only to wake up to absolutist repentance and nausea that would come on faster than you could say Manichean duality.

Drinking in Russia deserves, and in due course will receive, a separate chapter. But since we are talking about social acceptability, it's important to note straight away that it wasn't just how much, but what and in what way one drank that mattered. The redemptive arrival of the consumer age was somehow being delayed throughout my childhood, and the acceptable urban middle-class booze included vodka (Stolichnaya for 3.07 roubles a half-litre bottle, Moskovskaya for 2.87), brandy (Armenian or Georgian 3-star for 4.12) and vile fortified wine named, as the spirit moved the manufacturers, port, cahor or jeres, all costing around 1.40 and bearing just enough resemblance to their illustrious namesakes to turn one off fortified wine for life.

The demographic disclaimer is necessary here because the rural population drank moonshine almost exclusively, while urban lower classes seldom elevated their consumption above 'white wine', which in their parlance was the cheapest vodka available, and 'red wine', which meant the vilest port going. These represented the upper limit of their beverages but not the lowest, which plunged into the area of liquids not manifestly designed for human consumption, such as floor varnish, methanol, antifreeze, cologne, deodorants and other arcana.

Benny Yerofeev, the late poet of Russian dipsomania, remarked correctly that while few people in Russia know what Pushkin died of, everybody knows how to prepare floor varnish for drinking. I hope you won't find it patronising if I divulge the secret to the uninitiated: you take a three-gallon bucket of floor varnish and empty a four-pound bag of salt into it. The salt will form a blob that will start sinking to the bottom through the dense liquid. As it sinks, the blob will get heavier with the oils, ethers and other impurities it has absorbed and dragged down to the bottom. In about four hours you will be left with a brownish liquid, which would be unlikely to cause any sleepless nights to the makers of Lagavulin and Remy Martin, but which can be drunk with relative impunity, at least in the short term.

Since I was definitely urban middle class, I stuck to regulation booze that, as etiquette would have it, was supposed to be consumed either from eight-ounce tumblers in one daring gulp or straight 'from the neck'. As a concession to one's wimpish origin one would have been allowed to empty the bottle in several pulls.

At the time I am talking about I once came home blissfully inebriated. To my poor mother this was a sight as repugnant – and frequent – as the Torah being stomped into the ground would have been to an Eastern European rabbi. Unlike the ecclesiastical gentleman, however, Mama usually responded to such instances with somewhat hysterical violence. As she did this time, attacking me with the gusto, if not the skill, of a middleweight boxer going after his prey.

That seemed hilarious to me, so I bobbed and weaved on shaky legs, laughing my head off. Doing so many things at the same time proved to be too taxing for a boy with a couple of bottles of chemically derived plonk under his belt. I fell down and just lay there supine, rocking with laughter. It's the laughter that must have really made her see red.

Mama grabbed a hatchet, which we had lying about even though no one had ever used it before for any domestic purpose, and took a violent backswing. She wouldn't have hit me in a million years, but I suppose she needed the backswing to register mandatory opprobrium. Unfortunately for all of us, Papa, who abhorred things loud and hysterical, was bringing up the rear, hoping no doubt to prevent some of the worse excesses. That conciliatory stance put him in an ideal position to catch the blunt end of the hatchet right in the middle of his mirror-like pate. We've already discussed the sanguinary potential of scalp wounds; and on bald heads they have an even greater visual effect.

Papa reacted with his usual stoicism. He wiped the blood off his head, quietly packed a small case, whispered he had had enough of this madhouse and walked out. I can't tell you what happened next because I passed out. But when I woke up the next morning, he wasn't there and Mama was in tears. Papa had vanished without a trace, and over the next few days we knew nothing about his whereabouts and couldn't even talk to him on the phone because his secretary said he wasn't there. Now much as I loved my father, he would have been perfectly capable of disappearing for ever – not out of heartlessness but rather out of his innate distaste for conflicts. In Russia, however, it's not so easy to disappear, not with millions of enthusiastic snitches ever ready to turn the fugitive in to the KGB or, even worse, his deserted wife.

Papa hadn't stayed on the out for more than a week when the well-wishers' network went into action, clasping chain links together until the last link led to the Smirnoffs, our neighbours from the flat down below. Mrs Smirnoff, whose daughter was a member of the celebrated harp quartet, sought out Mama and offered the following information: first, Papa was alive and well, which was the good news; second, he had moved in with a woman by whom he already had a five-year-old son; third, the woman was his co-worker, a Doctor of Science who loved Papa to distraction. Fourth, and most important, Mrs Smirnoff proffered the woman's name, patronymic and telephone number.

Much as I would like to say that Mrs Smirnoff's motives were noble, springing from love of truth or something as praiseworthy, one suspects she was driven by sheer viciousness and eager anticipation of a good show. That she got, for Mama wouldn't take the matter lying down. Instead she began to attack the poacher telephonically, the problem being that the only telephone she had access to hung on the wall of our corridor, within earshot of the snooping neighbours.

The situation clearly didn't call for circumlocution, but looking back I still think Mama went a bit too far. She would start in a very reasonable, almost placid way: 'Is this where Lenka [contemptuous name for Elena] is residing?' The woman would instantly understand what was what, but would still respond with dignity: 'Not Lenka, but Elena Alexandrovna. This is she.' Dignity was, in Mama's opinion, the last thing she was entitled to, and she wouldn't let her get away with it. 'Elena Alexandrovna, eh? You're no Elena Alexandrovna, bitch. You are a slut! You're a slag! Your mother's a whore!'

Since Mama was unaccustomed to such language, she used the polite *vous* form throughout, rather than the idiomatically appropriate *tu*. Partly because of that stylistic incongruity, I would roll on the floor with laughter while the neighbours would suddenly develop compassion for Mama and decide to help her as best they could.

They would all poke their heads out into the corridor, and when Mama's reserve of Russian argot was running thin, begin to prompt her with vile expressions that they handled with consummate mastery. Mme Flustov: 'Tell her, screw you in the mouth.' Comrade Renner, who by then had withdrawn murder accusations: 'Tell her, I'll rip your arse inside out.' Col. Tranchuk, trained in inspiring troops with rousing pep talk: 'Tell her, I'll pull your twat over your ears.' Comrade Shapsky, true to his noble birth: 'Tell her, she's a philistine.'

It's a measure of Mama's desperation that she would repeat all the suggestions dutifully, including the last one, and the somewhat one-sided conversation would continue for rather a long time, perhaps half an hour at a time. 'Don't you dare hang up!' Mama would pre-empt precipitate if logical action, and Elena Alexandrovna, dignity long since gone, wouldn't dare hang up, listening instead to a detailed description of the perverse reproductive practices Mama would like to perpetrate upon her, her brat and every relation she had ever had in the past or was ever likely to have in the future. With the neighbours happy to forgo the three-minute time limit for the entertainment value, Mama's language would be getting more and more baroque. Papa would stay on the sideline throughout, obviously weighing his departure in the balance and finding it wanting.

A month later he was back in the fold, tail between his legs. The official reason for his return was that he couldn't live without us after all, because we were part of his own body and soul. The unofficial, but obviously truer, version was divulged to me over a glass of beer: 'I realised I couldn't have any life there worth speaking of. Your mother was calling every night, effing and blinding, bugger this, screw that, all sorts of stupid things. I didn't even realise she knew expressions like that. I mean, even I don't know some of them, and I've been in the army. So I figured, what the hell, might as well go back. Sorry about that whole thing, but I thought you always wanted to have a little brother.'

Quite apart from the cynicism of this last remark, he was wrong. I never wanted to have brothers or sisters, realising that there was only so much love to go around in our family. So I said, 'Papa, you're wrong. I mean, even if I did want a brother, it wouldn't be a bastard you spawn on the side. In fact, to prove the point to you, I never want to see that brat in my life.' I stuck to that pathetic resolution for many years, which is more than I can say for some of the worthier resolutions long since forgotten, and only met and befriended my half-brother when Papa was on his deathbed.

What Papa didn't know was that I had saved him from a fate worse than a torrent of invective interfering with his domestic tranquillity. For in between two one-sided telephone conversations, Mama had sat down and written a long letter to Papa's boss, the minister (the same Dudorov, Papa's lifelong patron, who by then had fallen off the high perch of the Interior Ministry and been demoted to a less visible ministerial post). 'Letter', actually, is a wrong way to describe it; it was a straight garden-variety denunciation, describing Papa's shenanigans in excruciating detail and pointing out that his licentiousness and polygamy ill-behoved a Soviet man in a position of responsibility.

As a simon-pure child of the thirties Mama thought there was nothing wrong with denunciations. We were all in the same ranks, marching firmly to the glorious future, she had been taught, and any deviation, sexual or political, that made us break step was morally wrong in that it delayed the advent of the glorious global future. Denouncing the violator to the authorities might destroy his life, but this life wouldn't be wasted as it would have served its purpose as a stepping-stone of historical inevitability.

This sounds deranged, I know, but those people in my parents' generation who didn't think this kind of drivel made sense all died horrible deaths. Those who survived either toed the line or at least made a damn good show pretending they did. Thus, as a citizen of the beacon to all progressive mankind, Mama acted properly and in character. Where she made a mistake was in seeking my advice in the matter of style.

This I proffered with alacrity, pointing out that 'polygamy' meant having more than one wife at the same time; and even though Mama was Papa's fourth wife, he married them all consecutively and not simultaneously. As far as licentiousness went, I brightened Mama's narrative with a few graphic details and volunteered to post the letter. I then dropped it in the nearest dustbin, thus saving Papa his job and myself from having to work my way through university.

And speaking of university, my last coherent memory of the flat has to do with the party to celebrate my admission to an institution of higher learning that specialised in foreign languages.

It certainly was worth a celebration. In Russia, one had to pass entrance exams to be admitted. Depending on the university, there would be four or five exams altogether, sometimes even six. Each exam was scored on a five-point scale, with five being the highest mark and three the lowest (these days they use a different scoring system, but the principle is the same). Anything below three was not a passing grade, and the recipient of it was out of the competition until the next year.

If this abject failure happened to be a boy, he was in trouble. The usual school-leaving age in Russia was 17, the conscription age, 18, but university students were exempt. That meant a boy had just one whack at it, and if he failed he went straight into the army for three years. Considering that the suicide rate in the Russian army was higher than that of Sweden, a fellow paragon of socialist virtue, every point won or lost in an exam took on a monumental significance.

The combined score required for admission was established on the basis of the number of aspirants. In the year I was reaching for the brass ring, our university had something like 15 aspirants per available seat, which accounted for stiff competition and set the passing score at 19 out of 20. In English terms, this meant getting no less than three As and one B out of four exams, a difficult but by no means unachievable task, you may say – and you'd be right.

That is, you would be right if I were describing a place in which socialism hadn't yet emerged quite so comprehensively victorious as in Russia. There, a certain unwritten, or at least unpublished, quotient was applied to each applicant's score. For instance, a member of the local YCL (Young Communist League) committee was in automatically unless he failed an exam outright, and every effort was made to make sure he wouldn't do so no matter how hard he tried. The same went for any YCL member in good standing, which essentially meant a little shit who reported on his classmates to the authorities.

That activity laid a solid foundation for the personal file that floated from school to school and then from one workplace to another, documenting our lives from the age of eight or so till the moment we died. The first contributions to one's file were inevitably made by one's snitching classmates, and surely those devoted patriots rated preferential treatment.

A demobilised soldier could safely assume that in his case at least three points would be knocked off the official passing score. An aspirant with at least two years' work experience could count on minus two points. A member of one of the better ethnic minorities, a Kazakh, let's say, or perhaps an Adzharian, ditto – even if his Russian was a bit shaky, as it often was.

The zero-sum law would suggest that this kind of privilege would be counterbalanced by discrimination against less fortunate groups. And true enough, while being bad economics, zero sum operated very well in Russian universities. The unfortunate groups were, in that order, members of the undesirable ethnic minorities (Jews mostly, but also Tartars and Germans), non-YCL members, and people whose parents had done time for political offences. These unfortunates usually had to score at least a point over the passing score, sometimes two.

Now if you are any good at maths, you're likely to say, 'Right – if the passing score is 19, obviously anybody who scores 20 out of four exams has to be admitted, because it's impossible to go any higher'. That's perfect Aristotelian reasoning, except that in Russia one can take an unabridged volume of *Logic*, fold it five ways and put it where the sun doesn't shine. You forget what computer experts call the human factor. In this case you forget that examination boards were made up of people highly trained not only in their subjects but also in examination techniques. Part of their art was to make sure that the wrong kind of applicants never gave the right kind of answers, and they practised that art ad absurdum.

One instance springs to mind. A friend of mine, a son of a Turkish communist exiled to Moscow, was taking an entrance exam in the Turkish language at the Institute of Foreign Relations, one of the most desirable and prestigious places around. He was completely bilingual in Turkish and Russian, which meant his Turkish was quite a bit better than his examiners' – and yet he failed. I mean he didn't just get a four – he failed. The authorities were so anxious to bar a 'blackarse' (the affectionate term the Russians use to describe anyone born south of Kiev) from becoming a Soviet diplomat that they couldn't even wait until the exam in Russian composition where their action would have been more plausible if no less reprehensible.

Incidentally, a few years ago I read Zhirinovsky's autobiography and checked his experiences against my own. The future leader of Russia's loony-fringe right entered the Institute of Oriental Languages the year before I entered my university, and according to him the competition was a meagre three aspirants per seat, which effectively meant one was in if one hadn't failed any exams outright.

With all humility and respect, I have to say he is lying through his teeth. The Institute of Oriental Languages was a nomenclatura set-up, one of perhaps half a dozen Moscow universities where an aspirant needed a letter of recommendation from his local YCL Committee for his application even to be considered. In all such institutions there were two clearly demarcated streams of applicants: those who had already acquired work experience as KGB stoolies, and those who hadn't.

Zhirinovsky is right in saying that those in the former group, of whom he clearly was one, had rather lenient conditions of entry. But the poor yokels who had done enough to rate the magic letter, but not enough to get a seeding, had to compete in an open draw, where the competition was at least 20 per seat, which meant nothing less than straight fives was acceptable.

Unlike Comrade Zhirinovsky I was out before I came to bat because I already had three strikes against me, to use a term from American baseball: as a lad of largely Jewish ethnicity, I was a member of the least desirable minority; I was not a YCL member at all, never mind one in good standing; and my father had been exiled for a number of years for having been a POW during the war.

Now if you were to decide I needn't have bothered to apply, you would display sound reason. But Thomas Aquinas postulated that while reason is an important cognitive tool, it can get you only so far. Correction: in Russia, it can get you nowhere. For in the face of state oppression private enterprise tends to find loopholes. British subjects flee whenever – or soon after – a Labour government takes over. Americans hire crooked accountants whenever yet another war on poverty is declared. Dutchmen buy return tickets to Liechtenstein or Luxembourg on paydays. Russians bribe.

A bribe – or exchange of favours – was the starting point of most transactions at the time, including those not ostensibly replete with commercial potential. That system is still there, except that the bribes are now larger and denominated in different currencies. Also, they are not these days needed to buy things like clothes or food, which was the case when I lived in Russia.

For example, when looking for a pair of shoes, I would go to a shop, cast a scanning glance at the empty counters and then talk to a salesclerk. 'I'm looking for something, you know…' 'Yes,' he would commiserate, 'I understand, but with supplies being what they are…' 'Still,' I'd half-whisper in a conspiratorial fashion, taking a leaf out of Papa's book, 'if you could help me, I'd be grateful. Very grateful.'

That degree of gratitude usually meant a 50-percent surcharge on the official price. The salesman would take a long, penetrating look at my face, trying to determine whether I was the kind of charitable person who could find an appropriate amount of gratitude in his heart. If he was satisfied with the examination, he'd ask me what my size was, then disappear for ten minutes or so and come back with a dusty box of something wearable.

Law enforcement wasn't off-limits either. As any Russian driver can tell you, these days any traffic violation, including one resulting in injury or death, can be swept under the carpet for a price. If that's indeed the case, then the cops today are merely developing a rich tradition.

Once, I remember, I went for a ride in the country with my distant relation, a small-time racketeer who wanted company on his away trip to pick up some contraband. On the way back he was stopped for speeding, and the cop asked him what he had in his boot. To my horror, my relation was completely at ease. 'Oh, about 20 pairs of blue jeans,' he said. 'And you know what? One pair is for you.'

That's it, I thought, as various GULAG visions flashed through my mind. Now not only would I be arrested as accessory to black-marketeering, but there would be an additional charge of bribing a policeman. These fears turned out to be unfounded. The cop greedily rummaged through the boot, selected three pairs that looked roughly his size and went behind the bushes to try them on. A few minutes later, and a pair of Levis lighter, we were on our way.

In an even more interesting development, my neighbour the cab driver once picked up a drunk Georgian fare. Instead of giving a normal destination, the jaded son of the Caucasus offered my neighbour 200 roubles to drive him through Red Square. Now what you have to understand is that to say Red Square was pedestrianised means to say nothing.

This Soviet holy of holies had every access to it vigilantly guarded by policemen, lest an intruder might disturb the inner peace of the folk behind the Kremlin wall. When a Kremlin denizen was about to leave the Spassky Gate in his limousine, the square would have been cleared of pedestrians twenty minutes in advance. During the changing of the guard at the Lenin mausoleum, all life had to come to a standstill. In short, driving an unauthorised vehicle through the square was akin to relieving oneself on the relics of St James at Santiago de Compostela, but the consequences of the sacrilege would have been immeasurably harsher.

Nonetheless, 200 roubles was a princely sum, so the cabbie took on the task. Without slowing down he drove past a furiously whistling policeman onto the sainted cobblestones, zipped through the square, collected his reward, dropped the happy Georgian at the other end, then turned around and drove back to confront the gleefully awaiting cop. Before the latter could have described in detail the punishment to be meted out, my neighbour explained the situation and gave the cop 50 roubles. 'Your share,' he said. The policeman beamed from ear to ear. 'Listen, brother,' he said. 'You can drive through any time you like. Just make sure I'm the one on duty.'

Papa played the baksheesh system considerably better than Alfred Brendel plays the piano, but the trick was in finding someone in a position of influence to bribe. Had I decided to read chemistry or a related subject, it would have been no problem, what with my uncle a member of the USSR Academy of Sciences and my father quite well known in that industry. But languages? Who the hell did we know in languages? No one, as it turned out. But it just so happened that Papa's old girlfriend knew this chap, a medical doctor of sorts, who serendipitously was head of the outpatient clinic at the very university I wished to enter.

Did he 'take'? Of course he bloody well took; what did you expect the poor chap to do, live on 175 roubles a month? A contact was made, and after playing hard to get for three seconds or so, Dr Palatnikov agreed to mastermind my ascent to the ranks of the Academe for the very reasonable sum of 500 roubles, about Papa's monthly salary. For that paltry remuneration, and believe him, he was only asking for so little out of a genuine desire to help an obviously worthy young man, Dr Palatnikov agreed to act in the capacity of general contractor, wherein he would undertake to establish a confidential contact between Papa and the appropriate examiners, with whom Papa could then make separate arrangements. Dr Palatnikov didn't think the separate arrangements would go over 200 a pop, unless of course those thieves had upped their fees from last year, which he wouldn't put past them.

As we found out later, the thieves not only hadn't upped their fees from last year but actually had to kick half of them back Dr Palatnikov's way. The latter's professional credentials might have been weak but, as often was the case in Russia, he had more real power than his official status would suggest, since it was up to him to decide how many sick days professors were allowed to take, and how many free holiday vouchers they were entitled to receive. Power in Russia, as you'll have plenty of opportunity to see, doesn't derive from money or position; it's roughly the other way around.

The 1,300 roubles Papa had to pay in total went not only towards offsetting the imperfection of my CV but also towards covering my nonexistent academic attainments. My English, though decent, was certainly not up to the highest standards; my literature was weak in formal terms, even though I had been a voracious reader for 13 years; my history of the Communist Party was frankly pathetic, and my really strong subjects, drinking, carousing and hustling chess, cards and pool cut no ice with the examination board.

Making up the deficiency of my training in the month remaining before the first exam was a clear impossibility; the prospect of spending a month pestering girls in the street and drinking with my best friend Volodia Anikeyev was a sheer joy. So while other applicants were buried in textbooks I placed implicit faith in Dr Palatnikov's organisational talent and was buried in things that offered greater tactile delights, if less enlightenment.

The good doctor delivered, thus proving yet again that vice can always triumph over virtue, at least in this world. While my performance at three out of four exams was surprisingly not bad, meriting at least a four, if not necessarily the straight fives I did receive, it was the oral exam in Russian literature that made me appreciate fully Dr Palatnikov's clout within the academic hierarchy.

Though widely read in the Russian classics, I was a bit of a dilettante, in that I knew only what I liked and, more to the point, didn't know what I hated. As the luck of the draw would have it, the book whose literary and social significance I was expected to enlarge upon was Gorky's *The Life of Klim Samgin*. That I hadn't read the book was, in Russian parlance, 'half the trouble'; but the fact that I didn't have the vaguest idea of what the book was about spelled trouble with a capital T, as I wasn't even in a position to cover my ignorance with the smokescreen of verbiage.

This sad state of affairs became obvious to the examiner, a mousy little woman in steel-rimmed glasses, after 10 seconds of my incoherent mumbling. 'All right, young man,' she said, 'it's obvious you need some help. The Life of Klim Samgin is a what? Starts with an N?' 'A novel!' I exclaimed, happy to be engaged in some kind of dialogue. 'Good, good, good,' she said contemptuously and took her glasses off. 'Now what kind of novel is it?' she asked, squinting myopically. 'Starts with an E.' 'Epistolary !' I was on a roll, but her contempt for me deepened perceptibly. 'No, no, no, have another go.' 'Enigmatic? Effervescent? Ephemeral?' Desperation was setting in.

'Listen, young man,' my torturer said. 'I have neither the time nor the inclination to go over the entire vocabulary of the Russian language you possess. That might keep us here for an hour. I'll give you another clue. The second letter is a P.' 'Eponymous… Epic!' I exclaimed in a flash of revelatory zeal. 'Excellent!' she smiled, which almost made her look like a woman. 'Now tell me frankly,' she glanced at the examination sheet, 'Boot. Have you read the book?'

You know how it is. At some point a man must recover his honour at whatever cost. Honour can under certain circumstances be more valuable than life, which explains the charge of the Light Brigade and my answer to the mousy creature's question. 'No, I haven't,' I said. 'And I can promise you that I will never in my whole life read, whatever the provocation, anything produced by that crushing bore Gorky.' 'A literary critic, are we?' the woman became sarcastic again. 'Dismissed!' An English sergeant major would have a lot to learn from a Soviet professor.

I walked out into the hall, where Anikeyev was waiting for me or, to put it more precisely, for the drink I had promised to buy him if he stuck around. 'How did it go, old man?' Only noonish, but his speech was already slurred.

I replied with an obscene Russian colloquialism that can be roughly translated as 'I don't think I did at all well, actually.' 'Oh, well,' said Anikeyev who had just been expelled from our night school for drink-induced absenteeism, 'those are the breaks. How about Palatnikov though? The last-ditch man?' 'Listen,' I said, 'if the old bastard delivers on this one, I'll lose whatever illusions of justice I have.' 'If you have any left,' said Anikeyev affectionately, 'you're even a bigger arsehole than I thought you were.'

Ten minutes later, a man with a Chaliapin-quality basso announced the results: 'Avilova, 4; Astafiev, 3; Astakhov, failed; Batyuk 4; Bauman, failed; Bolin, failed; Boot, 5...' – and my faith in justice was for ever lost, a small price to pay for guaranteed admission to one of Moscow's better institutes.

Clearly a celebration was in order, or at least that was how Anikeyev summed up the situation. My parents concurred and, elated as they were, agreed to disappear 'to let the young people have a little fun', especially since it was also my seventeenth birthday.

The young people in question knew of only one kind of fun, namely getting drunk and then passing girls around as if they were pipes of peace, but my parents really thought that now I was being launched on an academic career, the occasion itself would impose a certain discipline and a tone of solemn restraint. They couldn't have been more wrong, as was clear to us from the very beginning and became even clearer in the planning stage. Mama had graciously agreed to cook 'something nice and healthy', which meant a few salads and the kind of main course the NHS would have endorsed had we fallen under its jurisdiction.

Anikeyev took it upon himself to plan the rest of the meal, with me and Boria Migailo acting in a consulting capacity only. The choice of beverage was agreed upon unanimously: vodka, in an amount calculated on our customary 'a bottle a snout' basis. Since some of the 'snouts' belonged to young ladies who seldom could keep up with the boys, and considering that my cousin Alec was a teetotaller, while his brother Gosha at that time didn't drink much either, the drinking 'snouts' were expected to pour down an amount guaranteed to make them senseless. Anikeyev said it was fine by him.

Boria, the Casanova of Gorky Street, undertook to make up the deficit in the number of 'heifers', our slang for girls; a deficit that was rather large considering that only Gosha and I could find 'heifers' to invite. Gosha's was Nina, the girl he was subsequently to marry and stay with until now, which can safely be assumed to mean for life.

Mine was a rather dazzling blonde I had 'cadred up' during the entrance exams, still hadn't scored with and was hoping to get at least a share of during the festivities.

Boria said no sweat, no deficit was too large, and when had he ever failed to deliver. 'Yeah, yeah,' said Anikeyev, 'but make sure it's something decent this time, not the three-rouble variety.' Boria assured us it was a piece of piss, and not to worry our pretty little heads about incidentals.

That left only one problem, that of table settings. Here Mama was to make yet another mistake she would regret later. Since my parents never entertained, and no alcohol was ever consumed except on birthdays, we had barely enough glasses for four people, so something had to be done to make sure the remaining 12 guests wouldn't have to drink straight 'from the neck', something nice people simply didn't do at home.

The mistake Mama made was to borrow a dozen glasses from Mrs Renner, with whom she had just restored diplomatic relations and who therefore was reluctant to enter another period of hostilities by saying no. Mama also insisted Papa and she would come back home no later than one a.m. but agreed to leave at half past five. That accounted for an early kick-off, which in hindsight wasn't necessarily a good idea, for it could have been confidently predicted we'd get legless and disorderly by nine or so, when most neighbours were still up and about.

Boria and the 'heifers' were supposed to show up a little later, and the evening started on a high note, with Bach blaring from the record player, Anikeyev reciting poems by Gumilev and Akhmatova, Alec pontificating on the finer points of Camus and getting cross because I pretended not to realise he was talking about Albert and not the VSOP. While conducting this learned discourse with one hand, I was trying to keep Anikeyev from drinking with the other, because Volodia's pugnacity when drunk fully matched his poetic sense when sober. However, all the good intentions became cobblestones on the road to hell the moment Boria appeared with a small herd of 'heifers'.

It became instantly clear the tenor of the gathering would be lowered for, while he had kept his word on the head count, he had reneged on the quality. The ladies were wearing chic western clothes, which to an Englishman would probably have looked as if they came from Oxfam or the NHS Procurement Unit, but which to us instantly identified the ladies as members of the profession that had a sacramental significance to the Babylonians. They were unquestionably hookers, of the type who worked foreigners, and as if to prove the point they had actually brought a foreigner with them, an Arab they 'simply couldn't leave for the night'.

Some of the people present were slightly prejudiced against Arabs, but this one was the nicest man you ever wanted to meet. He charmed everyone with a shy smile, put two bottles of Scotch on the table and kept his slender, elegant frame out of harm's way for the rest of the evening. A perfect, well-mannered gentleman he was, which still makes me blush at the thought of the bacchanalia he had to witness.

When the 'heifers' came in, restraint went out. Everybody, ominously including Anikeyev, got drunk quickly, and a hormonal interchange began. Some of the guests didn't have the heart for public copulation and were discreetly taking one girl after another either to the lavatory or to the bathroom, in full view of the neighbours who were gradually coming to a boil. Some of the others weren't so discreet, with Anikeyev consummating his affection for one of the hookers on top of the Flustovs' kitchen table. The scandalised owners were in attendance but – even though a couple of their plates got swept on the floor in the process – were either too disgusted, or, more likely, too terrified to stop the mating.

The only girls who would have none of that were Nina, Gosha's bride to be, and my date who, as she proved on another occasion, wasn't averse to collective efforts, but certainly not in a dingy communal flat. Her taste ran more towards the spacious, dimly lit abodes of the party élite. A few years later she was able to indulge her taste for the good life by marrying the Soviet ambassador to one of the Scandinavian countries, I can't remember which. One hopes she enlivened staid diplomatic affairs with her beauty and good common sense, which she displayed amply that night.

Meanwhile, the room was rapidly acquiring the look and smell of a cheap bordello in which most patrons practised coitus interruptus and most employees wore the cheapest scent they could possibly get. Alec, who would not demean himself by going all the way, reclined on one of the sofas, contemptuously clutching the breast of whichever hooker was taking a time-out and disdainfully explaining to her why Camus was a better writer than Sartre, but not nearly as much of an existentialist. The worst was still to come.

For Anikeyev, resplendent in his bottle-green three-piece suit, fancied Nina, a lovely gamine of a girl with a coltish figure, boyish haircut and slow grin. She must have been disgusted by that whole affair but had the *sang-froid* not to show it, and she displayed the same quality in warding off Anikeyev's advances without appearing rude.

Unfortunately for everybody present, Anikeyev mistook good manners for a come-on, and with each drink tossed down his bottomless throat he was beginning to see Gosha as the only obstacle on the way to happiness. Predictably, since I was the host, he wanted me to remove Gosha by getting him drunk, an impossible thing to do when a man simply won't drink. In the end, Anikeyev despaired and took the matter into his own hands, or rather his right hand, which he threw at Gosha's face without warning. That was the last punch he landed that night.

For Gosha was living proof that different personalities can be drawn from the same genetic pool. Where his brother Alec was bookish, he was a footballer. Where Alec was chubby, he was reedy. And most appropriate, where Alec was timid, Gosha was a vicious street fighter. He didn't look the part though, which proved to be Anikeyev's undoing. Mind you, Volodia himself was no slouch in such matters, and had he been sober his greater bulk and height might have triumphed over Gosha's violence and speed. But drunk he was, his legs were gone, and it was no contest.

Gosha threw a quick combination of a dozen short punches, all of which landed on Anikeyev's face, splitting it open like an Astrakhan watermelon dropped on the floor. Before Volodia could respond, Gosha executed a perfect hip throw, of the kind he and I used to practice endlessly as children, and Anikeyev hit the parquet floor with a tremendous thud. At that point, Misha Petrov, who was more friend to Anikeyev than to anyone else present, decided to intercede, and Boria and I had to push him aside. He fell, bringing the table down with him, with all of Mrs Renner's glasses shattering to bits.

Anikeyev, meanwhile, stayed down, kicking at anyone who was within kicking distance. One of the kicks hit the refrigerator, leaving a perfectly shaped imprint of a heel in the door. This assault on our property enraged me and I kicked back, but Anikeyev managed to grab my foot and bring me down on top of him. I landed with my elbow on his chest and pinned his right arm to the floor. Gosha, appraising the situation instantly, pinned the other arm, but Anikeyev was an agile young man who used to take fencing lessons. With his upper body pinned to the floor, he still managed to keep twisting and kicking at our heads with some accuracy, each time catching a fist in the face for his trouble. Trying to duck one of the contortionist kicks, Gosha yelled at his brother, 'Hold his bloody legs!' As Alec, who had just finished discussing the relative literary merits of *La Nausée* and *L'Etranger*, knew less about violence than he did about his chosen subject, he went about complying with his younger brother's order the wrong way. He leaned away from the site of the action, poking his toe at the swinging legs, much in the manner of a man about to plunge into icy water. That didn't do the trick and Gosha's scream was quite on a par with Joshua's battle cry: 'Fall on them, for Christ's sake!!!' That Alec did, with all 13 stone of him going splat across Anikeyev's legs.

The fight was over, and the horrified Arab could at last emerge from the wardrobe into which he had crawled the moment the first punch was thrown, displaying both the wisdom of his ancestors and the cunning of his contemporaries. He had stayed in the wardrobe for the duration, and peeked out only once, cautiously, his face reflecting the bemused distaste one often catches on the face of foreigners who observe Russians having a good time.

Now came the time to minister to the wounded, specifically to Anikeyev whose face looked as if someone had emptied a bottle of tomato sauce on it. This task fell to Nina who had in her heart the endless capacity for compassion so characteristic of Russian women. With Anikeyev still pinned to the floor just in case, she sat astride his chest, demurely pulled her skirt down, took Anikeyev's handkerchief out of his breast pocket and began to wipe the blood off his face. By now the fallen hero had quieted down and the original romantic impulse had returned. Tears were running down his face, prompted not so much by pain, to which alcohol taken way in excess of LD 50 must have anaesthetised him, but by Nina's kindness.

'Ninochka,' whispered his split lips, 'you're good. You're kind. You are a wonderful, pure human being – unlike this scum Boot. [It was his best friend he was talking about.] But for you, I would've pulled their twats over their ears...'

The last remark displayed clear insensitivity to the hard anatomic realities, but we were all happy to see Anikeyev in a more docile mood. Anyway, it was time to think of damage limitation, what with my parents' advent as imminent as the Second Coming, but more precisely fixed in time. We had about half an hour to do what we could, and there were only a few of us left: my cousins, Nina, Anikeyev, and of course the now forlorn host. The first order of the night was to get Anikeyev out, the second to tidy up the room, which had retained all the characteristics of a cheap bordello, but had now also acquired those of Hitler's bunker immediately after an Allied raid.

The latter proved impossible, the former, difficult. Anikeyev, having failed to express himself pugilistically, decided to display his dancing prowess, accompanying himself a capella: 'Cahm on, let's tvist ugain like vee deed lust sahmmer…' This was definitely preferable to his previous performance, but time was running short, and unfortunately his dancing had an element of striptease thrown in for good measure, in that he was rhythmically removing first his jacket, then his waistcoat, then his tie, unbuttoning his shirt… Before he descended to his trousers, we all began to talk to him as sweetly as we could, trying to restore the sartorial status quo. In that we probably would have succeeded but for my parents' arrival.

Mama wordlessly sank into the only chair still standing, but Papa remained upright and he was anything but wordless. He took a scathing, scanning look around, turned a colour that definitely wasn't on for someone with a heart condition and yelled at the top of his voice: 'Scum! Lowlife! Animals! So this is the kind of friends you have, Sasha?!? The same kind of worthless shit that you are!!! What have you degenerates done to the family bed?!!?'

This last turn of phrase, added to the fact that throughout this soliloquy Papa was pointing at Alec who was as innocent as a newborn lamb, broke me up and I burst out laughing. The laughter stopped short because I realised Anikeyev wasn't taking it all with equanimity. He kept muttering unfriendly things, such as '…brain bloody Daddy… throw the wanker out of the window…' and then he charged, like a bull attacking the famous matador Manoletto, the hero of a popular film that had just been released.

Papa, on the other hand, reacted in a way that clearly showed he was as unfamiliar with Manoletto's techniques as he was with

Queensberry's. He backed away, trying to cover his face with his palms. The gong for the last round had sounded, but the round didn't go the distance. Gosha and I grabbed Anikeyev's arms and threw him out, tossing his jacket after him. The last thing I remembered before passing out was the sight of my poor mother quietly sobbing as she was trying to wipe some unspeakable congealed muck off her bed cover.

The next morning I woke up with the kind of self-hating hangover that makes you promise yourself you'll never touch the stuff again. Nausea was rapidly rising from my stomach, getting mixed with guilt some halfway up my oesophagus. Papa made me feel even worse by saying, 'Son, I had to knock Mother out with a sleeping pill, you know how she is. But I did have a talk with her before she passed out, and we decided to offer you a deal. I mean, you're a growing lad, and we understand you have needs, God knows he-he-he I did when I was your age. So whenever you want Mama and me to, you know, go to the cinema for a couple of hours, I mean, perhaps I could just about swing it, though Mama is opposed. But we don't want any of that scum around, just you and your girl, and certainly not that degenerate Anikeyev. Him, I never want to see again, do we understand each other?'

We did. The next day I met Boria Migailo, and we decided to ban Anikeyev for at least a month, or ten parties, whichever came first – this despite Anikeyev having telephoned everybody present the night before and apologised profusely, 'Sorry, old man, I suppose I went a bit over the top last night… did I… shit!... and what else?... shit!... I did what?... bloody hell!...'

Banning our old comrade was a hard decision to take and we had to fortify ourselves to a point where we ended up at a party where we knew nobody and nobody knew us. The party turned out to be a crushing bore, and we left at around 5 a.m. without sampling any of the ladies present who looked like out-of-towners and didn't shave their armpits.

The sun was just popping up over the horizon, and Gorky Street was light but empty, the exact reverse of its usual bustling buzz. We were arguing bitterly about the length of the ban on Anikeyev, with Migailo acting in the capacity of Maximum John and me trying to emulate the liberal attitudes of today's British judges. Where we reached complete agreement was in the urinary area, what with our bladders about to burst and our back teeth floating, in Boria's elegant phrase.

If it had still been dark, any street corner would have provided deliverance, what with both public lavatories in central Moscow having shut for the night. As it wasn't, decorum made us seek a suitable doorway of a suitable block of flats. We found one quickly, a solidly built sample of Stalin's baroque, and walked in, unbuttoning our trousers on the way.

The massive oak door opened to your usual cavernous, echo-filled staircase of a Moscow building, complete with some broken furniture and several prams left out in the foyer to air during the night. I was about ready to do my business under the stairs, when Migailo began to relieve himself into one of the prams. 'Hey, are you nuts?' I whispered at the top of my voice. 'What the hell is the difference?' replied Boria, emptying his night's intake of red wine. 'The baby pisses in it, anyway.'

We were half a mile away from 1/12 Ogarev Street, where my parents were exercising our right to affordable housing.

THE RIGHT TO FREE EDUCATION

1

'FALL IN! RANKS OF TWO!' The order was sharp, masculine and military. Except that it came from a middle-aged woman, and we were not on a parade ground but in the courtyard of Primary School No. 133.

The Conservatory was right across Herzen Street. A bronze Tchaikovsky sat in a bronze chair in front of it, looking at us with that expression of shit-eating inspiration Soviet sculptors invariably put on the faces of canonised artists. What The Greatest Composer of All Time And Don't You Dare Think Otherwise saw in front of him was hardly inspiring. A hundred seven-year-olds were scampering around the courtyard trying to follow the first order on their first day in school.

'By height!' came the next command. The children understood and speedily arranged themselves right to left in the order of descending height.

Only one boy misunderstood the order and had to be contemptuously yanked out of the ranks by a teacher and shoved where he belonged, on the extreme left. The treatment was a little harsh because I hadn't gone to kindergarten and had no idea how to follow military – or for that matter any other – orders. On second thoughts, a few other boys and girls hadn't been anywhere near a kindergarten either, but they must have acquired the necessary knowledge by osmosis.

This was the first year that Russian schools had gone co-educational, a development about which I had mixed feelings. While I had little experience dealing with boys, I had practically none at all with girls. The mixture of my feelings was rich in fear and excitement, neither of which I could explain to my own satisfaction.

Another new development was the introduction of school uniforms for boys, and here my feelings were unequivocal: I loved it. The girls' uniforms were brown dresses with festive white or everyday black pinafores, and they looked pretty that day, 1 September, 1954. The boys wore military-style uniforms – none of those effete blazers the English sport.

We all had on peaked caps with patent-leather visors, tunics complete with stand-up collars and shiny brass buttons, black patent-leather belts with heavy brass buckles, trousers of the same grey fabric as the tunics, and sensible black shoes. The innovation had been announced in August, just a month earlier, and I had found out about it during my summer holiday at a military base near Tambov where my uncle Boris served.

'Our Boris', so called to distinguish him from his cousin 'Leningrad Boris', was Mama's younger brother. A mild, kind man, he was the least bellicose character I've ever met, and yet he was the only career officer in the family. When the war started he transferred from university, where he was reading electrical engineering, to an officers' school, where he learned how to handle mines, receiving his commission in time for Stalingrad.

Boris spent the next three years commanding first a sappers' platoon then a company, miraculously ending the war without a scratch but, predictably, with a chest full of medals. (The Soviets were generous with decorations, and many lowly officers ended up with more tinsel than Field Marshal Montgomery.) After the war, Boris was ordered to enrol in the Kuibyshev Military Engineers' Academy, from which he graduated with honours to become a professional soldier.

At that time the rhomboid pins of academy graduates adorned officers' tunics much less frequently than medals for valour. Thus you'd think that Captain Kudashev, who had both and was a dedicated Party member to boot, would have gone on to a glittering career. Rather, you would have thought so had you forgotten that a campaign against 'rootless cosmopolitans' (Pravda-speak for Jews) was in full swing. So Captain Kudashev, whose veins carried Turkic, Karaite but mostly Jewish blood, should have been thankful to be alive and at large, never mind contemplating a career. Thus he embarked on a life-long peregrination, starting with a derisory posting to the Tambov base where he was put in charge of the armoury.

At that time I knew none of those details, and our Boris was my idol. My feet never touched the ground when I walked down Gorky Street with him, his uniform somehow looking more dashing than thousands of other uniforms flooding Moscow at the time.

Those thousands were a nuisance to our Boris who, according to the ironclad regulations, had to salute all his superiors with unmitigated enthusiasm while not forgetting to return the salutes of his inferiors. Since every other man we passed was uniformed, Boris's hand was going up and down like a Baku oil derrick, and boy did I love it! The Marquis de Custine, who travelled in Russia in the 1830s, remarked with horror, 'The country is always on a war footing. It knows no peacetime.' Had he taken a walk down Gorky Street with our Boris and me, he'd probably have said, 'Plus ça change, plus c'est la même chose.' I admit though that what the Frenchman found appalling I found appealing as a five-year-old.

Like any Russian boy my age, I could identify not only the rank of a passing military man but also his branch of service. Boris would correct the odd error but even in the midst of doing so would stiffen and throw his hand up in a prescribed arc every time we passed a major or a lieutenant-colonel. Naturally it never crossed my mind that this insistence on formality was incongruous in the Red Army of Workers And Peasants.

Nor did this thought occur to our Boris. He'd snap to attention whenever an out-of-town major asked him for directions, and then soak his right hand in hot water after a two hours' stroll through central Moscow. When Boris himself wasn't satisfied with the salute he received from a man he outranked, he'd make him come back, pass us again and this time salute properly. I suspect he was so strict partly to impress me, and duly impressed I was.

In fact, few things could have impressed me more, as martial virtue reigned supreme in our society, which was more thoroughly militarised than any other in modern history. All those uniforms were in Moscow for a purpose. They all had jobs to do, and only some of them involved run-of-the-mill soldiering in the Moscow Military District, which was roughly the strength of a peacetime army.

To that you should add two KGB divisions stationed in or around Moscow, sizeable Interior Ministry troops, Kremlin guards, thousands of officers who manned military-studies faculties of which every university had several, employees of the Defence Ministry, General Staff officers, instructors and students of half a dozen military academies and a dozen officers' schools, and countless military reps at countless plants and factories.

All in all our city alone had more uniforms in its streets than most countries had ever seen. It was enough brass to make my head spin, especially since they all tended to converge in the city centre where we lived. After all, I, along with millions of other Russian children, had been weaned on stories of mass heroism displayed by Red soldiers in the Civil War and especially the Great Patriotic War, as the Second World War is called in Russia.

At that age I didn't know the names of Pasternak or Mandelstam but could easily reel off the names of a hundred assorted heroes. I didn't know how the great poet Tsvetayeva died but would have had no problem describing in minute, if possibly apocryphal, detail the exact circumstances of the death of Alexander Matrosov (threw himself chest first on a German machine gun), Captain Gastello (landed his burning plane on top of a German train), Lieutenant Talalikhin (rammed a German bomber over Moscow), Zoya Kosmodemianskaya (hanged by the Germans for sabotage) and dozens of others.

I didn't know Christ's dying words but could have recited in its hair-raising entirety the pre-mortem soliloquy of Commissar Klotchkov addressing the last remaining soldiers of the Panfilov Division: 'There's nowhere left to retreat. What we have behind us is Moscow!'

The pathos of these heroic words is somewhat diminished for me today by the realisation that, as both Klotchkov and his audience were mown down directly he had allegedly delivered the rousing message, there would have been nobody left to tell us exactly what he had said. But at that time such a seditious thought would never have occurred to me, or indeed to any grown-up of my acquaintance.

Nor did I know at the time that Matrosov, a petty criminal before the war, served in a penalty battalion and had nowhere to go but forward, what with the NKVD 'blocking detachments' aiming their own machine guns at his back.

Or that Talalikhin was conscripted into the Air Force straight out of a colony for delinquent orphans, having lost his whole family to Stalin's collectivisation programme.

Or that Gastello and his fellow pilots were actually trained to aim their burning planes at the enemy if hit. Suicide pilots before the kamikazes, many of them didn't even carry parachutes, and so their subsequent heroism wasn't always a matter of choice.

Or that Kosmodemianskaya belonged to one of the NKVD guerrilla units left behind the German lines to commit senseless sabotage. That stratagem was designed to turn German troops against the local population which, for the first time in Russia's history, was greeting foreign invaders as deliverers.

Or that even the magnificent Marshal Rokossovsky, the best commander the Soviets had during the war, went into action straight out of a Lubyanka interrogation cell where his toes had been flattened with a hammer.

Or that Marshal Meretskov was appointed Front Commander while still at Lubyanka where the interrogators had beaten him senseless with rubber truncheons and then took turns pissing on his head.

There was no one to tell me those things, for no sane adult would have shared such information with a child even had he known it. But there were lots of adults around to provide fantastic stories designed to turn me into an unthinking automaton ready to die for the motherland with relish. They, including our gentle Boris, ultimately failed, but not for any lack of trying. I still remember the shock on his face when we were arguing the virtues of universal conscription some 13 years later.

'If we didn't have it,' he asked, 'then who would defend the motherland?' 'This motherland?' I inquired with the sarcasm of a 20-year-old full of himself. 'I hope nobody will.' That was a true enough representation of my feelings but a cruel thing to say to a man who, at my age, had seen his comrades blown to scarlet bits.

Militarisation didn't just affect the appearance of my city, it pervaded the entire nation. The army embodied what Russia was all about, and even many of the mufti-wearing wimps who had never seen a live round in their lives tended to adopt military attitudes.

Factory workers and farmers were split into 'brigades', school children into 'squads' and 'detachments'. Bosses everywhere talked down to their 'men'. For instance, a factory manager, normally described as a 'production commander', would seldom ask a worker to do something, or even tell him to do it. He'd issue a military order, using the grammar and tone of voice designed to achieve that stylistic effect.

He'd say 'go and clean up that bloody mess', rather than 'will you go and clean up that bloody mess'. And he'd never resort to the gentlemanly 'would you please go and clean up that bloody mess', a subtle yet telling difference in our language.

Talking to a subordinate engineer, a fellow 'commander' but of lower rank, the manager would inevitably use the familiar *tu* form rather than the deferential *vous* the latter would use in addressing him. And he'd remain seated when talking, while the subordinate would be standing up until ordered to sit down. The conversation usually would end with 'expedite!'

By the time I grew up, Papa had grown in professional stature and he'd talk in that manner to engineers with 30 years' experience in the industry, something to which I once took exception, much to Papa's bewilderment. Of course, like any *nash*, he could take as well as he dished out, and his minister treated him exactly the same way as he himself treated his own underlings.

As an adult I came to detest this manic, ill-mannered militarism. But as a seven-year-old I was proud of my grey uniform that didn't quite make me look like our Boris, but close enough.

Papa, capitalising on his martial past, showed me how to polish the brass buttons and belt buckle with dentifrice. When Mama was looking the other way, he also showed how to loop the belt around my wrist and use the ballistic potential of the heavy buckle to inflict damage on an adversary. A couple of years later, when facing a similarly trained classmate, I tried to put that lesson into practice, suffered a split eyebrow and came home with my uniform stiff from the blood it had absorbed.

On that 1 September, I could have used another lesson, which I had never received: how to dress and undress myself. Alas, the first-day curriculum included PE. We were all taken down to the gym and told to don appropriate attire, which in my case was easier said than done.

Though getting out of the uniform was a doddle, my undergarments presented a difficult problem. Other boys wore the same underwear as their fathers, only smaller. But I wore what Mama considered to be more appropriate for a child: a suspender belt with stockings. This is a combination some men find sexy in women, but it can easily defeat the limited dexterity of an utterly spoilt boy of seven.

While the more worldly boys tried to peak into the girls' dressing room (eventually they abandoned subterfuge and kicked the door wide open, so even I caught sight of Natasha Bogdanova's precociously developed breasts), I was fighting with the suspender clasps trying to figure out where to shove the garments I had finally managed to take off. I could think of nothing better than to push them into my brown-paper lunch bag, which contained a half-eaten Antonov apple. By the time I took them out again, the fruit had gone brown, and the brown stuff had rubbed off on my underwear.

Since I was as squeamish as I was clumsy, putting the underwear back on after the class was out of the question. Much to the profanely expressed mirth of my new classmates, I had to pull the coarse woollen uniform over my sweaty gym clothes and put the shoes on my bare feet.

Our teacher, Tatiana Petrovna Kisselyova, noticed white skin where the bottom of my trousers met the shoes and told, nay ordered, me to put my socks on. I refused, politely yet firmly explaining to her that I wore no socks but had stockings which I couldn't put on for reasons beyond my control. She then pulled the brown underwear out of the soggy lunch bag and held it up for the class to pass comments on. I still remember the disdainful laughter in the girls' half of the class. The loudest came from Natasha Bogdanova, whose breasts had impressed me more than anything else on that day.

Having already sensed that I was a *ne-nash*, the *nash* boys soon branded me as a wimp, and that reputation is easier to acquire than to lose at any school. The only recourse was to do battle. For a small boy unwise to the ways and means of street fighting, the way to survive fisticuffs with bigger boys was to earn the reputation of a 'psycho', someone who could respond to innocent bullying with an incommensurate pen stuck in the eye or a piece of brick used as a knuckleduster. The bullies didn't mind rough action, but it could get messy and there was easier prey to be found. So, after breaking a couple of heads and earning two suspensions for 'hooliganism', I began to be beaten up no more often than once a month, which was par for the course.

2

Apart from the PE class, my first day at school presented no academic challenges. At that time in Russia most children were illiterate at school-entering age (seven), and the first couple of years were mostly devoted to the basic Rs.

Along with a few others in my class, I was literate and could already read *The Three Musketeers*, add up simple numbers and even write

'Grandpa is a shit' on the wallpaper (the subject of that graffito was laughing his head off as he spanked me painlessly). So I got top marks without trying, which wasn't conducive to developing solid work habits. But the Soviet educational system didn't care about that. The underlying assumption was that if I had the ability to develop skills that could advance the future that worked, I'd be forced to apply them diligently anyhow, and my natural laziness wouldn't be allowed to come into play. If, however, I didn't have the make-up required to design planes or build missiles, and if my nature led me towards the useless fields of literature and the arts, then the state didn't really care how lazy or industrious I was.

However, it did care about turning a *ne-nash* into a *nash*. This was communicated to me loud and clear on that first day, when I plonked my bag onto one of several spare desks. Tatiana Petrovna, who was at heart a kind, sympathetic woman, had her orders to follow and so she demanded that I share a desk with a classmate.

'I'd be more comfortable sitting on my own,' was how I couched my bourgeois individualism. The teacher would have none of that: 'No one here cares about your comfort, Boot. You're not here as yourself, you're part of a collective. That's all you are. You know what they say in the army? If you can't, we'll teach you; if you won't, we'll make you.'

That wasn't the last time in my school life that I heard parallels drawn with the army. I quite liked it: coupled with my paramilitary uniform, such references reinforced my illusions of being just like our Boris. I didn't mind living my life according to the much-touted principle of 'train hard, fight easy' and was prepared to sleep every night locked in a passionate embrace with my rifle.

What I however resented even then was the obvious disapproval of what I was, rather than of what I did. Under the influence of my doting mother I was happy with the way I had turned out and felt that, if any changes to my personality were necessary, I'd somehow effect them myself. No outside help was needed, thank you very much.

But the state was after bending my whole personality to its will, not after educating my mind. Following Rousseau's prescription it sought to replace all my loyalties with state worship. That's why the Soviets canonised not only Rousseau but also his devoted, if unwitting, follower Pavlik Morozov.

When Tatiana Petrovna mentioned his name on that first school day, it vaguely rang a bell. I knew he was some kind of hero but couldn't for the life me remember what his heroic deed had been. Tatiana Petrovna, speaking with the same fulsome solemnity with which the Muslims talk of the Prophet, filled in the missing details.

Pavlik, the patron saint of the Young Pioneers, a boyscout-type communist organisation to which all Soviet children belonged, was a 13-year-old peasant in the thirties. At that time the traditionally conservative peasantry was being forced into progressive collective farms. As an expression of historical inevitability, their grain stocks were confiscated, and they were allotted food in proportion to their enthusiasm for the new system.

Some peasants (most, as I found out later), led astray by their reactionary proprietary instincts and wilfully misled by deviationists from the Party line, didn't see the light immediately. Pavlik's father was one of them. Driven by the bourgeois-imperialist wish to keep his family alive through the winter, he hoarded some of the grain. The miscreant perversely believed it belonged to him anyway, just as Comrade Lenin had promised.

At that time the OGPU 'food squads' were ransacking the countryside, looking for hoarders and executing them on the spot. Pavlik, one of the first recipients of the same free education we all benefited from later, discovered the hoarded grain and was confronted with a Hamlet-like dilemma: to betray or not to betray? That wasn't even a question, as far as Pavlik was concerned.

It's testimony to the early successes of our educational system that he didn't hesitate at all. The Soviet hero dutifully shopped his father to an OGPU firing squad, setting a shining example for the generations to come. He was then lynched for his trouble by the outraged villagers led by the martyr's own grandfather who apparently didn't share Pavlik's strong views on the collectivisation of agriculture.

With the all-pervasive obtrusiveness so characteristic of the Russians trying to make a point, the grateful state placed portraits of Pavlik into every classroom of every school. It was at this icon that Tatiana Petrovna pointed as she asked each of us in turn if we'd be capable of similar selfless heroism in analogous circumstances.

'Ivanov?' 'Yes!' 'Bogdanova?' 'Well, yes.' 'Solovyov?' 'Of course I would.' 'Boot?' 'Yes,' I mumbled because I didn't want any trouble on my first day at school.

What I didn't realise then was that the first vetting of my life had taken place – and I had failed. For the state wasn't satisfied with half-hearted acquiescence; it demanded the chapter and verse of enthusiastic support. Since few people did support it enthusiastically, what separated the *nash* men from the *ne-nash* boys was the wide-eyed, open-mouthed readiness to fake it. That is to lie, cheat and dissemble not only with readiness but also with conviction.

By answering 'yes' to Tatiana Petrovna's inquiry I thought I had done enough to pass muster. But my shifty eyes, dropped head and quiet voice told her my heart wasn't in the right place. Thus the first entry into my personal file probably went along the lines of 'watch him, he is a *ne-nash*'.

In the subsequent 18 years of my life in Russia the file must have got fat with other entries proving that Tatiana Petrovna's original hunch had been correct. Now, after my 40 years in the West outside of the *nash* jurisdiction, that file is still lurking somewhere in the damp cellar of the KGB computer, or whatever that outfit calls itself now.

For Mother Russia isn't a cuckoo, she never abandons her young. When a man born to her runs away, she is robbed of her legitimate property. And she'll never have a quiet moment until the property is reinstated. Until that time there's no substitute for accurate records, to make sure the naughty child doesn't misbehave too badly. When he does, he is spanked – with poison, bomb or bullet.

This tendency, incidentally, didn't start with the Soviets. Since Russia became a unified state, around the fifteenth century, she has never tolerated her fledglings flying the coop. One celebrated case was that of Tsarevich Alexei, Peter I's son and heir. The youngster fled because he couldn't stomach the orgy of bloodshed unleashed by his father. However, tricked by Peter's emissary, Leo Tolstoy's ancestor, the boy grudgingly returned home. There he was tortured and then beheaded by the royal hand of his august parent, a firm believer in the maxim 'spare the axe and spoil the child.'

When I came home that first day, there was a party waiting for me. Mama, my grandparents and Inna, our Boris's wife, were sitting around a table laden with some of my favourite delicacies, including a glorious poppy-seed cake. Mama was horrified at the sight of my underwear peeking through the soggy lunch bag, but a trifle like that couldn't be allowed to mar the festivities. The grown-ups made me feel as if I had already achieved something.

3

Soon it was time to run for various public offices within the school hierarchy. Each class was divided into three 'squads', and each had to have a 'commander' who was entitled to wear one red stripe on his sleeve. The three squads added up to a 'detachment', the leader of which was identified by two stripes. All the detachments together formed a *droozhyna* (the old Russian word for troop) whose supreme commander proudly displayed three stripes.

The teachers nominated three candidates for each job, and we all voted for them in an open ballot. Generally, the nominees included *nash* semi-intellectuals, in preference to *nash* proles and to the entire *ne-nash* faction, who were thus disfranchised. The latter had only one office available to them, that of editor of the 'wall newspaper'. This indigenously Soviet invention was usually no more than a collage of articles and pictures clipped out of real newspapers, pasted on cardboard and hung on a corridor wall.

Every organisation in Russia, from primary schools to research institutes, had such a collage on its wall. It was the editor's responsibility to select the entries, arrange them in an aesthetically pleasing way and provide headlines and captions. Realising that this was the only path to social prominence open to me, I coveted and secured a nomination.

This was a nonelective office because most children really didn't care a monkey's who spent an evening each month putting the sheet together. So it was up to the teacher to select the most deserving candidate. Tatiana Petrovna suggested that each of us three nominees put together one issue on spec, and may the best entry win. The theme was the upcoming anniversary of the Great October Socialist Revolution, the most religious of all Soviet holidays, starring Marx as God the Father, Lenin as God the Holy Ghost and the current leader, at that time Khrushchev, as God the Son.

Luckily Papa was in town, and he used to edit a similar sheet at his university. Ably assisted by Mama who was a wizard with scissors and glue, Papa put together a retrospective of Lenin's life in pictures, from an oval photograph of the would-be leader as a curly-haired child to a reproduction of Serov's painting *Lenin Addressing the Congress Of Peasant Deputies*.

'*Finis coronat opus*,' said Papa as he inscribed 'edited by Alexander Boot' in the bottom right corner of the completed masterpiece. His handiwork carried the day, and within a week I received my only political appointment in Russia.

Meanwhile Mama, whose love was never entirely free of selfishness, realised that her importance in my life was diminishing: parents weren't allowed to compete with the state wanting to raise its youthful subjects in its own image. From that day on Mama redoubled her efforts to maintain the illusion of gentility she had so painstakingly created in the unlikely conditions of our communal home.

She also attempted to strengthen the bonds between us in the way that comes so naturally to mothers in general and Jewish mothers in particular: laying guilt. In this Mama often used the same language as Mother Russia, which also cultivated the sense of guilt in her children. 'I give you everything,' they'd both say, 'and what you owe me in return is unquestioning love and obedience.' Mother Russia was more successful than Mama. So successful, in fact, that even many dissidents and émigrés never got rid of irrational guilt feelings towards the motherland to which they had been so ungrateful.

Subtlety was never Mama's most salient feature, and she went about her task in a forthright way. A week after I started school, and was behaving towards her in a progressively beastlier fashion, she came down with flu. As I handed her a cup of tea, she grabbed my wrist and said in the voice of the *Lady With Camellias*: 'Everybody thinks it's flu but it isn't. It's cancer… I'm dying… and it's all your fault.'

That much guilt was more than even a blasé seven-year-old could handle comfortably. I burst into tears, begging her to reconsider the harsh diagnosis: 'Mama, please don't die, I'll be a good boy now…'

I lied. Survival was now the order of the day, and goodness was a hindrance, not an asset. I had to pretend that the non-stop attack on everything that made me such an obvious *ne-nash* was succeeding, so Tatiana Petrovna wouldn't mock me in front of the class. Actually, she wasn't a bad sort, deep down a bit of a *ne-nash* herself, but breaking children in was the most important requirement of her chosen profession. She had to be good at it to keep her job.

She kept summoning Mama to school, hoping to get to the roots of my stroppiness. In the course of those meetings the two women became friends, and neither could quite understand how such a devout communist as Mama could produce such an obviously *ne-nash* viper. However, because of this friendship Tatiana Petrovna left me alone and allowed me to persist, within reasonable limits, in my asocial behaviour.

Some people are born asocial, some have this quality thrust upon them. I fell into the second category, suffering from a modified version of the Groucho syndrome: I didn't wish to belong to any club that didn't want me as a member. In the eyes of the *nash* majority, I was an enemy, so I had to seek friends, or at least allies, among the *ne-nash* minority.

There were six of us, out of 40 in the class, and we stuck together not because we had a lot in common but because we had little in common with the other 34. It was a marriage of convenience or, if you will, a fortress under siege. The enemy tried the occasional direct onslaught, and we'd emerge bloodied but defiant. Attrition worked better, and in a few years half of us became *nash* turncoats, while the others learned how to camouflage their nature with put-on elements of *nash* behaviour.

Mama, however, continued to preach the abstraction of the communist brotherhood of man, insisting that I help the less privileged within the *nash* enemy camp. She singled out the family of our local street sweeper, a Tartar named Mamedov. His son was my classmate and namesake, Alexander, Sasha for short. (Sasha was a popular name in that vintage, and 40 percent of the boys in our class were my namesakes. This was one reason we usually addressed one another by surnames, in the style of English public schools.)

The boy lived in the basement of the same building in which our communal flat occupied part of the third floor. The basement stank even worse than the rest of the house, and Sasha carried that sour stench everywhere he went. I was morbidly sensitive to smells, but Mama believed that this friendship would have redemptive value for me.

Every day I'd share my lunch with Mamedov, who – with a cunning amazing in one so young – played my guilt feelings with the virtuosity of Oistrakh playing his Strad. Every time I gave him half of my cheese sandwich and Antonov apple, along with one of my two biscuits, he'd say, 'Boy, you must be well rich.' I knew we weren't, not in any absolute terms, but guiltily allowed that perhaps we might be rich relatively speaking. That was a concept Tatiana Petrovna was trying to explain to us at the time.

Each subject she taught us, be that reading, calligraphy or arithmetic, had an element of West-baiting to it. In reading classes, we'd be given texts about Negro boys lynched in Alabama by ghastly capitalists. In calligraphy, we had to write neatly 'Down with American imperialism' 20 times until we got the rightward inclination of the letters just so, and they were all linked in the prescribed fashion. In arithmetic, we'd tackle such challenges as 'British imperialists sent 12 spies across the borders of our motherland. Our valiant border guards shot four and arrested the rest. How many were arrested?'

And during a discussion period, Tatiana Petrovna explained that all those stories we might have heard about people in the West having a higher standard of living were nonsense, and subversive propaganda to boot. Yes, she admitted, there were rich people in the West, vampires who sucked their ill-gotten gains out of the blood of the toiling masses. But compared to those exploiters, the masses were poor, even though they might have cars and TV sets. Hence the masses were poor in relative terms, and relative wealth was all that mattered. That line of reasoning made sense to us. And it would have made even more sense if half the class didn't go hungry most of the time, in a shamefully absolute way.

Mamedov was one such child. Though he might have exaggerated his hunger when talking to me, hungry he was. Even though I never had any toys and had to wear the same pair of shoes all year round until they fell off my feet piece by piece, I always had enough to eat. Therefore I had to accept the burden of charity.

Mama suggested it would be a good idea if I invited Sasha to dinner, so 'the poor boy could get a proper hot meal.' The fragment of the Golden Horde came over the very next night. While Mama was in the kitchen, he inspected the room, which at the time we shared with my grandfather (Grandma had just died).

'Boy, you're well rich.' Mamedov uttered his favourite admonishment even more disapprovingly than usually. He then went up to the cupboard and pulled out the cutlery drawer. We owned four or five forks, and about as many spoons and knives, all made of paper-thin stainless steel that bent when coming in contact with the stringy fibre of Russian frozen meat.

'Boy, you're real fat cats,' he repeated, and my heart filled with a mixture of shame, pity and affection. 'Well, now,' I stammered. 'Not really rich... we are just, well, a family... you know... I mean haven't you got knives and forks?' 'We wouldn't have nothing to eat with them, mate,' replied Mamedov in his implicitly deprecating manner.

'But you do eat something, don't you?' I was grabbing at straws. 'Like what have you had today?' 'All I had, mate, was a piece of bread and butter at eight in the morning. My stomach is churning. Listen, you wouldn't have something to munch on while your Mum is cooking, would you?'

I reached into the window box, something I was under explicit orders not to do, and took out our last apple, hoping the member of the starving masses would let me have half. He scoffed the lot and, when Mama brought in dinner, ate two bowls of borscht and three meat patties with potatoes washed down with kissel, a Russian fruit drink with plenty of filling starch in it.

That, in my view, cemented our friendship for life, and I was surprised more than anything else to see Sasha Mamedov in the front line of the gang that ambushed me to administer my monthly beating the next day. The most merciless attacker, he continued to kick me even after the others had already been satisfied. The pain of his blows was nothing compared to the realisation that my friend Sasha hated me – not something I represented, but me personally, the brilliant Sasha Boot so loved by Mama, Papa and our Boris. My heart hardened.

The next day I got my own back. Mamedov always came to school early to do some homework. He couldn't do it at home, because the noise of his father beating his mother distracted him from computing how much money a capitalist would amass after stealing 10 dollars from each of 1,000 starving workers.

That morning I showed up early too and found him in our empty classroom. The events of the day before hadn't, in his view, changed the cordial nature of our relationship. He greeted me with his customary, 'Hi, mate,' accompanied by an extended hand. Ignoring the hand, I went into him with all my pent-up class hatred, landing chaotic blows with both hands.

For some reason, Mamedov didn't expect such savagery and backed off, his nose bleeding profusely. When he took a backward step, he tripped and fell down, splitting the skin on his head over a ribbed radiator. Disregarding the spurting blood, I jumped on top of him and continued pounding his face with both fists until Tatiana Petrovna, attracted by the noise, dragged me away. We were both covered with his blood and sobbing, he from pain and humiliation, I from realising that my gentle childhood was over.

Having listened to a long lecture on my 'savage hooliganism, unbecoming the son of such a cultured mother' and served my two-week's exclusion, I returned to the same class. Mamedov and I remained civil, even though there were no more shared meals.

The last time I saw him was 15 years later when, in his capacity of Post Office delivery man, he knocked on my door and handed over a parcel. We recognised each other and exchanged the few perfunctory remarks one would expect from two former classmates whose lives had taken different courses.

As we were saying good-bye, I casually put my hand in my pocket, wondering if I should tip him and if so, how much. 'Don't,' said his face, and we shook hands instead.

4

Four years went by. It was time to say good-bye to Tatiana Petrovna and move on to Secondary School No. 123, three blocks up Herzen Street. By now my life had changed: Mama had had to take a job at a library, and I was allowed by default to go out and play with anybody I wanted.

This was easier said than done, for Moscow was overrun by teenage gangs, at that time uncontrolled and possibly uncontrollable. Unlike their Western counterparts, these young thugs had little interest in mugging pedestrians, possibly because they knew that few had anything worth stealing. Their interest was in beating people up, especially young people. Walking the streets at the time was all one's teeth, and sometimes one's life, were worth. The only way was to seek some accommodation with the gangs, playing one against another or simply currying favour.

My saving grace came from the fact that Russians of their social stratum respect story-tellers, and many an 'intel' saved his life in concentration camps by telling 'novels' to his murderous cellmates. This ability to spin a decent yarn stood me in good stead in Moscow when I began to roam the streets on my own. To Mama's horror, I'd walk around our neighbourhood, surrounded by older boys with an average of three GBH convictions, and as many again for theft. They were all suckers for stories broadly based on *The Three Musketeers, Ivanhoe* and my other childhood books.

The stories had to be altered somewhat as my audience demanded juicy details that weren't always part of the original narrative. But one could hear so much urgent expectation in their wide-eyed questions ('Did Ivanhoe shag Lady Rowena?'), that it would have been cruel, not to mention imprudent, to reply that Sir Walter Scott had somehow left that particular detail out.

The only possible answer was, 'Of course he did. Every which way.' Such poetic licence would earn me grateful guffaws, some protection from rival gangs and a deep sense of satisfaction over the realisation that I had left at least some people the richer for having known me. As I grew older, the nature of my reading changed, but not the nature of the poetic licence I used when entertaining my potential murderers ('...and then Faust did Gretchen doggie-style...').

I was already attending the chess club at The Pavlik Morozov Palace of Young Pioneers, and was put on Board 2 in the new school's team. Chess at the time was taking up my every moment not spent on reading, which left precious little time for homework. Papa didn't mind because he was sure that one day I'd become champion of the world. Not to rob posterity of valuable archival material, he lovingly preserved the cross-tables of every tournament I played.

My future stardom was so important to him that after a while I began to show him only the cross-tables of the tournaments in which I had done well. Papa would highlight my results with a red pencil and file them away. Once or twice I falsified cross-tables to make my scores appear better than they were. Tragedy struck when Papa discovered the deception by chance. Close to tears, he tore up his entire collection, nay his dream of vicarious stardom, including the cross-tables of the tournaments I had won for real.

It was through chess that I discovered Tverskoy Boulevard, part of the boulevard ring that encircles central Moscow. The benches in the middle of it provided the site for an informal chess club, where dozens of people, most of them regulars, played knockout blitz (5-minute chess) for hours on end. The winner of the game would stay on and the loser would take his place at the end of the queue. There were at least 10 boards going at the same time, and the losers chatted while waiting their turn. *Ad hoc* friendships were formed, although they seldom spilled over into the extra-boulevard life.

By now, the boulevard has crystallised in my mind into the only unreservedly good memory of Russia. I started playing there at 11 and stopped 14 years later when I left the country. Throughout that time the cast of regulars remained unchanged, and... I almost said it probably hasn't changed much even now, but then I remembered that 40 years is a lot of water under the *Bolshoi Kamennyi* bridge.

The place had a buzz that's difficult to find in a more formal chess setting, and there were quite a few good players. In fact, at the risk of sounding chauvinistic, I'd venture a guess that the boulevard team of my memory would hold its own against the team of any British city, except London. Even Grandmaster Lein would make the occasional appearance and take on all comers in handicapped blitz games.

But one's popularity in the jolly boulevard crowd wasn't solely dependent on one's prowess at chess. What mattered even more was one's aptitude at 'bell-ringing', that off-colour barracking, usually more obscene than witty, which accompanied every game.

'I'm about to shag your queen,' one player would announce. 'Great game, chess, isn't it,' would retort his opponent. 'You should consider taking it up one day.'

As I was contemplating my next move, the chimes of 'bell-ringing' would penetrate my concentration with snippets of conversation the likes of which I had never heard before.

'...You play like a pigeon I told him...' – '...so how about a fiver on the next game' – '...if I shagged the way you play, my wife would divorce me'... – 'I buggered him three times on the trot in the Ruy Lopez...' – 'A rouble a game, and the game is not the same...' – 'Tal [the rising star of Soviet chess] will do your Botvinnik [reigning World Champion] sideways and backwards...' – 'The Queen is like a Georgian lass, let us shag her in the...' – 'Riga [Tal's birthplace] is about to be re-named Tal-Aviv...' – 'You're one pathetic git and your game is deep in shit...' – 'Look at that kid, he can't wank yet and he's already screwing adults…' 'Don't listen to him, lad, he's jealous…' 'Don't rape the position. Be gentle – it'll spread its legs all by itself…'

5

At the time of my transfer to the new school, the hours I spent on chess were having a less than beneficial effect on my studies. Physics was especially painful, as the homework took time, and my time was spent either playing tournaments or hustling on the boulevard.

Thankfully, our teacher Matvei Ivanovich was a chess buff himself and didn't lean on me too heavily. In his subject we were using the official textbook by Pioryshkin and Faleyev, which defined the atom 'as the smallest and further indivisible particle of matter.'

This was roughly 35 years after Rutherford had split the atom, and about 12 after his discovery had been used to such a well-publicised effect in Japan. That fact was once pointed out to Matvei Ivanovich by my *ne-nash* friend Zhenia Mayachenkov who unlike me was a wizard at things like maths and science. Matvei Ivanovich evaded a scholarly debate by ordering Zhenia to shut up and tell his mother to come and see him.

What he could have told us was that nuclear physics was a bourgeois science that didn't pass ideological muster. But the need to liberate the world from the shackles of capitalism had made that branch of science hard to ignore in practical life. So, while Matvei Ivanovich was teaching us his antediluvian wisdom, more successful physicists, such as the dissident-to-be Sakharov, were cranking out hydrogen bombs like hotcakes.

Our biology teacher wasn't far behind. She taught us the Lysenko version of her science, explaining that there was no such thing as genetics. She didn't quote Stalin who had once referred to genetics as 'Yid crap', but never diverged from this terse definition in spirit. The official term for that bourgeois perversion was 'Morganism-Weissmanism', derived from the names of its two famous practitioners.

The teacher would describe those gentlemen in the terms people in the West normally reserve for child molesters. Clearly, they had no place in our school. Instead, the walls of the biology classroom were decorated with a row of portraits where the ubiquitous Lenin competed with Pavlov of the dog fame, Lysenko and also with Michurin. That 'biologist' had put Lysenko's theories into practice, grown giant fruit and, according to a Moscow quip, had been killed by falling off a strawberry.

The teacher effortlessly reconciled Lysenko's theories with the new passion for maize Khrushchev had developed when visiting the great farms of Iowa. Upon his return he ordered many of Russia's traditional rye and wheat fields uprooted, and maize planted instead. In his red-hot passion for that cereal the current Great Teacher on Agricultural Matters had somehow forgotten to ask Iowa farmers if maize could grow as bountifully close to the Arctic Circle as it did in Iowa.

That oversight augmented the drive towards the cultivation of the virgin lands of Kazakhstan at the expense of the traditional breadbaskets of central and southern Russia and the Ukraine. In inverse proportion to food gradually disappearing from the shops, our textbooks contained more and more assurances of how the two great developments were firmly rooted in science. Every day we had to repeat Michurin's words: 'We cannot expect mercies from Nature. Our task is to take them from her.'

If that was the diet on which we subsisted in science, you can imagine the nature of our education in the more subjective humanities. Years later I read a book by an American 'educator' whose name, if memory serves, was Thorpe. The book, titled *What Ivan Knows of What Johnny Doesn't*, compared Soviet education favourably with American. While Johnny, enthused the author, reads about a bunny rabbit going hop-hop up the hill, Ivan learns how to calculate the diameter of the hill and analyse its mineral composition.

What the author didn't tell us was that little Vania was made to learn those wonderful things not out of abstract love of knowledge, but because he was expected to grow up being able to dig the hill empty of uranium or turn it into a missile silo. Reading the book at the university, I thought Johnny got the better deal, on balance. It would have been more fun to read about bunnies than to write essays on the subject of Eugene Onegin, as a Manifestation of Moral and Socioeconomic Decay in the Class Structure of Tsarist Russia, or else Lenin on Imperialism as the Highest and Final Stage of Capitalism.

Thorpe also remarked that 11-year-old pupils in Russian schools read more complicated English texts than American pupils did at the

same age. Not having studied at American schools, I don't know if
our texts really were more complicated but, taking a stab in the dark,
I'd venture a guess they were different.

That is, unless you're prepared to maintain that Johnny Q. Public
also learned his English grammar from stories about a Comrade
Petrov. A member of the regional committee of the Communist Party,
he supervised the activities of Comrades Ivanov and Sidorov who had
been entrusted with the task of organising the collection of scrap metal.
That activity was of paramount importance to the long-term success
of the Soviet economy.

'Good evening, Comrade Petrov.' 'Oh, I say, good evening,
comrades. Jolly wonderful to see you. And how much scrap metal have
you collected today?' 'Twenty tonnes between us, Comrade Petrov.'
'I say, that is smashing news! Actually, great news for the advancement
of socialism.' 'Yes, Comrade Petrov, we are well on our way to
overtaking America in the per capita production of pig iron, and
Comrade Sidorov and I are doing our best.' 'I know you are, comrades,
I know you are. Keep up the good work, what?'

The history we were taught, apart from the obvious propaganda we
were expected to know but even the teachers didn't expect us to
believe, was Russocentric. By that time the drive for Russian 'priority'
in science and technology had somewhat abated, and we were allowed
to know who James Watt was. But Russia was still presented to us as
the saviour of the world from time immemorial. Our borders didn't
just separate Russia from other countries; they separated good from
evil.

At the same time the entire Russian history was presented as a
succession of revolutionary movements, from peasant uprisings led
by such obvious brigands as Razin and Pugachev to the coup d'état
attempted by aristocratic officers in December 1825. The officers led
their regiments to Petersburg's Senate Square where they ran into the
troops loyal to the tsar. After a short standoff the loyal troops loosed
off a few salvos, and the rebels dispersed. The aftermath of the
uprising, in which many noblemen had been implicated, turned into a
field day for the bloodthirsty tsar. He sentenced five ringleaders to the
gallows, and a few dozen others to imprisonment and exile.

We were fed endless stories about the tsar's conversation with
Pushkin, many of whose friends were on their way to Siberia. 'Where

would you have been on 14 December,' asked the inquisitive monarch, 'if you had been in town?' 'I would have been in the square, Sire' replied the courageous poet. For that death-defying reply he was savagely banished to his country estate for a few months.

We weren't told that throughout the turbulent nineteenth century the bestial tsars executed all of 997 criminals, including murderers. By contrast, during the five-year reign of Lenin, 1,861,568 were judicially shot by the Cheka – on top of the millions murdered extra-judicially. This before the advent of Stalin whose monstrosities Khrushchev had just exposed in his 'secret session' speech of 1956.

However, though we didn't have many contradictory facts at our disposal, we had enough to produce reasonable understanding. How about just five death sentences as a result of an armed uprising against the legally instituted authority?

When during Khrushchev's reign unarmed workers in Novocherkassk took to the streets demanding food, hundreds were shot on the spot, with an additional couple of hundred executed thereafter. An armed uprising would have resulted in hundreds of thousands of deaths, including not only the rebels themselves but their families, all their acquaintances and most of their co-workers.

We weren't encouraged to think for ourselves, or to draw any historical parallels. Just the opposite, we were expressly forbidden to do so – or else. The threat was no longer as clearly enunciated as it had been in the previous generation, but it was no less manifest. The state didn't want us to think outside of the officially approved channels or, for that matter, ever to learn how to do so. And the state succeeded, with few exceptions.

By lying to us against all evidence about the indivisible atom or about the horn of plenty that Soviet agriculture was, and insisting on our acquiescence, the System knew it was forging the New Man. That breed could then be kept in line even without the boot camp of communism. The System was right, and not many Russians believe these days that the 'collapse of communism' represented meaningful change.

We knew we were being taught nonsense, but had to pretend we didn't. It took a first-rate dissembling talent to do so without ever slipping. I either didn't have that talent or else was too proud to use it, having been taught by Mama that I was the apex of creation.

That meant I didn't get along with most teachers, even as in my adult life I could never get on with most figures of authority. But I began to get on better with my classmates. And since they hadn't changed, then I must have done. Still, the changes didn't run deep and I remained a conspicuous failure of our great educational system. Though I didn't exactly learn how to think for myself when in Russia, neither did I lose those lobes that are responsible for acquiring this ability.

The *ne-nash* minority had quite a few misfits like me, though not so many as it's fashionable to believe these days. Some of them still live in Russia, but not one can be found within the ranks of those men of 30 to 70 who now run the country. For all their verbiage, any Russian *ne-nash* knows these 'leaders' for what they are: *nash* slaves to their bone marrow. And slaves who see nothing wrong with their condition are bound to impose it on others, or die in the attempt.

6

On my first day at the secondary school I befriended the only boy in our class who went on to become a celebrity, although not in any usual way. Sasha Solovyov, a former classmate from the previous school, took me for a round of introductions in the new school, where he already knew everybody. More important, he knew which of my new classmates habitually carried knives and should therefore be treated with respect.

There were a lot of perfunctory handshakes, and then one boy came up to me of his own accord. Already at age 11 he was going bald, and his unsmiling dark eyes stared at me out of a small face crowned by an unrealistically high forehead. He just stood there without saying a word until Sasha pushed him aside.

'That's Vitia Raskin' he said. 'When he looks at you that way, just punch him in the snout. He'll go away.' I didn't quite understand why the boy should be punched for looking at me in an odd way but nodded, pretending I too was a *nash*.

Later that day I chatted with Vitia, or rather we exchanged the semiotic signals Russians utilised to tell those who could be trusted from those who couldn't. He was all right, I thought, well-read and clearly a fellow *ne-nash*, if perhaps a bit strange.

We talked, swapping general information about ourselves. His father, he told me, was a famous lawyer; his mother was a psychiatrist. He didn't mind being friends, if that was fine with me. It was, especially since his was the sort of lineage Mama found acceptable.

A week later he suggested we go to his place after school and play. I cleared that invitation with Mama and got an enthusiastic endorsement. So the next day I found myself playing with an elaborate train set and a few other expensive toys. A radio buff, Vitia also showed me a set he had assembled himself. That made his stock drop in my eyes: a budding man of the humanities, I affected contempt for 'technocrats', as we called the scientifically minded.

Unlike me and most other children I knew, the Raskins didn't live in a communal apartment. Vitia's parents weren't at home and we had the whole one-bedroom flat to ourselves, a luxury to me in those days. But it was getting late and, fearing Mama's wrath, I began to inch my way towards the door.

'Wait,' asked Vitia. 'Stick around for another half hour? There's something I want you to help me with.' He fumbled in a toolbox, produced two hefty hammers, gave me one and took the other for himself. 'What are the hammers for?' I was afraid he was going to ask me to fix something in the house, a feat of which I was as incapable then as I am now.

My fears were ill-founded: 'We need the hammers,' he explained in that haughty tone he often put on, 'to kill two superfluous people.'

My first reaction was to think he was suggesting a new game, and my question had an unsuspecting, innocent quality. 'Who?' 'Oh, my parents, of course.' To Vitia that must have gone without saying.

'When they come through the door, you take on Mother, I'll take care of Father. Bang, bang, they'll never know what hit them.' The offer came out of the blue, but I declined it as fast as it had come, thinking the lad was more than a little unhinged.

Since that episode our friendship cooled off, but we remained cordial for the next three years. Occasionally we saw each other socially, but always in the company of other children, which prevented him from renewing his offer. Then we parted ways for a couple of years, with Victor transferring to another school and me going on to a technicum, a rough equivalent of a British polytechnic.

At age 17 we found ourselves in the same classroom again, this time in 10th form of Night School No. 75. Most other students there were thirtyish fathers whose jobs as turners or bus drivers had prevented them from completing secondary education at a normal age.

Being an oasis of enlightenment in a cultural wasteland, we greeted each other as brothers and went out for a drink. In Moscow at that time this meant buying a 'blockbuster', a big bottle of vile fortified wine, and consuming it 'out of the neck' in some piss-sodden doorway. Vitia insisted on buying.

Chasing the chemical taste with a slice of processed cheese, he inquired casually if I had maintained my links with the local gangs. (I had never had such links but pretended otherwise as a possible deterrent to violent attacks.) 'Why?' was my cautious reply. 'Oh, well, I was just wondering if you could help me get a gun.' Vitia still spoke with the same casual flippancy I remembered from the old days.

'What the hell do you need a gun for?' 'I need a gun,' he explained, 'to kill two superfluous people.'

Memories came flooding back and yet I felt I had to ask, 'And who might they be?' 'Oh, my parents of course. Why?' This sounded like the most natural thing in the world, but that's not how I took it.

'Listen,' I blew up, 'when we were eleven and you said the same crap, it was funny. Now we're adults, and I don't want to hear that crap from you ever again.' 'Just help me get a bloody gun, will you?' He wouldn't be sidetracked. I finished the bottle off, gagged and walked out into the street.

This time we didn't remain cordial and stopped seeing each other socially. After we left school we didn't see each other at all for a year or so, and then I ran into him in Herzen Street. He was so pale, almost green, that I had to stop and talk to him. 'Vitia, long time no see. What the hell's happened to you?'

Speaking as if every word was causing him pain, he answered, 'My parents have just been murdered.'

A complex thought rushed through my mind, featuring aspects of bewilderment, pity and suspicion. I did have to say something though, and what on earth does one say to a man after an announcement like that? 'What... who... how,' was all I could manage.

'All I know is that they were murdered brutally and I'm left all alone in this world. The cops don't have a clue who murdered them – they even thought I'd done it.'

The same thought had crossed my mind as well, one of those rare occasions when the law enforcement authorities in Russia and I were on the same wavelength. 'They realised of course it was ridiculous, and I had an alibi anyway, so they apologised and let me go.'

That put me to shame. I cursed myself for being an unfeeling bastard and muttered, 'Listen, I don't know what to say. I mean if there's anything you need, anything at all, money or something, I…'

'That's all right, old man, I'll manage. They asked me to name everyone I know, and I mentioned you among others, so they may want to talk to you, hope you don't mind…' 'Not at all, old man, not at all,' I hastened to reply, thinking selfishly thanks, mate, that's all I bloody well need.

However, no one wanted to talk to me in any official capacity, and I was beginning to forget the whole thing. A month later I ran into Sasha Solovyov, another blast from the past. He was walking absentmindedly down Herzen Street, his pimpled face bespeaking shameful absence of a regular sex life.

After perfunctory greetings, I said, 'Hey, have you heard about Raskin's parents?' 'Yeah,' he responded. 'And d'you know who done it?' In a flash, I realised I had known all along, which made his clarification redundant.

'He done it himself. Know what, I'm on my way to his trial. Want to tag along?' Tag along I did, out of the same scavenger instinct that makes drivers slow down to get a better view of a crash site with a few mangled bodies strewn about.

There he was in the dock, his head clean-shaven, his accomplice, an obvious thug named Sapronovitch, sitting on his right. It was the last day of the trial, and Sasha had to fill me in on the details.

'He wanted to marry that bitch Tamara, right? There she is, second from the left in the front row? And his father said no way, you're too young, and anyway you're not marrying that bitch, she's a slag.'

I thought that the scholarly Raskin Senior would have been unlikely to express any thought in that particular language, as Sasha continued. 'Over my dead body, he said, and that gave Vit'ka this idea. But you know he always was a wimp, so he needed a helper. It just so happened he knew this guy, Sapronovitch. His elder brother was doing time for murder and he himself just stole a motorbike.

'So Vit'ka blackmailed him over the bike, saying you don't help me I turn you in. And if you do help me, we'll split my inheritance fifty-

fifty. Flat, car, dacha, the lot. Sapronovitch said why not, great idea, and they rode the bike to the dacha, put gloves on their hands, nylon stockings over their shoes and knocked on the door.

'His mother said, who's there, and Vit'ka said, Mama it's me. She opened the door, Vit'ka grabbed her and jammed his hand over her mouth while Sapronovitch stabbed away, forty knife wounds. His father heard the noise, ran into the room and yelled, "Vitia, what are you doing?" Sapronovitch hacked him on the head with an axe.

'On the way back to Moscow they dumped the gloves and stockings into a ditch, but a cop saw them do it and took a good look at Vit'ka. So they knew about him all along, but just waited for him to make contact with the other bloke. They nicked them both in a restaurant, arguing about the loot. Now what d'you call a boy who killed both his parents?'

'An orphan,' I yawned, spoiling his fun. It was a tired old joke.

Meanwhile, the court was going through its formal business, with Vitia sitting in the dock and gazing at his feet. Then suddenly he looked up and our eyes met. He kept staring at me, and it was I who finally looked away. For some reason I was feeling embarrassed and even guilty. Then it was time for his last word.

'As I loved Tamara,' he said, ' I couldn't understand how my parents who supposedly wanted the best for me could stand in the way of my happiness. Having said that, I think now that what I've done is unpardonable. I am a moral cripple, and creatures like me don't belong in the Soviet Union, the most just and crime-free society the world has ever known. Therefore I am not asking the court for mercy. There is only one possible punishment for what I did, death, and that is the verdict I am asking for.'

The court promptly obliged, and Victor somewhat inconsistently went on to appeal the very sentence he had requested. The appeal failed, and the papers, which were devoting at least a page in every issue to the case (*The Nylon Footprint* was the running title in the Moscow Pravda), told us a fortnight later that the sentence had been carried out. At the time of his crime, Victor hadn't quite reached the legal execution age of 18, but Soviet courts seldom let such incidentals bother them.

Was he already in love with Tamara, I wondered, when he was 11 years old?

Looking back on those years of secondary school, all I remember is a non-stop struggle in science and maths. This was accompanied by an ever-growing disgust over the way the subjects I loved, literature, history and English, were taught.

When it came to the Russian classics, not only were we not expected to read them, but in some cases we were explicitly told not to. Instead Valentina Borisovna, the literature teacher, would interpret the entire Russian literature in terms of class struggle and on-going revolutionary activity.

We wrote essays on Eugene Onegin, the Superfluous Man (which is where Raskin got his description of his parents), Leo Tolstoy As the Mirror of the Russian Revolution, Chekhov And the Rotting Away of the Landed Gentry, Gorky the First Proletarian Writer, Lermontov the Victim of Tsarism and so forth.

At night I'd pull a blanket over my head and read *War and Peace* or the Karamazovs with a small torch, hoping that my parents, whose bed was separated from mine by a curtain, wouldn't see a ray of unauthorised light shining from under my blanket. At the time Andrei Bolkonsky, the proud aristocrat, was my role model. When I grew older I realised I wasn't at all like him. Pierre Bezukhov was the most I could hope for.

When I got home from school, Mama and Papa were usually still at work. I'd furtively pull a volume of Maupassant from the bookshelves and read descriptions of the activity that was starting to interest me, though I was still in the dark about its mechanics. As I read, the bodies I saw in my mind's eye belonged not to *Bel Ami*'s sultry mistresses but to my classmates, especially Sveta Gorshkova with whom I was in love.

However, she favoured Yura Razgonov who talked to her about American fashion and rock'n'roll, and was closer to her own height. Sveta was growing out of her school dress, and her skirt was getting shorter and shorter. I would drop my books on the floor to steal a naughty peek at the top of her stockings – only to bump heads with that wretch Razgonov who always got the same idea at the same time.

Sveta tolerated me because I'd often do her English homework. My English was better than hers as, from the time Mama hadn't had two kopecks to rub together, she had been paying for a private tutor, and a fair amount of English was spoken at home anyway. I resisted, as all those gerunds and past participles were cutting into my chess, football and reading.

Over my objections, Mama persisted, and at age 12 I was perhaps more fluent in English than Valeria Nikolayevna, our teacher. More important, I had begun to read simple books in the new language, gradually building up my vocabulary to a point where I managed *Three Men in a Boat, Ivanhoe* and, in the privacy of my torch-lit blanket, *Lucky Jim.*

My reading in Russian was getting more involved, and I was already attracted to books on philosophy and theology. I didn't have any channels through which I could obtain the books themselves (most of them weren't for sale and required a special permit at the Lenin Library) and had to satisfy my *ne-nash* curiosity with volumes of criticism. Those I had an unlimited supply of thanks to Mama's job at the library.

Some of the books were excellent, written by *ne-nash* men who had not only the mind to grasp the issues involved, but also the diplomatic skill to veil their scholarship in the usual cant of Soviet criticism. Thus, while outwardly exposing the reactionary bourgeois nature of Aquinas, Kant or Pascal, they described the thought of their subjects in great detail, easily understandable to those who possessed the essential Soviet skill of 'reading between the lines.'

I was also a voracious reader of the Russian poets of the Silver Age: Mandelstam, Pasternak, Akhmatova, Tsvetayeva and their less illustrious contemporaries, such as Nadson, Kuzmin and Severianin. Long out of print, these books were available only in the black market to which I had no access and where I wouldn't have had the necessary king's ransom to buy anything anyway.

So I was fortunate to have Volodia Sergeyev as my chess partner. His maternal grandfather, a close friend of Mayakovsky, had known most of those poets personally and owned signed copies of their books. Volodia would let me read them in his flat during the day, and we talked poetry after sating our chess appetites with our usual diet of 50 2-minute blitz games.

Volodia had grown up in a truly cultured family. While Mama merely mentioned those half-banned names, his mother encouraged him to learn the entire Russian poetry by heart. His best friend was named Alec, a posher version of Alexander than Sasha. Alec, whose background was similar to Volodia's, was studying art. Years later he went on to become one of the few émigré Russian painters to have a lucrative career in America. There he made a success of painting sarcastic pseudo-classicist pictures of Stalin as a wreathed Greek god or Lenin as Zeus.

At that time Alec was already a master of that light-hearted, irreverent banter on serious matters that separates fine minds from ponderous bores. Volodia, of course, spoke the same language. Having had to stew in my own juice all those years, I didn't have much to contribute to their repartee. And when I attempted to do so anyway, I was cut down to size in epic style.

I especially remember one of Alec's putdowns: 'What you're saying has been known to be nonsensical since the time the primary substance was as fresh as a young maiden before a thunderstorm.' Volodia also treated me mercilessly, but I soon learned to hold my own.

In Moscow *ne-nash* circles, the intellect was used as an offensive weapon, a blunt instrument with which to bludgeon victims. Without going too deep into the psychological aspects of this intellectual thuggery, the obvious explanation for it was the realisation that we were all losers in the general scheme of things. Thus we had to channel our competitive impulses into the only avenue open to us: the company of the like-minded.

Our language was full of slang and we spiced almost every sentence with swear words, which the 'philistines' didn't do quite to the same extent. We were probably influenced in our proclivity for invective by the general style of Soviet propaganda, which we rejected rationally, but which had to affect us subliminally.

Soviet newspapers never pulled their punches, and the historian Avtorkhanov once compiled this list of epithets used in just three issues of the Pravda (some may not sound pejorative to you, but were contextually used in that spirit):

Fascist, social-fascist, reactionary, magnate, enemy agent, spy, destroyer, pickpocket, hypocrite, cynic, thief, millionaire, Jesuit, demagogue, cretin, throw-out, dollar diplomat, imperialist, crook, imbecile, rascal, rogue, charlatan, corruptible, adventurer, sell-out, trash, cheat, mercenary, ambush, liberal, provocateur, sadist, parasite, reptile, Trotskyite, fleecer, scum, horror, dog, Janus, saboteur, coward, dolt, microbe, ass, bandit, schismatist, lord, speculator, Yankee, Fritz, gangster, degenerate, scamp, ignoramus, oppressor, torturer, blackguard, inquisitor, idiot, traitor, executioner, riff-raff, assassin, cosmopolitan, slimy rat, salacious viper.

This method of discourse eventually influenced intelligentsia even in places beyond Russia's immediate control, such as England, where conservatives are routinely described as fascists. Since we were closer to the epicentre of this linguistic explosion, we had to suffer more, *pari passu*, from its fallout. That's why our slang frequently included most of the terms you've just read – plus those that at the time were considered unprintable.

The mixture was designed as shibboleths by which we could identify one another and keep outsiders out. As the Moscow saying had it, 'not everybody who uses a lot of four-letter words is an intellectual'. This meant that all real intellectuals did use such words, and one could commonly hear pronouncements like, 'Vivaldi was a talentless wanker. You know, if it's Baroque don't fix it, if it's Tuesday it must be D-minor. I'd rather eat shit than hear another bar of The Four bloody Seasons.'

Years later I horrified a respectable New York poet by opining that the abandonment of rhyme and meter had buggered poetry sideways. Though he agreed with that thought in principle ('When modernists become the establishment, you know it's the end of the world', he once said), the poet could under no circumstances countenance the way in which it had been expressed. What he didn't know was that the subject of our conversation had made me relapse into the English translation of Moscow jargon.

Debate, or rather abusive argument, was the only way we knew how to discuss matters of the mind. That encouraged outsiders to butt in, hoping to divide and conquer. But they didn't realise that they were allowed to listen and admire but not to offer any views – even those that agreed with ours. When they violated that unspoken rule, the warring parties would unite against them, and the intruder would be told in no uncertain terms to keep his stupid mouth shut. This treatment was reserved for those who in our view weren't entitled to membership in that exclusive club of *ne-nash* Moscow intelligentsia.

Occasionally, we played cruel tricks on the uninitiated, and regrettably I was rather good at that sort of thing. Once, I remember, somebody brought to one of our gatherings a cute Pushkin-loving girl who yearned to belong to what she thought was the intelligentsia upper crust. She also expected to hear some penetrating insights that she could then use to impress her usual circle. Sensing her burning need, I said, 'I wonder why it is that when you throw up after getting pissed on beer, the puke smells worse than after vodka. I last puked three days ago and my bathtub still stinks.'

'Hell,' contributed a friend who was quick on the uptake. 'You mean you haven't puked for three days? I puke every night and morning, before brushing my teeth.'

By now everybody but the victim had realised what was going on. The conversation continued to be devoted exclusively to emesis until the cute status seeker decided that this must have been the 'in' talk of the higher circles. 'Oh, yes,' she butted in girlishly, 'I also puke every day...' 'You do?' I asked indignantly. 'How revolting!' – and started talking theology. The girl turned red, soon left and we never saw her again.

If you feel such behaviour was barbaric, you are absolutely right, and the fact that we were rather cultured lads has nothing to do with that. When in Russia, I was worse than most. As a relative Johnny-come-lately, I had to prove myself by acting in a more-vicious-than-thou way towards those deemed to be outsiders. But in spite of my zeal and some aptitude, I must have been striking wrong notes all over the place, as one inevitably does. As a result, my friendship with Volodia Sergeyev eventually petered out and one with Alec never got off the ground.

I had to do my apprenticeship in the minor leagues before winning promotion. And in the minor league I was invited to join, another Volodia, Anikeyev, reigned supreme. But before that happened my life had gone into a tailspin.

8

When I was ten, Papa was finally allowed to move back to Moscow. Or rather the reprieve came a year earlier, but he was waiting for Grandpa to die, as he didn't cherish the prospect of living in the same room with the old man. So Papa added patience to petulance, waiting for Grandpa to smoke himself to death. The latter obliged, and our family reunited in the same old communal flat.

On circumstantial evidence, I don't think Papa liked what he saw. Mama was unreasonable every time he came home smelling of scent. And I – having more or less grown up without him – treated him without excessive respect. A year or two later, we grew accustomed to each other and became friends, with Papa telling me jokes that grew progressively dirtier, and recounting time and again his war exploits. Occasionally, we'd play some chess, and Papa loved the ease with which I routed him.

His arrival expanded our social options, since we now got regular invitations from Papa's brothers and sisters. One of his brothers, Uncle Cement, you remember, was a member of the Academy of Sciences, the other – the truly successful one in the family – ran a grocery shop. They were both married to peasant women, and Mama regarded going to dinners at their houses as slumming.

I didn't, because we got Lucullan feasts there, especially compared with the bland fare we had at home. They ate so well because neither of them ever had to buy any of the food available to the wide masses. The successful *nash* never saw the inside of a grocery shop with its endless queues and plebeian merchandise. Instead they took advantage of a complex system wherein the state rewarded their dedication gastronomically.

To that end, there existed a chain of special distributorships that were in fact limited-access, heavily subsidised shops for the *nash* elite. In 'the most egalitarian state ever', even those distributorships were hierarchical. The highest stage was open only for the Kremlin, the second highest for Central Committee members and so forth. From there they went all the way down to the lowest privileged stage, to which Papa was eventually granted access a few years later. 'The People and the Party Are United!' proclaimed the ubiquitous posters. 'Too bad the shops are separate,' quipped the Muscovites.

Uncle Cement, whose rank was implicitly equal to that of a minister, had access to the second highest stage. And as Uncle Grocer knew everybody in the food business, he didn't need any special privileges to eat well. But, as often happens in this unfair world where the rich get richer, his wife worked at the Kremlin distributorship and could purloin those few things she wasn't allowed to buy.

As a result, while Mama waged a daily losing battle trying to buy a bit of frozen meat and rancid salami, my uncles' festive tables groaned under the weight of unimaginable delicacies. The dull grey of freshly cured beluga caviar competed for our attention with the pale pink of salmon roe. Salted ceps (for which most Russians would do a Faust any day) clashed orgiastically with marinated chanterelles. Sturgeon in aspic gleamed in its impeccable whiteness punctuated by the golden gleam of lemon slices, while roast beef had this special burgundy colour that only the best of filets can boast.

In winter, when less fortunate Muscovites had no fresh vegetables other than potatoes, cabbage and beetroot, fresh tomatoes and cucumbers would be flown in from Uzbekistan to form a careless heap on the table. And of course there was no shortage of every pickled vegetable you can imagine. For no self-respecting Russian would down a shot of iced vodka without chasing it with a crisp pickled gherkin or a baby squash or perhaps some sauerkraut with onions and cranberries.

And that was just *zakuski*, the starters! We gorged ourselves on those, with adults drinking vodka openly and me surreptitiously, and no one was hungry hours later when the women would bring in a steaming dish of roast goose stuffed with apples, or whole sturgeon stuffed with its own caviar.

This wasn't the kind of food one ate to slake hunger. These were masterpieces demanding veneration. We'd dig in, spurring our appetites with viscous liquid drizzling out of bottles frozen into blocks of ice. Afterwards, we'd be too full and tipsy to negotiate the Metro, and Papa would spring for a cab, adding to the festivity of the occasion.

What invariably subtracted from the festivity of the occasion was the embarrassment I felt about Papa's performance. As the most gregarious of the Boots, he was always appointed toastmaster. In that capacity he would time after time, year after year, repeat the same platitudinous mock-Georgian toasts most Muscovites knew by heart. Papa would deliver a couple of those, each time to a tumult of applause, and then a couple more – and then more. At that point someone would shout, 'Mayakovsky! We want Mayakovsky!'

Papa's knowledge of verse was restricted to two poets only. One was Mayakovsky, the hack who after the Revolution devoted his rhyming talent to West-baiting and the bloodthirsty glorification of the Red terror. The other – bizarrely – was Robbie Burns in Marshak's translations. However, what Papa lacked in breadth, he more than made up for in depth, being able to recite his favourites for hours on end.

He'd easily switch from Mayakovsky's unemployed Americans jumping into the Hudson from Brooklyn Bridge (an impressive athletic feat, considering that Brooklyn Bridge spans the East River, not the Hudson on the other side of Manhattan), to Burns's McPherson going to the gallows with joy. He must have anticipated that one day his name would have to be stressed on the last syllable to make it rhymeable in Russian.

After his core programme, Papa would take requests for encores. The only request he ignored would be my stifled, 'Papa, please. Please, Papa, enough's enough.'

On the way back Mama would create a scene. She'd tell Papa she hadn't brought me up in the spirit of the highest intelligentsia so that I'd be exposed to red-faced vulgarians proposing four-letter toasts and, which was worse, reciting Mayakovsky. Papa's response usually ran along the lines of 'if you're so smart, how come you ain't rich'. And Mama had to acknowledge that his family was immeasurably wealthier than hers.

Uncle Cement's income was perhaps twenty times the average wage, which was small beer compared to what Uncle Grocer raked in. Not in salary, mind you – his income came from the spirit of private enterprise that the Russians weren't at the time allowed to express legally but found ample opportunities to express illegally.

Uncle Grocer's salary was 200 roubles a month. But, according to Papa, he had to spend about as much every day to bribe numerous inspectors, whose good will was all that separated him from prison. Some of the bribe money went to the state distributors who were responsible for classifying his merchandise. A hundred here or there, and a 20-tonne shipment of apples would be classified as 'second sort' rather than the 'first sort' they actually were. Uncle Grocer would buy them as 'second sort' wholesale, then sell them as 'first sort' retail and pocket the price difference of one rouble a kilo.

The profit of 20,000 roubles was more than Papa made in three years at the height of his earning power. Yet this formed but a tiny brook flowing into the mighty river of Uncle Grocer's income. The trick, of course, wasn't simply to do that kind of business but to do it and not get caught – and he was exceptionally good at it.

A sapper, according to our Boris, makes but one mistake in a lifetime. But Uncle Grocer survived his one mistake back in the early fifties. Having infuriated an inspector with a mean bribe, he went straight to jail, Monopoly-style. But his three-year sentence was reduced to six months for good behaviour. That is, the good behaviour of his wife who used her Kremlin contacts to bribe him out. He made no more mistakes.

Uncle Grocer didn't attempt to influence my life, as he was aware of his own educational shortcomings. Uncle Cement did, and his arguments were rather persuasive.

'Remember,' he'd tell me, 'you're a *ne-nash*. That means you'll never get anywhere in life without help. I know you like your books and music,' he contorted his thin Germanic lips in a contemptuous smile, 'but you can enjoy them in your spare time. Professionally, you should go into the only field where your father and I can offer tangible help: construction materials.

'If you do, you know I can get you into my university practically without any entrance exams. Then you'll just have to get by somehow, and you'll be guaranteed a post-graduate position. Three years later you'll have your doctorate, between your father and me we'll find you some well-paying sinecure, and you'll be laughing. Think about it.'

I did and, since I was young and stupid, the thought appealed to me. So, when I finished seventh form at age fourteen, I let Papa place me into a polytechnic that specialised in construction materials. Both Papa and Uncle Cement felt this would look good on my CV as a prelude to entering the Mendeleyev University of Applied Chemistry, and I thought I was jumping onto a springboard to a painless life. Instead I found myself on skid row.

The entire humanities curriculum from the last three years of secondary school was compressed into one year at the polytechnic. And the teachers were even cruder: one, for example, explained that the recently erected Berlin Wall was designed to keep at bay all those West Germans clamouring to settle in the East. 'And vice versa,' I suggested with the reckless abandon of youth. The teacher turned crimson and demanded a retraction, which I proffered abjectly.

Nevertheless, I was doing well in those subjects. Where I was failing miserably was in the core curriculum: analytical chemistry, calculus, resistance of materials, cement manufacturing and so on *ad nauseam*. At fourteen I could speak passable English, had read (though not always understood) *The Critique of Pure Reason*, Mandelstam, the Republic, Pasternak and bits of *Summa Theologiae*, had thought of God and the meaning of life.

What I didn't know was how deeply I loathed all those analytical chemistries. At school I could just about get by in sciences without applying myself. But at the polytechnic they demanded their pound of flesh. That I wouldn't give them; and only my name, which in that field had the same ring as Rutherford's would have had at Cambridge, kept me from being expelled.

Apart from that I quite liked the polytechnic. We were treated as adults, which of course most of the other students were. They aged from 17 to 25 or older, most had a few years' experience working at cement or glass factories, and they all regarded the polytechnic as the apex of their educational aspirations.

I wasn't bullied and was treated as the baby of the class. This consisted of a dozen boys, or shall I say young men, and three girls. One was Masha Fokina, whose plain face was offset by sensational legs, a rarity in Russia at the time. (Pushkin wrote, 'You won't discover in all Russia three pairs of shapely women's legs'. If true, in the early sixties one of those three pairs belonged to Masha).

The other two were Lena Kurochkina, whose thin body struggled to support a 42DD bust, and Lyuba Lee, a pocket-sized North Korean girl whose father had flown MIGs against the Yanks.

Every day, when a sharp bell announced the end of the class, the instructor would walk out, the boys would wedge the back of a chair under the door handle and surround the girls. They would then partly undress the young ladies and feel them up, stopping just short of rape.

Of the three, Masha submitted to the abbreviated gangbang with boys-will-be-boys resignation. Lena welcomed it with enthusiasm, unbuttoning her blouse and unhooking her bra without being forced. On the other hand, Lyuba, who had been raised in a strict Oriental fashion, wouldn't submit at all. So Ghena Kalachov and Yura Kononov always had to pin her down to the desktop before the others could have their bit of fun.

Being by far the youngest of the group, and imbued with Mama's standards of right and wrong, I wouldn't join in. But neither would I leave, deriving shamefully voyeuristic pleasure out of those rites of passage.

One day Ghena grabbed me by the wrist and stuffed my hand inside Lena's unhooked but unremoved brassiere, with the girl giggling contemptuously, and the other boys cheering on. That was the first time I had touched a woman's breast, and the sensation was so strong I still haven't got over it. Lyuba would incessantly complain to the management, even producing red marks on her wrists as evidence. But the boys testified this was nothing but her fantasy. As the other two girls were better endowed and still claimed nothing untoward had been happening, Lyuba's case always collapsed.

Mercifully I wasn't asked, as otherwise the code of 'thou shalt not grass' would have clashed with some other codes I had been taught. The Korean had to endure her plight for another year, at which point she actually did get raped one night after classes by two of the more adventurous students. Though she again couldn't prove her case, she secured a transfer to another polytechnic.

At just about the same time, I had run out of excuses and was expelled for academic failure, smashing to bits Papa's hope of continuing a construction-material dynasty. Uncle Cement was also upset, as there was no other Boot to continue the family tradition. His own son Zhenia had a few years earlier been trampled to death by a rampaging crowd at a Moscow soccer stadium.

Hooliganism, incidentally, was rampant at stadiums. My relation Leningrad Boris, was once caught in a full-blown riot at the Kirov Stadium. The riot started with a drunk running onto the pitch and trying to help the Leningrad goalie. The cops got hold of the fan and threw him rather high up into the stands. The football lover retaliated by tossing an empty vodka bottle at a policeman. The cop deftly caught the projectile and tossed it back. After that all hell broke loose. Bottles rained on the cops (one inadvertently caught Boris on the temple, and his subsequent recollections were rather hazy), fights flared up all over the stands, and the arena was torn apart. Every bench and both goals were demolished, police cars and ambulances overturned, a fire engine set alight. The riot only quieted down after soldiers were rushed in and one of them fired a warning shot through a fan's head.

My expulsion left me at a loose end at a silly age of 15 and two months, with no hope of resuming my education until the start of the next school year. Luckily, Papa delivered on his promise of a sinecure, though not in the same spirit in which the original promise had been made. He got me a job as laboratory assistant at the Ferro-Concrete Research Institute.

The lab manager was Papa's old friend who agreed to take me on despite knowing that my contribution to the cause of ferro-concrete research would be nonexistent. But the paltry 60 roubles a month he was paying me didn't make a dent in his budget. And even if it had, that would have been the least he could do for a Boot.

In the first couple of months there I started two friendships, of which one, with the oversexed Boria Migailo, took off immediately and lasted until I left Moscow 10 years later. The other, with the talented poet Grisha Gorin, took a few years to germinate but has persevered to this day.

Boria, Grisha, I and a couple of other boys spent our days in the basement, drinking and talking to the boiler operator Alexei, a crusty old geezer who was perpetually drunk and talkative. 'Look at me,' he'd say. 'Just bloody look at me. What the hell do you think I can do these days? Bugger-all, is what I can do.'

He'd down another glass of vodka and reconsider the frank self-assessment. 'Well, maybe I could still go on a reccy mission behind German lines.' The vodka would then bring on a touch of self-pity leavened with realism. 'Yeah, yeah, some bloody reccy that would be.'

Boria kept bragging about his amorous conquests and invited reciprocity on my part. 'My dick is like a legend,' he'd say. 'It's passed on from mouth to mouth.' Unfortunately, all I could have contributed to such a conversation was a pack of lies, and I wasn't secure enough to attempt those, fearing that my ignorance would shine through.

In my third month there, however, I got my education in that same basement, behind the boiler, from a 23-year-old co-worker Tania who combined sexual curiosity with respect for clever boys who talked poetry. That first time was more memorable for me than I'm sure it was for Tania. Laudably she didn't let on that five seconds was perhaps an unsatisfying duration for an act of love.

Then of course she was a *nash* Russian woman raised on a steady diet of *nash* Russian men. Those chaps tend to regard premature ejaculation as a sign of virility, and sex itself as either punishment they inflict on unwilling women or, alternatively, as a reward they can grant for good behaviour and withdraw for a transgression.

In my last couple of years in Russia, when I was deprived of daily contact with the *nash*, I often chatted with cabbies who are as forthcoming there as everywhere else. I relied on them for a bit of *vox populi* wisdom, and was always rewarded handsomely.

'I told this bitch,' one of them shared with me the troubles he was having with his wife, 'to give me real food, like borscht with fresh meat and vegetables. And what does the bitch do? She stuffs my face with macaroni and potatoes. So I don't shag her for that.'

Another driver told me, 'My cousin came to stay from the village, and I only have one room in the dorm, and one bed. So I tell her fine, you can stay until you find your own place but I want you to keep the room tidy and cook all my meals. First night I come home from work, there's no food on the table and the place looks like a pigsty. I tell her "Right. Since this is the first time, I'm just gonna shag you. But next time I'll kick you out into the street." '

One of my last dialogues with Russian cabbies started with the driver asking, 'You're smartly dressed, I see. Going on a date?' 'I am actually,' I replied readily. 'Taking a girl to the cinema.' 'Good,' he said. 'I'm going to see a movie myself after work.' 'With your wife?' 'What the hell should I take my wife to a movie for? She puts out anyway.'

With such attitudes, it's not surprising that *nash* Russian men are horrendous lays, while their women are among the best, or at least the most eager, lovers in the world. That dichotomy is often resolved, to the best of their ability, by *ne-nash* men who tend to be more sensitive and therefore seldom have a shortage of willing partners.

The mating ritual, which we called 'cadreing up', as in 'last night I cadred up a great heifer', amounted to chatting up girls in the street. Girls welcomed those approaches and usually handled them with aplomb and good humour. After my initiation by Tania, Migailo and I often went hunting as a pair, an ideal arrangement as girls usually promenaded up and down Gorky Street in twos. I was there in a purely auxiliary capacity, with Migailo putting his swarthy good looks and gift of the gab to good use.

It was as simple as, 'Excuse us, ladies, do you mind not rushing so we can keep up with you? Do you mind if we talk? You see, my friend and I have a problem, and since you look like kind, sensitive human beings, we hope you can come to our assistance in our hour of need. The problem is that we have a flat, in the centre of which there is a table laden with the most exotic gifts of Georgian countryside and Moscow distilleries. Unfortunately my friend and I have no one to share this repast with and it is therefore likely to go to waste. Can we presume...'

As often as not we could. On those few occasions he was rejected, Boria would shrug philosophically. 'If the mountain doesn't go to Mohammed,' he'd say, bending the phrase ever so slightly, 'it can go screw itself.'

The problem with my initiation was that Tania practised the rhythm method, and arithmetic wasn't her forte. Nothing like the pill was available then and still isn't, at least not to the majority of Russian women. Their favoured method of contraception is abortion, and few haven't had theirs running into double figures. My distant relation's wife, for example, had had more than her fair share by the time she left Russia for the States. Having settled in New York, she went to see a gynaecologist for a minor complaint.

The doctor took one look at her scarred insides and asked in a gentle medical voice, 'And how many abortions have you had, dear?' 'Eight,' she said with modest contrition. The doctor replied with the righteous indignation doctors often assume but seldom feel, 'That's insane! Irresponsible! Don't you know how dangerous that is?' In fact, she had had not eight but 28, a figure a bit on the high side even by Russian standards but not at all unheard of.

I objected to Tania getting an abortion and suggested marriage as an alternative. She laughed and, as a responsible adult, pointed out I wasn't quite 16 years old and the baby might not be mine anyway. The resulting trauma left a mark, but not a deep one, and I continued my gay bachelor ways in the company of Boria Migailo and a few other derelicts like us.

But as the new school year approached, the matter of my further education began to loom large. The only avenue open to me was a night school. But the few I had talked to told me they'd take me no higher than into eighth form, since I had completed only seven full years of primary and secondary school. My year and a bit at the polytechnic counted for nothing, as far as they were concerned.

By now I was 16. All my former schoolmates were about to start tenth form, and the thought of lagging two years behind them was humiliating. This time it was Mama's connections that came into play. She networked among her friends until she found one who at the time was Headmistress at Night School No. 75, at the corner of Herzen Street and Tverskoy Boulevard. Mama, who like most Russians was superstitious, took the location of the school, a few short blocks away from our house, as a sign of divine benevolence.

She chatted with her friend and, their reunion unmarred by the fact they hadn't seen each other for 15 years, explained to her my predicament. Even though the friend wasn't sure Mama would ever be in a position to scratch her back, she nevertheless agreed to scratch hers. I was admitted to tenth form.

10

It was on my first day there that I met Volodia Anikeyev who was 18 going on 30. A tall, powerfully built lad, he looked 10 years older than his age. That impression was reinforced by the green three-piece suit he always wore with a white shirt and tie. Like me, he was obsessed with poetry. Unlike me, he was also obsessed with alcohol.

We all drank, of course, as it would have been more socially acceptable for a boy to wear a frock than not to spend his whole disposable income on vodka or its surrogates. *Ne-nash* parents discouraged early manifestations of dipsomania but *nash* men didn't.

'My boy is great,' yet another cabbie bragged to me once. 'Just seven, you know, but the little bastard can down a tumbler of vodka and walk away sober as sober can be.' Paternal pride in his voice was unmistakeable.

I had done my share of imbibing. A couple of times Migailo had to bring me home from work in a taxi, drag me up the stairs and hand me over to Mama who'd always take delivery with gratitude but without much joy. Once or twice I failed to make it home under my own steam and had to catch a nap on a park bench. Muscovites, unmoved by the familiar sight of a boy with vomit on his shirt sleeping on a bench, wouldn't disturb me. After a refreshing nap I'd stagger home.

My self-preservation instinct was strong though, and I didn't really drink as much as it might have appeared. Anikeyev, on the other hand, had no self-preservation instinct whatsoever. By age 18 he had become an alcoholic, a condition at which *ne-nash* men tended to arrive at a slightly later phase of their lives. What was worse, Volodia was a violent drunk who brawled regularly. And he was never deterred by the opposition's numerical strength or indeed official status in such institutions as the police.

By the time we met he had already served four summary 15-day sentences that hooligans received at police stations without any state money being wasted on lengthy court proceedings. Each time the cops also beat him to a pulp, and once he received special treatment. 'The garbage' (common name for policemen in Russia) tied his wrists to his ankles behind his back, picked him up by the knot thus formed and dropped him on the floor from a height of four feet.

'I pissed blood for a month after that,' confided Anikeyev with pride. 'I suppose I shouldn't have kicked that cop in the balls when he asked me what my name was.'

His taste both in literature and in life ran towards the romantic, and he was vicariously in love with every consumptive heroine ever to have crossed the pages of Erich-Maria Remarque. That German novelist was obsessed with tuberculosis. His favourite trick was to have his witty, loyal, hard-drinking protagonist fall in love with a witty, loyal, hard-drinking beauty only to have her die in his arms spurting tubercular blood.

Anikeyev insisted on his life imitating art, drank hard and was tragically in love with a nice *ne-nash* girl. The similarity ended there, as his beloved was in rude health and wouldn't give Anikeyev the time of day on account of his drinking. That rejection completed the vicious circle by making Volodia drink even more.

'I told him,' she said to me once over a cup of coffee, 'listen. We've had a hundred dates over two years and I've never once seen you sober.' 'I was under the impression he took to drink because you rejected him.' I felt I had to stick up for my friend. 'Don't ever believe anything you hear from that creep,' she said. 'He has never been sober for at least five years.'

In the absence of amorous reciprocity, Anikeyev had to compensate by re-enacting the emotional fabric of Remarque's novel *Die Drei Kameraden* in my presence. The mode of expression he favoured was drink. As Remarque's characters drank tokai, kummel and cognac, Anikeyev always pretended that's what he was drinking as well, as he gulped down foul-smelling vodka.

There were no bars in Moscow, and we usually drank in the attic of an apartment block in Gorky Street. A rafter ran across the attic, and with a little imagination we could pretend it was a zinc bar somewhere in Hamburg (Remarque), Paris (Ehrenburg) or Madrid (Hemingway). Such leaps of faith came easily to Anikeyev, and indeed to most Russians who had no option but to live off literary allusions.

'This bitch Galka [his unrequited love] isn't at all like Pat [Remarque's TB sufferer],' he'd start in his witty, loyal, hard-drinking way. 'She's not kind, the bitch has no kindness whatsoever. She's tormenting me for the hell of it, and what do I do? Instead of kicking her arse and telling her to bugger off, I am suffering and drinking myself to death. So here's to you, Boot, may you rot in hell.' Aware that the last contribution was based on a bad Russian translation from the German, I took it in the same loving spirit in which it had been offered.

We talked about the finer things in life as well, such as jazz, which meant a lot to Anikeyev, and had heated debates on the relative merits of Pushkin ('doggerel', according to yours truly) and Mandelstam ('too bloody philosophical to be a real poet', according to Anikeyev).

Our friendship went beyond drunken discourse, as friendships between Russian men invariably do. Friendship to a Russian always has a strong emotional aspect. It's closer to a Western love between a man and a woman (minus the sex, as I hope you understand) than to what a Western man would describe as friendship.

Ask anybody who knows Russian what the Russian for 'friend' is, and he'll tell you it's 'droog', the word Burgess's characters used in their pidgin-Russian argot. In fact, these words are second cousins thrice removed, to borrow Twain's phrase.

'Droog' means someone with whom I can share my innermost feelings, the last rouble, the last drop of vodka, the last girl. 'Droog' is someone I'd give my life for and would only denounce to the KGB under duress. 'Droog' is my *alter ego*, my emotionally connected Siamese twin, my *doppelgänger*.

But to a Westerner 'friend' essentially means nothing more than 'someone I see occasionally who has done me no harm'. Even 'my dearest and best friend' comes nowhere near to the voluminous concept of a Russian 'droog'. That word, therefore, is not in its true sense translatable into English. Can it be it's not needed? I think so, as the English tend to operate within a much narrower emotional band than the Russians.

They don't love so tenderly, but then neither do they hate so deeply or so instantly as the Russians. They aren't so kind, but neither are they so cruel. Not so selfless, but then not so selfish. Not so disinterested, but then not so greedy. Not so charitable and not so perfidious. With the reticent English you usually know where you stand, to a certain extent, while with the effusive Russians you don't. But, and that makes things worse, you may think you do.

Marquis de Custine was one of the few Western travellers who almost understood the Russians. Anikeyev managed to get a mimeographed copy of his book, and we both nodded vigorously while reading the yellowing sheets in the same old attic.

The Marquis was spot on in most of his observations, we agreed. But then he travelled to Russia in the 1830s and wasn't ideologically predisposed in its favour, as, for example, the Webbs and GBS were a hundred years later. He saw the duality of the Russians but mistook it for duplicity. This was where Custine went wrong: it's just that in the Russian character good and evil are so sharply polarised they form a suspension, not a solution. They exist as separate fractions that come into play as the situation demands.

In a situation Custine described, a Russian took in a passing pilgrim and shared with him his supper and his hut – only to kill and rob him in the morning. Custine thought that the hut-owner's kindness in the evening had been a ploy to set up the sanguinary morning. But it's much more likely that in the course of a few hours the Russian's emotional pendulum swung a full sweep, and he was equally true to his character in both instances.

The Russians tend to see life as either a tragedy or a comedy, with nothing in between. Hence transition from mirth to tears, then back again comes easily to most Russians and takes no time at all. Westerners, for many of whom the ship of life sails at a more even keel, often marvel at the Russians' emotional spectrum that has only two polarised colours.

Many, especially Americans but also the French and sometimes even the English, find this incontinent emotional extremism appealing; émigré salons in the West are full of Russian groupies. I met quite a few American and English girls in Russia who never went to bed with their compatriots anymore, instead buying expensive junkets to Moscow. One often heard girlish gasps along the lines of 'Oh, you Russians! You are all so romantic!' Romantic Russians may be, but even as German romanticism fed not only Brahms but also Hitler, Russian romanticism isn't all about Turgenev and Tchaikovsky.

At that time my Russian upbringing hadn't been expunged yet, and Anikeyev was definitely a 'droog' to me. I felt his pain in addition to my own, and his smouldering eyes conveyed the heart-breaking sorrow that was also mine. I never got to the bottom of his drinking, which I should have done because even in Russia it's not normal for a boy of 18 to be an alcoholic. There was probably some real anguish there for which I didn't offer enough solace. Instead I just drank with him and participated, half-heartedly, in his silly re-enactments of Remarque.

Before long we started to use the school as a meeting place only. We'd show up there, consume our first 'dose' in the canteen and then wander off to other 'doses' life had in store for us that night. In our less sombre moods we relieved boredom by various pranks, with ubiquitous cabbies often figuring on the receiving end.

Anikeyev, imposing in his green three-piece suit, would raise his hand and a cab would cut across three lanes of traffic to brake screeching at our feet. 'Are you free, chief?' he'd inquire in his regal manner. 'Yeah,' would be the cabbie's impatient reply. 'Long live freedom!' we'd yell and disappear into the crowd.

Another possibility was to reply, 'So come out and let's have a dance,' which we favoured less but used occasionally to break up the monotony. Sometimes, we'd actually get into the cab and reply to the driver's 'where to' with either 'none of your business, arsehole' or 'what the hell, let's go to your place'.

Pharmacy assistants, especially young and pretty girls, were also a frequent target. We'd ask a mark, 'Excuse me, Miss, do you have any condoms?' 'Yes,' she'd say. 'And for sale?' we'd ask innocently. As a variation on the theme we'd pretend to be making a complaint. 'How come your condoms never used to bend and now they do?'

Another area of opportunity came from the telephone, an endless source of hilarity. Bell's invention arrived late at our shores and was by no means widespread even in the sixties, when the waiting time for a private phone was at least five years (it usually still is, by the way). This novelty appeal drove many Muscovites of all ages to spend hours on infantile wind-ups. I prided myself on my mastery of those, what with my ability not to give the game away by laughing at a critical moment.

I'd dial a number at random and say, 'May I speak with Vassia please?' 'You've got the wrong number, citizen,' was the statistically probable reply. 'Oh, I'm so sorry.' I'd be effusive in my politeness. Then I'd dial the same number right back: 'May I speak with Vassia, please?' 'Citizen, you're still dialling the wrong number.' 'So sorry. I must check my records,' I'd apologise, hang up and redial.

After 15 minutes of that torture the victim would start screaming abuse, focusing on the sexual behaviour of my mother. At that point I'd hang up and wait for about 10 minutes before redialling the number I now knew by heart. 'Hello, this is Vassia,' I'd say in a changed voice. 'Do you have any messages for me?' And our evening would be made bearable.

Another trick was to tell a randomly dialled respondent that I was from MosTelefon; we were running an extremely important survey and could she please measure the length of her telephone cord. One out of three marks would agree to do so, go off to fetch a ruler, then announce the length was 83 centimetres or some such. 'Splendid,' I'd intone in my best official voice. 'Now fold it five ways and stick it in you know where.'

Again, after the appropriate 10-minute interval I'd redial, this time sounding stern: 'This is the police. There's a band of obscene callers operating in your area. Have they by any chance phoned you?' The vindictive victim would be only too happy to oblige: 'Yes, they have, officer.' 'How long ago?' 'Oh, ten minutes or so.' 'Sorry, citizen, you'll have to be more precise than that.' 'Well, ten minutes ago. No more than eleven.' 'Good,' I'd say, and Anikeyev would put his hand over his mouth trying not to spoil the punch line. 'You can take the cord out now'.

Eventually I brought Anikeyev together with Migailo, and he introduced me to his own friends. Before long we formed a close-knit circle into which I tried to draw Sergeyev but failed, as collectively we were even more low-brow for him than I was individually.

'Anikeyev isn't a romantic hero but a drunken swine,' he told me. 'He's on an accelerating downhill slide, and if you don't watch out he'll take you with him.' I knew he had a point. That's why I told him to shove his snobbery, together with his advice, into the telephone-cord receptacle of my pranks. He shrugged his shoulders, and that was the last I saw of him until a chance meeting in the university library five years later.

My self-preservation instinct eventually prevailed over droogship, and Anikeyev and I parted ways a year after I had gone to university and he had been expelled from Night School No. 75. I had miraculously escaped the same fate a few months earlier.

In fact, four months into tenth form I was indeed expelled, and only Mama's interference saved me. She went to see her friend the Headmistress and begged her tearfully to reinstate me. 'But, Nyuta, dear,' commiserated her friend. 'Your son hasn't attended any classes for four months. And when he shows up he is drunk and abusive.'

Mama begged, beseeched, implored, she wailed and wept, she told her old friend about Papa's shenanigans that, according to her, had had a severe emotional effect on me, she promised I'd reform – and her friend relented. I was reinstated conditionally and, the old self-preservation instinct kicking in, actually started to attend classes and do some homework. As a result, I got my diploma, with only the mark for foreign language (English) entered as 'excellent'. Every other mark, including conduct, was a barely adequate 'satisfactory.'

Anikeyev and I went on a wild celebratory bender financed by the sale of a few volumes from our library, something Papa neither forgot nor forgave. Moscow was full of second-hand bookshops that willingly paid top rouble for most books, except for the overproduced 30-volume Dickens, which could thus be found on most Moscow bookshelves. In fact, those 30 greenish volumes were the only ones that could be found in Anikeyev's bookcase. The rest of his mother's library had been converted into vodka a long time ago, thus giving a whole new meaning to the concept of liquid assets.

Then university life sucked me in, I moved up the *ne-nash* social ladder and, as often happens to upwardly mobile people, left my old friends behind. In this case that was justified by Anikeyev's behaviour that was frankly getting out of hand. When two years later I heard he was in prison, doing a fiver for aggravated assault, I felt crestfallen and, in my typical fashion, guilty. I thought that perhaps I had failed him, as I might have failed Raskin earlier.

11

Most institutions of higher learning specialising in foreign languages attracted more girls than boys. The exceptions were The Institute of Military Translators, The Institute of International Relations, The Interpreters' Department of the Institute of Foreign Languages and the Institute of Oriental Languages.

These highly privileged institutions provided obvious training grounds for the KGB and the GRU. Few of their graduates ever chose, or were allowed to choose, a career path that bypassed various branches of the intelligence services.

Most of those admitted there, I'd say at least 90 percent, were either children of the *nash* elite (KGB, GRU, Party, government officials) or else self-made shits who had already distinguished themselves in the junior leagues of the KGB by snitching on their friends and classmates. The remaining few seats went to aspiring *nash* semi-intellectuals and a few crypto-*ne-nash* intels. They had to compete in the rough-and-tumble of entrance exams where nothing less than a 100-percent score assured admission. And there were instances when even some of those overachievers didn't get in.

Our university didn't dangle the carrot of a guaranteed steeply ascending career path upon graduation. But then neither did it bang one on the head with the stick of nearly impossible admission standards.

About 90 percent of all students in the English department were girls. Many of them, in the Soviet version of primogeniture, came from the same families as their brothers who went to the KGB hatcheries I've mentioned earlier. Most students had 10 years of specialised English-language schools behind them and were already fluent. The others had got in on the strength of family connections based either on friendship or, as in my case, bribery.

Of the 12 boys in our first year, two or three came from *nash* elite families. They had chosen our university because, while the academic standards there were as high as in other places, there was marginally less backstabbing. Upon graduation, these lads were either posted abroad straight away or went on to train at the KGB 'diplomatic' school.

Another two or three were hard-working demobilised soldiers who had got in on the Soviet equivalent of the American GI bill. One of them was a short, tongue-tied man who found it difficult to express himself even in his native language. His hobby was bodybuilding, and he incessantly exercised every part of his anatomy, including the intimate one. Actually, it wasn't as intimate as all that for Slava would often demonstrate his athleticism in the men's lavatory. There, much to my envy, and to the thunderous applause of the packed audience, he'd lift increasingly greater weights with his penis. His personal best, as I recall, was 20 kilos.

Then there were five hard-core alcoholics in their twenties. As each had a certificate explaining away his boozing as a medical condition, they were as hard to expel as they were to promote beyond the first year. Thus by that time those perpetually unshaven individuals had been disgracing first-year classrooms for an average of eight years.

Then there was I, and you won't get any prizes for guessing which group attracted me most. The Alkies, as they were affectionately called, along with a larger group of easy-going goodtime girls, were a lot more fun than either the other boys or the serious, academically minded young ladies.

One of the Alkies drank less than the others and, at 22, was quite a bit younger. Before deciding to obtain a higher education he had been a waiter for a couple of years, which occupation, he explained to me, was a licence to steal.

'Listen,' he told me once over a jar. 'I need this university like I need a hole in the head. I worked the restaurant at the *Ukraina* hotel for four years, and I lived like a king.'

'Salary or tips?' I wanted to know.

'Sod the salary, sod the tips, that's just 200 a month, your health,' winced Misha Balandin and downed his eight-ounce tumbler the proper way, pouring the vodka down his gullet without swallowing.

'How then?' insisted Sasha Boot, downing his tumbler the wimpish way, in several gulps.

'How much time have you got?' The drink made Balandin's irony drip from every word.

'First, there's the old caviar trick. Punters order four portions, you take three, split them into four, that's two-fifty right there. Do it twenty times a night, that's fifty. Then there's the brandy trick. Three-star is ten roubles a bottle, right? The name brand is twenty. A shitkicker from Siberia wants to impress a girl, orders the name brand, I pour three-star into the right bottle, cover it with a towel, make a show of opening it at the table but under the towel. That's another ten for Uncle Misha. At least three of those a night, that's another thirty. You've got to be careful, some shitkickers can actually tell the difference, but that's where experience comes in.

'Then, of course, there's overcharging, but again you've got to be careful. Georgians, especially when pissed, are a sure thing, they have so much dosh they don't give a tinker's damn how much the bill is for. But any punter is a good bet when pissed. All together, you do forty covers a night, two roubles over on each one, not to be greedy, that's eighty.

'How much is that so far? Hundred-sixty? That's every night, normal, without counting a shitfaced punter leaving his wallet behind, or a rat-arsed Georgian slipping me a hundred to add brandy to his girl's wine, and another hundred if I let him do her in the pantry. All told, if I didn't pull down three grand a month, that was one crap month. I had to kick five hundred back to the maitre d' each month, but what the hell, you can't be greedy. I was in line to become a maitre d' anyway.'

'How many waiters did you have?' I was always interested in precise data. 'Eighteen. Your health,' said Balandin, and a second 'dose' irrigated his lead-lined stomach.

'So why did you decide you needed all this aggro? Exams and all.' I especially wanted to know the answer as I had calculated that in backhanders alone the maitre d' was making eighteen times Papa's respectable salary. 'So I could work Intourist restaurants,' explained Balandin. 'They demand two languages there.'

He lived in a basement 'corridor system', 400 feet of musky maze with rooms on either side and cobwebs on the ceiling. Balandin shared his room with his 75-year-old epileptic grandmother whom he treated without much respect. Once, I recall, we took a couple of girls to his place and Balandin told Granny to take a walk for an hour.

'I'm not going,' she replied categorically. 'You're going to shag.' With her innate peasant cunning she had seen right through us.

For a misguided second I thought she objected to amorous activity on moral grounds, which ill-founded suspicion she went on to dispel. 'So it's gonna be like last time. I was locked out for five hours.' 'Not at all like last time.' Balandin was making an heroic effort to control his temper. 'Just an hour, that's all. We have to leave in an hour anyway, the young ladies have to attend to their studies. Go on, Granny, please.'

The magic word did the business. She relented and shuffled outside, threatening to start knocking on the window 60 minutes later on the dot. 'Yeah, yeah,' promised Balandin and bolted the door.

The grandmother was as good as her word. Exactly an hour later she started beating on the window what sounded like the percussion section from Ravel's *Bolero*. I got up.

'What are you getting up for?' asked Balandin. 'Well, your grandmother...' 'Sod the old bitch, she's used to it. C'mon, no need to rush.' The old lady stayed locked out for another three hours and was let in only when she began to have a fit outside.

Soon afterwards Balandin married his first cousin, which doesn't constitute incest in Russia. His new wife came from his native village and 'knew what a man needed', a *nash* phrase used to describe a woman ready to spend her life in the kitchen with a mattress tied to her back. Alas, she offset that fine quality by being daft. Balandin soon tired of her and, according to Kolia Lanovoy, another of my colourful Alkie friends, the marriage went sour.

'He slaps her around-slaps her around,' he told me in his inimitable manner, 'she screams-screams, Grandma starts rolling on the floor, frothing at the mouth, nightmare-nightmare.' Lanovoy was in the early stages of *delirium tremens*. That often made him say the same thing twice in rapid succession, accompanying each word with rhythmically twitching colourless eyelashes.

'The girls-the girls,' he once machine-gunned at me, 'in my class-in my class. Let's have a party-let's have a party they said, coz Kolia isn't integrated in the collective-in the collective. So they invite me over-invite me over, one of the bitches has this great flat-great flat. They have lots of food-lots of food, see, but who needs bloody food-bloody food, right? All the bitches have is two bottles of red for twelve people-twelve people, and I spill more than that-more than that. So I finish one, they finish the other-the other, then one bitch says maybe Kolia hasn't had enough-had enough, and another bitch goes, I wouldn't mind another drop myself, she says-she says.

'So they do a whip around-whip around and give me eleven roubles-eleven roubles. Kolia, they say, would you mind terribly if we asked you to go out and buy some wine-some wine. No problem I say-no problem. So out I go-out I go and come back two hours later-two hours later pissed as a fart and no bottles-no bottles. Half the bitches are gone, the other half say where's the wine Kolia-where's the wine, and I say nightmare-nightmare, I killed a man-killed a man, he attacks me-attacks me, I start hitting him with the bottles, nightmare-nightmare, he's dead-he's dead, every bottle broken-bottle broken, I'm sorry-I'm sorry, nightmare-nightmare.'

Either the bitches in question, well-spoken young ladies from good families, hadn't believed the story, or they had. In either case, Lanovoy received no more invitations designed to draw him into the collective of well-spoken young ladies from good families. He had to make do with his best friend Nikita Kryuk, the oldest of the gang, and also the most harmless.

The onset of 'white fever', the common term for delirium tremens, had left him partially paralysed and very reticent. He lived with his old mother on whom he doted and, having drunk away everything in the house, was having prolonged bouts of self-analysis so characteristic of the mysterious Russian soul.

The moral dilemma that was goring Nikita with its horns revolved around his mother's winter coat, the only remaining liquid asset available to him. To sell or not to sell, that was the question Kryuk finally had had to answer in the affirmative. Now he dreaded the arrival of the inclement Russian winter, which threatened to do to his mother's health what it had done in the past to the armies of Napoleon and Hitler.

'Mama, poor Mama, in the cold, outside, without a coat...,' he'd complain in a tearful bout of drunken remorse, and then drink to her health.

The most agreeable lad in the bunch, Tolia Dostenko, was in the same class as I. Unlike the others, he always showed up every morning, toting his ubiquitous guitar and a tattered briefcase containing two bottles of red. He'd sit in the back row, quietly plucking the silvery strings, taking the odd pull from the bottle, not bothering anyone and being seldom bothered himself, except by our conscientious phonetics instructor.

Of the six periods of practical English we had every day, four in that first year were devoted to phonetics. We had to learn pages upon pages of English texts by heart and enunciate them as closely to the received pronunciation as we could manage. Most texts featured as the principal character a fictitious Mr Sanford, the local rep for the communist paper *The Daily Worker*, as *The Morning Star* was then.

'I say, Mr Dixon,' we'd intone dutifully. 'Do you receive *The Daily Worker* at all?' 'No, I can't say I do, old chap, can't say I do.' 'Oh, what a shame! Surely you wouldn't mind trying it for a month or two, what-what?' 'Not at all, old chap, not at all. Oh bother, it looks like rain.' 'It does indeed, it does indeed. Terrible nuisance, that.' 'Well, the English climate isn't at all changeable, is it, Mr Sanford? Ha-ha-ha…' No one told us that people who employed the diction we were trying to emulate were unlikely to flog *The Daily Worker* door to door, although they were perfectly capable of funding it behind the scenes.

The phonetics instructor faced the tall order of reshaping our speech-producing organs, inured to throaty Russian. To that end this pleasant, blue-haired lady would stick her nose into our mouths, making sure our tongues were properly retracted in the direction of our hard palates. She attempted that trick with Dostenko a few times, only to be thwarted by the industrial-strength smell of good vodka and bad teeth.

Before she gave up on him she once asked if he could recite Text Five by heart. The question was posed in English, but the reply came in Russian: 'Fraid I can't.' 'Well, Text Four then.' Galina Stepanovna wasn't getting the message. 'Can't do that one either.' 'What can you do then, Tolia?' demanded Galina Stepanovna in a Russian as pure as Dostenko's own. 'I can sing you a song,' he offered. 'Please do, by all means,' said the instructor with what she thought was devastating sarcasm.

Undevastated and undaunted, Dostenko strummed his guitar and went into a hoarse, drunken rendition of the Russian folk song *At the river, the river, the o-o-o-other bank, Marusia was washing her darling white feet.* He knew it in its never-ending entirety. Galina Stepanovna, who had never heard anything quite so surreal in her 40-year career of hard-palate searching, was so stunned that she stopped the song only after four verses, each followed by the eponymous refrain.

Petia Shuruyev, the fifth musketeer, once made a pass at another phonetics instructor, a beautiful girl who had just taken her degree and was several years his junior. When rejected, Shuruyev, a wayward offshoot of a good *ne-nash* family, took revenge by employing his rare talent of being able to vomit at will.

Every time the comely Liudmila Nikolayevna demanded some kind of performance from him, be that reciting a text or pronouncing a phrase, he'd gag theatrically and throw up his daily intake of red and white wine into the aisle. As the girls in his class knew he was going to perform that charming trick, they'd sensibly take their seats as far away from him as the smallish classroom allowed.

Before long Shuruyev was summoned to the dean's office and asked to account for his behaviour. 'I can't help it,' he explained in his refined Moscow accent. 'It's an involuntary reaction, comrade dean. Every time she calls out my name, it just happens. Hard as I try I can't keep it in.' The dean dismissed him, saying it was more than high time something was done about him and the other four degenerates who belonged in front of a firing squad, not in a university auditorium.

To their credit, the Alkies never got drunk unless there was an important occasion to celebrate. It was just that in the Russia of my youth there was at least one such occasion every day. All one had to do was open the calendar.

Some, such as May Day, November 7 (Revolution Day), February 23 (Red Army Day), March 8 (International Women's Day) were huge national holidays when no one worked. Some were less important: Printers' Day, Railway Workers' Day, Scientists' Day, Teachers' Day, Steel Workers' Day and so forth, *ad infinitum*.

And that wasn't all. For we also had anniversaries: of every battle in the war, of every speech Lenin ever delivered, of every important Party Congress (such as the Tenth in 1921, when all opposition was banned), of – well, you get the gist. There was a pecking order to the anniversaries, and there was a sacrosanct protocol involved in the festivities.

Once our university's Party Secretary ordered that on such and such day we were to present ourselves at the conference hall to commemorate the 60th anniversary of the 1905 revolution. An occasion of that magnitude clearly called for a rally, not just a piss-up. And no rally of that type could have been complete without at least one eyewitness of the glorious event, proudly displaying himself in the presidium on the stage.

That was the tough part: what with the average life expectancy for men stuck at 57 and declining, finding a superannuated veteran was no mean task. But, according to Lenin's well-known pronouncement, 'there are no fortresses that Bolsheviks can't storm.' Impressive detective work by the Secretary tracked down a senile octogenarian Cossack. The veteran swore he had been an active participant in the 1905 revolt before covering himself with glory in the ranks of Budyonny's cavalry during the Civil War.

When the hero staggered onto the stage, even the Party Secretary's face showed some doubt. The man had a vacant look that suggested he wasn't in complete command of his faculties. That impression was enhanced by the saliva dripping out of his toothless mouth and onto his already dirty tie.

But beggars can't be choosers. The Secretary braced himself and got the ball rolling by delivering a formulaic half-hour speech at the end of which he introduced the veteran. 'So let's give a warm welcome to Maxim Ivanych!'

We clapped enthusiastically, anticipating some good fun. Maxim Ivanych didn't disappoint. He got to the microphone, tottered a bit but then straightened himself up.

'I remember that day azh if it wazh yeshterday,' he said and tottered again. 'There wazh a rally in the shquare. Lotsh of red flagzh, all shorts of people, shtudentsh, workerzh. They wazh all shouting, one Jew climbed on top of a shoap boksh to give a shpeech.' He smiled apologetically for having inadvertently identified the orator's ethnicity.

'Then the shquadron commander yelled "Shabresh out! Charge!!!" And,' he ended on a triumphant note, 'we chopped 'em all up to ribbonzh!!!'.

In the ensuing tumultuous ovation Maxim Ivanych was whisked off the stage by the despondent Secretary whose face had turned beetroot-red. The poor sod had made a career-ending mistake: he hadn't checked the facts, having satisfied himself that the Cossack had indeed fought with Budyonny. It escaped his attention that Maxim Ivanych had only seen the Bolshevik light in 1917, not in 1905 when he had been doing his normal Cossack service in the imperial security troops.

The Alkies celebrated with added vigour that night, with me keeping up my end. The sheer inertia of Anikeyev *et al* had carried me straight into the shaking arms of the five musketeers.

Though I could still coast academically on the baggage of those private lessons Mama had bought in the sweat of her brow, I was drinking more and more, and attending classes less and less. It was a stroke of luck that the unlikely cardiovascular disease from which I then suffered acted up, no doubt exacerbated by heavy alcohol intake.

I landed in hospital for several months, missing much of the curriculum. As a result, I had to come back the next year and start my course from scratch. By that time the dean had kept his promise and finally got rid of the five Alkie musketeers.

Shuruyev was the first to go. He was discreetly summoned to the dean's office and given the good news. For most people, expulsion would have been a tragedy, and no doubt that's what it was for Shuruyev, what with ten first years of university going down the drain. His reaction, however, was different from most other people's.

The Alkies, you see, routinely pestered other students with requests for small loans, a couple of roubles or so, which they needed to buy booze. Such loans were proffered, however reluctantly, because the Alkies had nowhere to hide: the next day they'd be back in the classroom. Eventually they'd have to pay back. And anyway, that practice was common in Russia where friends and family were at the time the only credit providers available.

Thus, when Shuruyev polled everyone he knew for a few roubles, he managed to put together a tidy sum before disappearing into the sunset, never to be seen again. When the next day the news of his expulsion spread, his lenders knew they had been had.

The other Alkies went the Shuruyev way soon thereafter, so on my return there were no black sheep I could milk. The only influence on my life came from a delicate girl from a professor's family who miraculously fell in love with me and married me a year later. Guided by her cultured hand, I began to study in earnest and went back, after a fashion, to the *ne-nash* ways Mama had tried to instil in me.

Towards the end of the first year all the students stratified into social classes, with the distinctions being based on their career prospects. As with any hierarchy, those at different levels developed different behavioural patterns.

At one end of the spectrum, the *nash* sons and daughters of the KGB elite knew they didn't have to do anything special to ensure a bright future. But while they didn't have to win the prize, they could still lose it by doing something unspeakable, like raping an instructor, punching the dean or, even worse, reading *The Cancer Ward* without authorisation. That explained why they developed typical upper-class manners, cordial yet conspiratorial to their own kind, affable yet aloof to hoi-polloi.

At the other end were the déclassé *ne-nash*, who tended to behave like normal people because, no matter how hard they studied or how enthusiastically they played lickspittle to the *nash*, they weren't going anywhere anyway. The brightest prize their careers had in store for them would be a decent teaching post.

One could find most students in between the two poles. Though not entitled to anything by birthright, they knew that, if they worked hard on their careers and even harder against everyone else's, they could perhaps get that coveted posting abroad without which one was a big fat zero in our profession.

As with most class structures, one could get on easily with the two extremes. But the upwardly mobile philistines in the middle were boring because they lacked either the social ease of the uppers or the amicable resignation of the lowers. In Russia they were also dangerous.

For it was from their ranks that the KGB recruited most of their 'tappers', informants who'd tap on some secret door and shop their comrades. Recruiting them was a doddle, and the process followed a simple binary path. I'm familiar with this technique because Valeriy, my pianist friend, once had the gall to record his telephone conversation with a KGB recruiter. The man sounded as if he was going through a mantra that he himself found tedious but knew it worked:

1.   'Do you consider yourself a Soviet man?' 'Yes.' [If the answer is 'No', you join the lumpen *ne-nash* – or worse.]

2.   'Are you prepared to do everything you can for the motherland?' 'Yes.' [If 'No', see 1.]

3.   'Do you accept us as the voice of the motherland?' 'Yes.' [If 'No', see 1.]

4.   'So you do realise that by helping us you'll be helping the motherland?' 'Yes.' [If 'No', see 1.]

5.   'Are you then ready to help us?' 'Yes.' [If 'No', see 1.]

6.   Then came the cruncher: 'So you won't have any objections to signing this paper?'

The paper was an employment contract, the documentary evidence of the signatory's Faustian downfall. Most signed their lives away on the spot. Some would prevaricate and try to talk their way out by saying that, while in principle they were eager to help, they weren't quite ready, for irrational reasons, to sign any document to that effect.

The ruse seldom worked. Their inquisitors would simply slide down the spiral back to the beginning and go over the whole litany again: 'Do you consider yourself…' KGBists were good at what they did and had all the time in the world.

That recruitment procedure only came into effect when they were out to catch hesitant souls. However, most souls came to them of their own accord, volunteering information in that open-hearted, almost disinterested way first made popular by Judas, but without suffering the same unpleasant fate. Nor did they suffer the fate of their progenitors, the 16th-century snitches from the time of Ivan IV, aka 'the Terrible'.

When I was little, Ivan was second in popularity only to Peter I. As Stalin saw himself as a ruler in the same vein, he ordered that the two tsars be canonised. So all children my age had to watch at least once a year films portraying the two gentlemen as fair and far-sighted rulers, if occasionally harsh on those subjects who didn't always see the light.

Ivan was the true trailblazer. He was the first Russian ruler to create a service, called *oprichnina*, whose sole function was to wage war against their fellow Russians. Here is not the place to describe their methods, such as frying people alive for the crime of starting a sentence with 'if I were the Tsar…' – this irrespective of what followed the seditious clause. Suffice it to say that those methods, many developed by the Tsar himself, were highly imaginative.

Then too people were encouraged to inform on their friends – and, more important, discouraged from not doing so. If, for example, a wretched criminal sharing a drink with his friends were to say something like, 'If I were the Tsar, I'd be even more strict with traitors,' and one of his friends would snitch to the *oprichniks*, then not only the evil-doer but all the other friends who knew but didn't tell would be tortured to death.

All this was similar to our times, but there was one critical difference. The first man tortured in the times olden and golden was the informer himself, as the oprichniks wanted to make sure he hadn't borne false witness. Only after a prolonged and savage torture of the informer (I'll spare you the details in case you're about to have your supper) were they satisfied that they indeed had an airtight case.

While the KGB generally followed the fine examples set by their precursors, including the use of torture, torturing grasses was a practice with which they dispensed. After all, they didn't care how sound the accusations were; their motto was 'give us a man, we'll find a case.' Thus our contemporary grasses risked nothing except of course the salvation of their souls. But they didn't believe in such nonsense.

Whenever there was a shortage of volunteers, the KGB would start their recruitment drive. When that happened, few in my generation, and none in my parents', were able to resist the cajoling of those well-trained serpents. Many of those who, like me, can proudly say that they never snitched for the KGB, were simply never asked.

(This reminds me of several quasi-dissident, and therefore unpublished, writers cornering the official, and therefore fêted, scribe Konstantin Simonov. 'We don't sell ourselves!' they proudly declared. The celebrity, who was short on moral fibre but long on wit, replied, 'Has anyone ever tried to buy?')

Komitet did buy or otherwise procure, but it had its quota of informers, about 15 percent of any sizeable group. They filled it effortlessly and didn't necessarily want to waste their time by generating overproduction. After all, each denunciation had to be processed, filed and acted upon. In common with government officials the world over, they avoided tasks that were likely to give them trouble.

Mostly – though by no means invariably – they fished in the quiet waters of the ambitious middle class. However, occasionally they needed to bag a big catch, such as a famous *ne-nash* 'intel' or a known dissident. That task *komitet* usually accomplished by simple coercion (their favourite threat to imprison father/mother/spouse/children seldom failed).

The upshot of all this is that most Russians who had successful careers at that time, and indeed are running the country now, either were KGB stoolies or could have been had they been asked – a practical but not moral difference. Thus it's not surprising that the country's government is made up of KGB officers, ably led in the best traditions of his *alma mater* by Col. Putin himself. And if you insist those government officials are only ex-KGB, you'd be arguing with the good colonel himself. For, when once queried on the subject, Putin proudly declared, 'There's no such thing as ex-KGB. This is for life.' The same no doubt holds true for volunteer snitches who then inundated Russia.

In 'ideological' universities, such as ours, the 'tappers' were probably even more numerous than 15 percent. The resulting realisation that every word one uttered in company was likely to be reported somewhat reduced the conversational ease within every class but the *ne-nash* no-hopers. We could afford a bit of leeway, as we had nothing to lose anyway. That's why we'd gather in the smoking area under the staircase, cast furtive glances about and start telling politically incorrect jokes.

Some of those were indeed political, some implicitly but not overtly so. Falling into that category were *chastushkas*, peasant four-line ditties sung by folk choirs whose members wore high boots and brightly coloured silk shirts girded with rope belts. In those days one couldn't turn on the box without watching those people put on silly faces and sing some folksy trash in the throaty voices that are as essential to the genre as *bel canto* is to Italian opera.

Their repertoire included a prescribed mixture of genuine folk songs and pastiches, and I never met a Russian with an IQ north of the average bust size who'd listen to those performances with anything but contempt. However, Western tourists flocked to their concerts in droves, thinking no doubt that those sideshows provided a shortcut to the ultimate understanding of the mysterious Russian soul.

Chastushkas are genuinely Russian, and one could hear these, often improvised, ditties at any village gathering. Those performed officially were denatured; but, just like the English limerick, the unofficial ones tended to be off-colour. Driven to distraction by the intrusion of Russian folksiness into their already bleak lives, the Moscow *ne-nash* would come up with endless viler-than-thou parodies of those ditties. These they mixed with the more obscene of the genuine article and served this cocktail to one another, never failing to drive their audience to gut-busting contortions.

If at that time you had walked up the stairs of our university past the smoking area, you could have overheard exchanges of this nature: 'Hey, have you heard this one? Past my mother-in-law's house I don't walk without a trick: either moon her with my buttocks or else flash her with my dick.' Uproar of laughter, everyone present choking on the acrid smoke of raw tobacco.

'Now how about this one: Our garden's full of muck, in the muck my father's stuck. I sneaked up through the morass, did my father up the arse.' Hilarity reaches apoplectic levels, laughter goes into a crescendo and begins racing up to a rousing finale.

'Up... the... arse... my father... fantastic. Now I've just heard this one: Even though my loved one's dead, I still dragged her to my bed. Even dead she's still the same, I believe she almost came.'

At that point either a professor would pass by, looking at us disapprovingly, or else a known 'tapper' would attempt to join in with a ubiquitous, 'What's up, boys? Heard any funny ones lately?' We'd wipe the tears of laughter off our faces and deny that we had ever heard a funny one in our lives.

'Well, I have,' he'd volunteer. 'These two rich Russian merchants, you know, back in the good old days, are drinking heavily in a smart Paris restaurant, feeling bored and maudlin. One says, "I'm going to go and shit into that piano." The other merchant pats him on the shoulder sympathetically and says, "Don't, Porphiriy Ivanovich, it's no use. These heartless savages, they just wouldn't understand." Good one, eh?' 'No,' we'd say and walk away. The party had been pooped.

The question anyone who lived there at the time has to ask himself is, what would I have done had I been asked to 'tap'? One likes to think that there would have been enough testicular fortitude stored in one's inner reserves to tell the serpent to go crawl into some other hole. But one never knows. That's why I don't think we should judge those people too harshly, a tendency especially pronounced among the philistines who have discovered that pouring scorn on those wretches somehow elevates their own stature vicariously.

I knew two 'tappers' well. One was my first cousin once removed 'Leningrad Boris', so called to distinguish him from 'our Boris'; the other Volodia Kramer, the English-speaking poet who was my partner in the wind-up of the century I'll describe in a subsequent chapter.

Leningrad Boris was a compulsive wag, a figure common in Russia. His speech was one continuous string of jokes, mostly borrowed from the satirical novel *Twelve Chairs*, the omnipresent source of good lines for those Russians who couldn't come up with their own. That quality, added to the gifts of fruit and sweets he brought me, always made me look forward to his frequent visits to Moscow when I was little.

When I grew up I realised there wasn't much substance behind Boris's gaiety, and his jokes began to sound a little banal. But we remained close, and I often went to Leningrad to visit Boris, especially since he was a fanatic of the city, knew every stone of it and was an eager guide.

Since I, along with most of my coevals, never had a place of my own, when I grew older I started to use his flat for occasional weekend trysts. Under those circumstances I often wished his love of the city were more moderate, as every morning at eight on the dot Boris would exuberantly burst into the room I shared with the young lady.

'Enough of this degeneracy! Get up! There's a great city out there! This one hasn't seen it yet!' he'd scream. Protests, no matter how forcefully or obscenely expressed, never had any effect. Often Boris would simply yank the blanket off, watching my beloved hastily cover the strategic bits with her hands.

In short, a worthy gentleman – except for one thing: he was a 'tapper' all his life. Leningrad Boris was recruited in the thirties, when refusal to co-operate was tantamount to instant suicide. Given the free choice between painful death and his signature, Boris chose the second. Perhaps he didn't feel he was losing his freedom because every Russian knew that the great Lenin had defined freedom as 'acknowledged necessity'. Leningrad Boris acknowledged the necessity of signing his life away, thus acquiring what, according to the vagaries of Soviet rhetoric, was the freest freedom.

Parenthetically, Lenin's school diploma was on exhibit at the Moscow Lenin Museum. Every time I was dragged on a school outing there I'd notice with malice that, while the Great Leader's marks were generally good, he almost failed 'logic'. His weakness in that subject must have been responsible for most of his authoritative pronouncements, such as 'Marx's teaching is omnipotent because it's true.' We used to quip that the adage would have made more sense the other way around.

Since his downfall, Boris turned in his friends and colleagues all his life. A man not without conscience, he always wept after a 'dose' or two, and I've never seen repentance as burning and sincere. But the next day he'd go back to snitching, because the KGB was the kind of merry-go-round that never stopped, so getting off would have been fraught with palpable, neck-breaking risks.

In the end Boris turned into a pitiful old man. Now you know the story of his life-long misery I invite you to cast the first stone – and pray that you yourself will never have to face the choice between martyrdom and a life of soul-destroying decrepitude. My hand, as it fumbles for that stone to cast, goes on strike. And while I feel some mild contempt for Leningrad Boris, I can't find it in my heart to feel any of the stronger emotions.

Which is more than I can say for Kramer. He was recruited to do the Judas work in the late sixties, when one could find tactful ways of turning the KGB down. Mind you, those people didn't take rejection easily, and the rejecter could kiss any meaningful career good-bye. But it was unlikely that he would be killed. And someone like Kramer didn't need a career to parlay his excellent English into a comfortable life, what with tutors and translators always in demand. No, he didn't need a career. But he desired it, and boundless ambition has been known to lead even better men to perdition.

That's why, following a chance discovery of his 'tapping' sideline, I broke up with him on the spot. That was a pity because he had been a close friend for a while. Ethnically German, he could have passed for a silent Swede just as easily as he once passed for an American in our epic wind-up I'll describe shortly. I tend to distrust silent types because I always wonder what it is that they have to be silent about. In this case, we got the answer to that question, but even before we did Kramer had often acted out of character.

The very fact that he had chosen as his poetic idol Nikolai Gumilev, the most sensual of the Russian 'acmeists', was a dead give-away that there was more to the lad than met the eye. Be that as it may, he wrote excellent Gumilev-inspired verse and once, for the first and probably last time in his life, even tried to act romantically.

The object of that unlikely outburst was the violinist Lidia Beryozova who belonged to another physical type I distrust: swarthy women. However, if you don't mind the type, she was good-looking, and talented to boot. The problem with their union was that they were not only physical but also emotional antipodes. While Kramer, with his slow Nordic burn, took a long time to fall in love, he'd stay there for the long haul.

Lida, on the other hand, fell in love with anyone who went to bed with her, and many of those who didn't. And once she decided she was in love, she'd act like a woman possessed, raving and ranting all over Moscow, phoning her beloved at odd hours, dragging him with her on lengthy Siberian tours, dissolving her very being in his and demanding that he give of himself as totally as she did.

In that Lida reminded one of the heroine of Chekhov's story *Sweetheart*. Except that the love of her life never lasted longer than a month or so. Just as easily as she had conflagrated, she'd turn herself off, and woe betide any man whose rhythms didn't coincide with hers. It's not that she'd suddenly break off the affair – she'd stop recognising him in the street. And if he dared remind her of the torrid love consuming them just a week ago, Lida would honestly fail to understand what he was on about.

We all knew about that remarkable quality of hers, and those who did go to bed with her never did so without practising the essential art of emotional self-defence. But as Kramer was a latecomer to our circle, he knew none of that. We had neglected to warn him, and he walked into Lida Beryozova head on.

For a month we watched Lida dart offstage to the phone the moment she took her last bow and irrigate the receiver with tears of emotive obsession. Step by step, she dragged Kramer into the same frenzy, which in his case looked particularly pathetic. He'd wait at her doorstep through the night, spend days on the train to hear her play Wieniawski in Vladivostok, lavish her with gifts and drive himself to feats of sexual athleticism that made him lose 20 pounds in a month (dieters, take note).

Then she went abroad for a week and returned with excellent

reviews but without any semblance of love. Now she too regarded Kramer's ravings as pathetic and complained to us that the creep simply wouldn't leave her alone. The creep couldn't; he was on fire; he demanded one last meeting, one last chance to explain to Lida that life simply didn't make sense without her. She reluctantly agreed to come to his place because that seemed the only way to make 'that wanker shut up', as she elegantly put it.

The meeting took place, with Kramer going down on his knees and begging Lida to stay. When she told him he wasn't making any sense, and who did he think he was, stalking her that way, Kramer got up, grabbed a razor blade and began slashing the outside of his wrist. 'Turn your wrist over,' advised Lida and walked out.

That far he chose not to go, and we consoled him by fixing him up with another violinist whose robustly expressed sexuality came with no strings attached. A month later Misha Polsky was summoned to the KGB and threatened with a fiver in a particularly nasty camp over a short story he had just finished writing. Kramer had the only copy.

The discovery hit us with the same impact as a positive HIV test would have on a homosexual. We knew what was in the air, and what kind of activities put one at risk, but somehow we never thought that we ourselves were in danger. Someone else, perhaps everyone else – maybe. But not Misha the writer, not Grisha the poet, not Valeriy the pianist, not – most important – a certain A. Boot. We saw ourselves as the ultimate untouchables, and the risibility of that notion had just been hammered into us with skull-crushing force. The *ne-nash* had a turncoat in their midst.

There were many such Kramers at the university, *nash* or freshly co-opted *ne-nash* boys and girls willing to help the devil take the hindmost. But most students didn't have to sacrifice a pound of flesh to the KGB. *Komitet* were the fishers of souls, not necessarily of bodies, and in most cases they were prepared to satisfy themselves with unreserved acquiescence. That was the absolute minimum required for a successful career, and it was with bemusement, though in those days not yet with detachment, that I watched the mad scampering of our human ants as graduation drew nearer.

One of the popular stratagems was to strike useful friendships, a time-honoured university tradition that crosses geographic boundaries. The salient difference is that, while at Balliol or Yale the concept of a useful friend wouldn't necessarily include the child of an executioner, at our university it more or less included no one else, and not always figuratively speaking.

One such potentially useful friend was my classmate Tania whose father, in his capacity of State Prosecutor, had just put away a few dissidents in a widely publicised trial. Consequently, he was castigated among the *ne-nash* intelligentsia.

Tania was, against the run of play, a nice girl, as many of her class were. The wield didn't object to their being nice because they had nowhere to go but straight into the works of the machine. Thus any serious effort to convert them to rank *nash*ness would have been redundant. Also against the odds, Tania wasn't at all promiscuous, and those of us who knew her well were her friends, and that was that.

Occasionally she'd invite a bunch of us home, to the palatial seven-room apartment whose size and contents would have put many an American millionaire to shame. There Tania would treat us to such rare delicacies as caviar, filet steak and real champagne (the first time I ever tried it).

The arrangement was reciprocal, yet all Tania demanded in return was interesting conversation that could include any witticism we wished but no references to her father's occupation. That wasn't easy, for her father's name was at the time about as topical among us as Eichmann's was among the Jews in 1944. Yet we had managed to restrain ourselves somehow, until Dima Proskurov blew it.

Before that calamitous night we had never actually seen the Pontius Pilate of the KGB, for the flat was so spacious that he never had to float into view. That time, however, he made an appearance as he needed to get something out of the large room where we were sitting. He greeted us standoffishly, picked up a book and walked back to his study.

In common with many *nash* climbers who liked to pretend they were something other than just that, Dima would often make dissident noises, especially with a 'dose' under his belt. The apparition set him off and he declared that he was going to tell the prosecutor off for his role in the trial. We tried to talk him out of it, but those of you who've ever tried to talk Dima out of anything will be aware of the sheer futility of that task. Sure enough, we failed. Dima shook off a couple of tackles and heroically went to his Calvary. We were left behind fearing that his perdition would also spell ours by association.

When he failed to return after 40 minutes or so, we decided that perhaps the satrap of the regime had taken on the additional duties of executioner and had carried out his own death sentence on Dima. Having been delegated to investigate (Tania had refused to take sides in this conflict), I tiptoed to the study door, found it ajar and caught the tail end of Dima's last question, very different from what we had feared he might be asking: 'And have you tried maggots as bait, Ivan Trofimovich?'

Before I got married I had been going out with another student, the daughter of the Deputy Minister of Something or Other. Actually, 'going out' is a misnomer, as we were simply friends who had many talks and long, untactile walks.

At some point I introduced her to my parents and, after she had left, Papa said her name rang a vague bell. Was she perchance related to the Deputy Minister of Something or Other? On finding out that she was indeed related, Papa reacted a bit like Comrade Alliluyev must have done when he discovered that his daughter Nadia was dating Comrade Stalin.

'And how well do you know this young lady?' Papa had never before referred to my female friends with so much deference. 'We're friends, Papa, that's all.' 'What do you mean that's all? She's a good-looking girl, you must have…' 'Papa, maybe I have and maybe I haven't. Why such sudden interest in my private life?' 'I think you should marry this girl, that's why.' 'Why on earth would I want to do that?' 'Well, you said you were friends, and she's attractive, so I figure why not…' 'Papa, there's one good reason why not. I don't love her.'

I hadn't often seen my father so agitated. In fact, he reacted a bit like Comrade Alliluyev might have done had he discovered that his daughter Nadia had turned Comrade Stalin down. 'Love! Love!!! Who gives a damn about love? This marriage could set you up for life! And you're talking about love?! What kind of pea-brain are you? You can always get love on the side!'

I didn't heed my father's advice, resigning myself to playing outside observer of the race being fiercely contested by the students who had some hope of a career. One could always tell those who already had it made from those who hadn't. The former would put on the enigmatic airs of a Gnostic; the latter would brag about having established a meaningful contact at the Ministry of Foreign Trade, the International

Trade Union Organisation, the International Youth Committee or other KGB offshoots. We knew they were fibbing. If their contacts really had been meaningful, they wouldn't have talked about them.

Dima Proskurov, for example, never talked, but everybody knew he had a couple of solid irons in the KGB fire. So his posting to Tanzania after our third year didn't really surprise anyone. However, after only one month there, he got drunk at an embassy party, punched someone and was expelled back to our academic fold. That didn't particularly surprise anyone either, for we all knew how Dima was after a couple. It was a pity, though, that his three years of hard work had to be thrown away like that.

Misha Nepomniashchiy never talked either, yet everybody knew he wouldn't stick around to be posted to some godforsaken school. His father was one of the directors of the *Novosti* Press Agency, a position that conferred dynastic privileges on his offspring. At about that time Nepomniashchiy Senior got involved in an embarrassing incident, which it took Misha a long time to tell us about because he couldn't stop laughing.

Apparently his father was away on a business trip abroad when one of his senior colleagues died the death any Russian male would have described as honourable: in the saddle, on top of his desk, terrifying his secretary who couldn't understand why the old stallion had stopped bucking. The next morning Nepomniashchiy *père* received a telegram summoning him to Moscow to deliver a eulogy at the funeral of his libidinous friend. Critically, the telegram didn't mention the circumstances surrounding the event, and Nepomniashchiy was blissfully unaware of them as he had missed a connection at JFK, arrived late and was driven to the cemetery straight from the airport.

The address had to be delivered off the cuff, but not to worry. Nepomniashchiy had been around the block, and the standard communist litany was at his fingertips. He rubbed the corner of his eye with a panache worthy of Sir Laurence Olivier in his immortal portrayal of Othello and orated, his voice breaking up in all the right places, 'Our comrade remained a communist until his dying breath.'

At that point he had to stop because a ripple of sniggering was developing in the crowd, where everybody but him knew the cause of death. Putting the laughter down to a series of nervous breakdowns, he continued bravely, 'As a true Leninist, he remained at his battle station until the very end…' The ripple was becoming a mighty wave, and even the bereaved widow was fighting hard not to laugh out loud.

'He died as he had lived, protecting with his life the values all progressive mankind hold so dear… Now what the hell is going on?'

The last remark was precipitated by everybody present, including the widow, having burst into open paroxysms. Nepomniashchiy's aide whispered something in his ear, the director angrily described some of the perverse ways in which he'd like to have sexual intercourse with everybody present and their mothers, got in his car and left.

Fulfilling his early promise, after his third year his son was sent as an exchange student to Prague University, a huge bonus in those days. His stint there lasted until 1968 when it was interrupted by Soviet tanks rolling into Prague and making Russian exchange students somewhat unpopular. That invasion cost Misha Nepomniashchiy more than just a couple of cushy years abroad.

His father was sent to overfly the Czech capital in a helicopter, dropping propaganda leaflets designed to soften any possible resistance. But a characteristic break in communications had occurred, and the Soviet soldiers on the ground hadn't been told what was going on. One of them didn't like the look of leaflets raining down from a chopper and loosed off a long burst in the direction of the flying machine. It's a tribute to the standards of marksmanship in the Soviet army that one of the bullets went through Nepomniashchiy's forehead. A few days later it was he who was being eulogised. This time no one laughed.

According to Stalin, class struggle intensifies as socialism advances. I don't know if he was right about that, but struggle for good postings was definitely intensifying at our university as graduation drew nearer. All graduates in the Soviet Union were posted to jobs assigned by the state, which they had to take for a minimum of two years as payment for their free education. Not a bad deal on the surface of it, but the trouble was that for a Muscovite to be posted out of the city meant losing, irretrievably, the Moscow residence permit – a tragedy today almost as much as it was then.

Nothing like an impending disaster to focus the mind. So every out-of-town student was desperately trying to marry a Muscovite thereby qualifying for the coveted permit. Every *nash* was feverishly boning up on Marx and Lenin to score the highest marks in the Scientific

Atheism exam. Every 'tapper' was tapping with such abandon that his knuckles turned blue. Every tappee was quaking in his boots. Every bookworm was burrowing even deeper into the few remaining tomes, hoping that his zeal would somehow be rewarded with the ultimate prize (fat chance). And every confirmed *ne-nash*, such as that nonperson A. Boot, was quietly trying to avoid the worst.

It didn't work in my case. As I was married, they couldn't kick me out of Moscow, but the posting I did receive, to teach English at the night school of the Likhachev Auto Works, was a bit derisory for someone who had graduated in the top three or four. I didn't bitch about that too much: after all, I knew what was in store. Someone brought up by my mother deserved everything that came his way. And anyway I knew that Papa's connections would somehow get me off the worst hook.

Sure enough, Papa delivered as he always had done, and my last three years in Russia were spent in a gentle academic environment. It was so agreeable, as a matter of fact, that as I walked through Manhattan shortly thereafter, wondering where my next meal was going to come from, I felt sorry I couldn't have stayed.

But that soon passed.

THE RIGHT TO FREE MEDICAL CARE

1

HE WAS A NICE MAN. In our hospital that meant he was resigned to his fate, never whined and didn't use his impending death as an excuse to get the nurse's attention ahead of the patients with a longer life expectancy. A quiet and desperately ill man, he just lay in his bed, staring at the water-stained ceiling.

Mind you, the rest of us weren't necessarily paragons of rude health either. That's why we had been placed in Ward 13, known to the superstitious Russians for a death toll that approached, in percentage terms, that of a field hospital in the battle of Stalingrad. But this nice man was in the last stage of lupus compounded by renal failure, and that combination beat my *polyarteritis nodosa* hands down.

One day, as we were holding an animated discussion of our nurse's breasts, we noticed the nice man was even quieter than usual, while his gaze was perhaps a bit too steady. Alexei, an ex-sniper in the Soviet infantry, conducted a brief examination and pronounced his verdict: 'Hey, the bloke's dead!'

'Why do they always have to croak just before lunch?' inquired Stasik, my chess partner. He too had lupus, but a milder version. The skin on his lean face looked as if it had received several grafts, though in fact it hadn't.

'Maybe because they know we get no other cold meats,' joked Sarkis Ovanesian. He was dying from periodic disease, a genetic blight that in the Soviet Union afflicted only Armenians – regardless of whether they had ever been anywhere near Armenia, which Sarkis hadn't. If the out-of-focus photograph on his bed stand was any indication, his skin and hair had formerly both been dark. But loss of pigmentation meant they were now the same white colour with a yellowish tint.

'Let's get the stiff out of here before lunch. I don't want it to be like the other day.' This contribution came from Pyotr Ivanovich, an old peasant with a crusted purple nose. He was my fellow sufferer from *polyarteritis nodosa*, but his case was more serious, affecting the kidneys and rendering his prospects bleak.

'And the day before that.' This from yours truly, a 17-year-old student whose moon face was the result of daily handfuls of prednisolone. Soviet doctors used that steroidal drug in huge doses to combat not only most diseases but even minor ailments.

'So why don't you buzz the nurse?' Irony coloured every word uttered by Nikolai, a victim of the traditional Russian pandemic of cirrhosis. His sense of humour was usually directed against the non-Slavic minorities. This quip was an exception, but you probably didn't get the joke. That's because you don't know that each bed in Ward 13 had its own bell, but none worked.

'Yeah, yeah, yeah,' said Pyotr Ivanovich who got up from his bed, went to the door, stuck his head out and yelled at the top of his voice, 'Nadia-a-a-a-a!!!' The sound reverberated nicely through the long corridor, bouncing off the beds of the less fortunate patients who hadn't rated a place in a ward.

'Oh, shut up,' advised one of them. 'I'll bust your mug,' promised another anonymous patient. 'Is it really necessary to squeal like a pig in an abattoir?' This came from an obvious 'intel' whose bed was next to Ward 14, and I made a mental note to check him out. 'Intels' were usually good for a game of chess or cards, if not necessarily elevated conversation.

'You shut up, bloody arseholes,' countered Pyotr Ivanovich. 'We have a stiff on our hands. Nadia-a-a-a-a!!!'

'What do you wa-a-ant?' came a distant echo from the other end of the corridor. Nadia, the big-breasted nurse on our floor, was obviously in one of her moods. That wasn't unexpected considering she had about 120 patients in her care.

'The bloke in bed Number Eight?' Pyotr Ivanovich's voice was now positively booming. 'He's dead!'

'So what do you want from me-e-e-e,' reverberated a reasonable question.

'Get him out of here? Before lunch?' Pyotr Ivanovich realised how presumptuous that request was even as he was bawling it.

'...zee?' came the tail-end echo of Nadia's rhetorical question 'Can't you see I'm busy?'

That was that. We knew we had to have yet another meal in the presence of a rapidly setting *rigor mortis*, and didn't particularly mind. I thought, however, that it might be a good idea for a doctor to show up and make sure the nice man really was dead. As if by ESP magic one did make an appearance half an hour later, some time after the main course of mystery patties and just before the watery tea.

He quickly performed the necessary formalities, covered the body with a bed sheet, said he'd heard of my prowess at chess and perhaps we should have a game some other night when he was on duty. He then left, having politely wished us all bon appétit. The corpse under the sheet stayed behind, providing a backdrop to yet another conversation about sex. This had been set up by the prior discussion of Nadia's formidable breasts that sloshed about freely inside her regulation white gown.

Sarkis volunteered the information that it was possible to push a girl's breasts together and use the slot thus formed as an alternative penile receptacle. That technique was known as 'ant's knot'. Nikolai took exception to that practice, observing that this was just the sort of thing one would expect from a representative of a blackarsed nation of perverts and pederasts.

That triggered off an angry reply from Sarkis, featuring a threat to smash Nikolai's cranium with a bottle. Nikolai's retort centred around the promise to pull Sarkis's metaphorical twat over his ears. What ensued was another round of jokes based on the alleged homosexual tendencies of Armenians.

'What's every Armenian's dream? That fortune turn its back on him.'

'What do you do when you drop a rouble coin in an Armenian street? You kick it all the way home.'

'This Armenian comes to a doctor and says he has a pain up his arse. The doctor tells him to get down on all fours, sticks his fingers up the Armenian's arse – and pulls out a rose. "You've got a rose up your arse," he says. The Armenian goes, "It's for you, doctor." '

'Radio Yerevan is asked if a man can get pregnant. They reply, "We don't know, but experiments are being conducted all over Armenia."'

Each new joke was met with an outburst of hilarity, and a great time was had by all. The only possible exception was Sarkis who suddenly acquired a slight Armenian accent, an unusual development for someone who had spent his whole life in Moscow. My own laughter was strained, as Papa had told me all those jokes quite a few times in the past.

The patients then went back to exchanging stories of their amorous conquests. As usually is the case with the broad Russian masses whose mystical souls appeal so much to Westerners, most of those stories revolved around rape, vaginal mutilation or, typically, a combination of the two.

Stasik got the ball rolling by volunteering the information that the best way to hold a woman down was to sit on her head (making sure she wouldn't suffocate, as otherwise there would be a lot of screwing around with cops.) That way you only needed one mate to help you, whereas any other method of restraining a thrashing female would involve at least two, or else the kind of violence that made legal trouble hard to avoid.

Nikolai contributed the insight that the first stage of VD treatment was beating up the bitch who had given it to you. We all laughed for we knew, some from experience, some from hearsay, that such diseases were catastrophic. For the first thing any Russian VD clinic did was send a notification to the man's place of employment. The culprit then had to appear at an office meeting, with all his colleagues in attendance, and repent publicly.

By all accounts, the treatment itself consisted of a long series of inhumanly painful and degrading procedures administered over several weeks by doctors who treated their patients with contempt. The alternative was to seek a discreet private doctor. But they were squeezed by taxes so much that the only way for them to stay afloat was to charge huge amounts, out of most sufferers' reach.

The ex-sniper Alexei then provided proof that generous doses of saltpetre in army food didn't quite do the job. His stories usually fell somewhere in the middle of the range, being less savage than some and more so than others, with rape the ever-present component.

My contributions to that kind of talk were on the passive side, and the others must have thought I was a virgin. For my part, I wondered what percentage of their wild stories were wild fantasies, then decided it was irrelevant. After all, though Freud probably shouldn't be believed in most cases, the nature of our fantasies must provide an insight into our souls.

Inevitably the conversation would shift from romance to booze, another popular topic. For my wardmates this craving was less platonic than the other one, and could be satisfied without leaving the confines of the hospital. The key was the parcels that all patients received from the out, without which we would have gone hungry as hospital food wasn't just revolting but also came in mean portions. The parcels usually included fruit, a rare delicacy outside and legal tender inside the hospital, what with the towering presence of Tamara Petrovna, the Head Nurse.

Tamara Petrovna, a middle-aged but remarkably zestful woman, always wore her white gown with the sleeves rolled up to expose her sinewy forearms. Her upper lip was adorned with a moustache that was thicker than mine, and she had a deeper voice. And, like most Russians, she had more than one facet to her personality.

The Mr Hyde side was a martinet who enforced hospital regulations in a masterful, if a bit heavy-handed, way. In the evening, at nine sharp, she'd go from ward to ward and, over the protests of the more bookish patients, turn every light off. If she heard as much as a whisper coming from any inmate after 9.30, the culprit received a stern admonition and was told to shut the hell up or get the hell out of her hospital. If a patient asked for a urine bottle without Tamara Petrovna being satisfied he really was unable to walk, he was told in no uncertain terms to crawl to the shithouse if he had to.

As you've probably guessed, Tamara Petrovna didn't learn her manner of self-expression from the Russian translation of *Debrett's Etiquette for Girls*. Both her language and approach to medical care were moulded by the war, during which she had served as field nurse in a tank regiment. The problems I had with her began in my first week at the hospital, when she was detailed to take me to another wing for chest X-rays.

My disease mostly affected the legs. When I stayed in the horizontal position, I felt a constant ache, which turned into unbearable pain the moment I put my feet on the floor. Walking in those first few weeks, before prednisolone kicked in, was out of the question, and Tamara Petrovna grudgingly accepted that. She had agreed to wheel me over to the X-ray room, but once there had insisted that I stand up on the machine.

'I can't stand up, it hurts too much,' I complained. 'You know what we say in the army?' barked Tamara Petrovna. 'If you can't, we'll teach you; if you won't, we'll make you.' With that bit of homespun wisdom she dragged me out of the wheelchair with one hand and dumped me onto the machine. The ensuing pain was so sharp I passed out, fell down and got a slight concussion. Later Tamara Petrovna was reluctantly apologetic, which didn't prevent her from describing me as a wimp to Nadia of the big breasts fame.

All that was the Mr Hyde part. But Tamara Petrovna also had a Dr Jekyll streak of charity, compassion and camaraderie so characteristic of Russian women. She knew that men, ill or not, needed their vodka. To satisfy that need Tamara Petrovna always kept in her office several bottles of medical alcohol, which was in such ample supply that no one at the hospital minded her purloining it.

Other nurses would simply sell it outside for one rouble per 100 millilitres (or 'grams', as the Russians refer to alcohol measures). However, Tamara Petrovna preferred to serve not just Mammon but, by relieving the suffering of the patients in her charge, Aesculapius as well.

Her going rate was one rouble or a Prokofievan three oranges for an eight-ounce tumbler of the warm liquid. (In case you didn't know, the chemical reaction between pure alcohol and water releases heat, which knowledge most Russian males acquire empirically before reaching puberty.) As a gesture of good will, Tamara Petrovna would throw in half a teaspoonful of strawberry jam to stir into the liquid, changing its colour and making it look innocuous to a passing doctor.

Not that doctors passed often. Hospitals in Russia (except those nowadays that cater to 'new Russians') are grossly understaffed, and even ours had no more than one doctor for 50 patients. I say 'even ours' because Clinic No. 24 was not an ordinary fleapit but one of the best teaching hospitals in Russia. Its medical staff was headed by Prof. Tareyev, a signatory to the fraudulent autopsy report issued a week after Stalin's death.

Once a week the venerable professor would lead a gaggle of thirty or forty students to the most interesting cases, of which I was one. Since the medical profession was among the lowest paid in Russia, most of the students were girls. Some of them were pretty and most of them compassionate enough to leave their phone numbers for the moribund young man who didn't mind over-dramatising his condition to make the best of a bad situation. A few of the young ladies moonlighted as night nurses, so the consummation of the budding romances didn't always have to wait until my discharge. (Tamara Petrovna had kindly exchanged a duplicate key to her office for another three of the ubiquitous oranges and a promise to keep my bloody gob shut.)

Other patients, especially the younger ones, also organised their lives as best they could. One of them, Volodia Apresian, another sufferer from periodic disease, while also availing himself of Tamara Petrovna's office, had obtained a key to the main auditorium. We regularly used it for a nocturnal game of cards.

Four of us would sneak out of our wards at night, tiptoe into the auditorium and spend a pleasant night drinking, smoking and playing preference. Since they were social players and I was approaching the end of a dissipated youth largely misspent on hustling, these nights were quite profitable, even at the puny stakes of a kopeck a point on which they had insisted. That stinginess on their part seldom produced more than five roubles a night, which was roughly what our doctors made in a day. But every little bit helped.

It was one of those underpaid doctors who put an end to the game when she was on night duty. What gave us away was dense cigarette smoke seeping into the corridor from under the auditorium door. The doctor realised what was what, used her skeleton key to open the door and beheld the scene of four young patients enjoying themselves in a way that contravened accepted medical practice.

What angered her more than anything else was that a few hours before the game she had treated me for an attack of kidney stones (a problem that often accompanies the prolonged administration of gargantuan doses of prednisolone) and had told me to take it easy for a day or two. As a result, we lost our duplicate key, having loyally refused to divulge its provenance.

Her wrath was understandable, but then so were our transgressions. After all, we were young men who had to spend significant chunks of our lives in virtual incarceration. For in Russia one didn't stay in hospital. One lived there.

The minimum stay was a fortnight, which was how long it took to process routine tests of blood and urine. If these showed nothing fundamentally wrong, often the patient was discharged. But even in

Russia more sophisticated diagnostic techniques were available, with biopsies and spinal taps being the techniques of preference. However, there were waiting lists for those and also for the more involved tests of renal, pulmonary, hepatic and cardiac functions. And it seldom took less than six to eight weeks for the tests to be completed.

After that the actual treatment would begin, always provided that by that time the patient hadn't acquired new maladies, necessitating a new round of testing. That was often the case, with pneumonia, sepsis from dirty needles (disposable needles haven't seen the inside of many Russian hospitals even now, 40-odd years later) and various skin conditions amply represented.

You already know that massive doses of steroids gave me kidney stones, a complaint that half the patients could legitimately make. And Tamara Petrovna's brutishness gave me a concussion – again not a unique incident. All things considered, a patient suffering from a chronic disease seldom went home after less than four months – only to return after just a few agonising months on the out.

All in all, I spent almost two of my 25 years in Russia in hospitals, most of the time at Clinic No. 24, always bumping into old friends. For example, Nikolai and I had shared at least two wards before we found ourselves in Ward 13. That unlucky number is often assigned in Russian hospitals to wards for 'last-leggers', an arrangement that dispels any illusions of a good prognosis that the patients might otherwise have.

Nikolai was the only one who didn't avail himself of the clandestine bar run by Tamara Petrovna. His face was the colour of ripe lemon, and even a drop of alcohol caused sharp pain to his calcified, cirrhosis-riddled liver.

This was probably the last time, he told me, that we were to find ourselves together in the same ward. He wanted me to know he had always thought I was an okay bloke for a Jew. My good soul made him rethink his overall assessment of that accursed race, which, before he met me, he felt sorry hadn't been completely eradicated by Hitler. And so he was sorry I was about to, well, not to cut too fine a point, croak.

Compliments of that nature always made me see red back in Russia, and I told him cruelly that he was a moron even by ethnically pure Russian standards. And when I died of old age I'd see him in hell as a resident of long standing. I was to regret those unkind, if understandable, words many times in the next 40 years, feeling ashamed that my prophecy turned out to be true, at least in its last part.

Nikolai died three weeks after our conversation, and in the good tradition of Ward 13 he did so just before lunch. I, on the other hand, was miraculously cured of my incurable disease the moment I left Russia. That contributed to medical science the solution to the problem of collagen diseases – even though my discovery that they are caused, or at least triggered, by the future that works has yet to make medical journals.

2

Most of the patients in Ward 13 were in pain of various degrees of intensity. Yet we always made a great effort not to moan because the others would have had the noisy wimp evicted to a corridor bed.

Russians in general have an excellent tolerance to pain, especially not their own. I recall being beaten up at age 12 by a couple of thugs, while my protectors from the local gang looked on with supreme indifference. A friend of mine was passing by, and he tried to enlist their help to save me from the assault. 'This is Boot,' he pleaded, 'you know, the bloke from 1/12 who tells you all those stories about the Count of Monte Cristo.' 'So bugger'im,' was their languid reply.

Doctors told us we shouldn't knock pain, as it gave them valuable diagnostic clues. Just how valuable those clues were is difficult to judge, considering that every patient I knew, including myself, had received extensive treatment for misdiagnosed diseases before the doctors figured out what the problem was. In my case, the doctors had treated me for what they felt was a dermatological rather than cardiovascular condition, before stumbling on the right diagnosis by accident when, in their opinion, I had only a few days left to live.

My mother died in the same hospital 22 years later, and no one could understand why she'd do anything so terminal, considering that she was being treated for nervous nausea, a minor problem. After she died, however, the Russian equivalents of Harley Street specialists found a malignant growth the size of a cricket ball in her stomach. The tumour was so big that it had blocked the passage out of her stomach, hence the nausea.

Papa was so upset that he did something unthinkable for a man who had spent his life in awe of authority – he wrote a letter of complaint. 'I do not comprehend,' he wrote, 'how it would have been possible not to see on a simple scan a cancer so highly developed...' and so forth.

Papa just didn't understand how those things worked. In all likelihood, no scan, simple or otherwise, had been done – may not have been done even had the equipment been available, which it probably wasn't. Russian doctors like, or perhaps have, to rely on impressionistic diagnoses. They trust their own ability to apply the mystic powers of the Russian soul to solving medical problems, despise Western doctors for their over-reliance on kit, and seldom ask themselves the question, 'What if I am wrong?' So if they felt Mama was suffering from nervous nausea, then that was that. And if facts eventually contradicted their judgment, then so much the worse for the facts.

'Have you heard the one about this medical congress?' asked Stasik. 'Seems like delegates from different countries are comparing notes, and this English bloke says, "Last month we were treating a patient for emphysema, then he died, and the autopsy showed he had lung cancer." "That's nothing," says the Frenchman. "We treated a woman for acute indigestion, then she died, and the autopsy showed she had a perforated ulcer." "That's nothing," says the Russian. "We treated this bloke for jaundice, then he died, and the autopsy showed he was a Chink." '

The outburst of laughter that greeted the story suggested that none of us had much trust in the doctors' ability to diagnose accurately – even when assisted by the patient's pain. That's why we felt we'd rather not have any and frequently begged for relief. The doctors usually obliged, thus proving they were prepared to comply with the Hippocratic oath, at least with the part that swore compassion. The part that gave them trouble was 'do no harm', as it was at odds with the remedies they had at their disposal.

The only OTC painkillers that existed in Russia were aspirin and Analgin, a paracetamol-type drug. Though not a patch on their Western equivalents in efficacy, large doses of them did produce some kind of analgesic effect. But large doses were expensive, and indiscriminate administration of them would have made an unacceptable dent in the hospital's budget.

Morphine derivatives, on the other hand, were dirt-cheap. So the old syringe, whose hygienic condition a King's Cross drug pusher would have found embarrassing, saw the light of day a lot. In lesser hospitals, anyone suffering from chronic pain would be turned into a drug addict within a month. Our doctors knew better than that – and still morphine flowed freely.

Many of us ended up with the habit and I myself, having received regular shots for several months, had to go cold turkey afterwards. That experience, incidentally, wasn't anywhere near as horrific as it's described by addicts who really don't want to quit. Then again, there must be something in me that resists chemical dependency.

That innate quality was tested to the limit a couple of years later when I went on the first honeymoon of my life. My wife and I arrived at our hired room at Piarnu, Estonia, in the evening. That very night I had one of those diabolical attacks of kidney stones creating the kind of pain experts rate as being stronger than the pain of childbirth. I needed an ambulance straight away, but out in the Soviet sticks it was easier said than done.

There was no telephone in the house, and no public phones anywhere around. All my wife could do was walk out and start ransacking the whole town in search of a hospital. Considering that Piarnu is a sizeable place, and yet not the kind of bustling metropolis where you can meet people in the street at two in the morning, I was fortunate it took her only three hours. While she was thus doing the sights, the pain was throwing me from the bed to the floor, into the armchair, then back onto the bed.

Finally she returned, accompanied by a young blonde thing who spoke broken Russian and wasn't a doctor at all but just a medical student moonlighting in the ambulance service. She had the compassion to sympathise with my suffering, the honesty to admit she hadn't got as far as kidney stones in her studies, and the humility to ask for my medical advice, based on much first-hand experience with the condition.

In my state I wouldn't have been averse to DIY amputation, so I proffered the advice with alacrity and slight acrimony. 'First check it's not appendicitis – if you know how, that is.' Ignoring, or perhaps failing to understand, the crude sarcasm, the blued-eyed Balt assured me she was capable of such a test and proceeded to administer it. 'Zis is not appendicitis,' she pronounced. 'Right,' I moaned. 'In that case, give me a shot of painkiller, the stronger the better.'

The young lady was on safe grounds there. She whipped a syringe out, filled it with what later turned out to be three times the recommended dose of Demerol and injected it with considerable panache.

'Are you feeling better?' she asked, pulling the plunger up. The stone moved somewhere in my urethra, pain shot through my back, and I muttered in a semi-conscious haze, 'No. Give me another.' The compassionate student complied with that irresponsible request and injected me with another triple shot, and then one more in the way of a nightcap. As a result, I recovered from my kidney attack but during the four weeks of our holiday had trouble controlling the muscles of my lower jaw.

At our hospital, once the pain subsided, boredom set in. Even nocturnal trysts of one kind or another failed to relieve it, and the patients looked for various ways to solve the problem. Mine was to read bagfuls of books. That indulgence was made possible by Mama's job as librarian and her readiness to do anything she could to 'save her baby's life', as she put it with a characteristic touch of melodrama. In addition to heavy loads of books, she also brought me enough food to subsist on without having to resort to the muck one got at the hospital.

The hospital had a strict policy on visiting rights, with only an hour allowed every other day. But all one needed to visit a patient was to put on a white gown and pretend one was a doctor or, in my friends' case, a medical student. Thus I got frequent visits from my friend Anikeyev who brought real vodka, as opposed to Tamara Petrovna's concoction, and Java fags, the mildest of Russian cigarettes.

As often as not he'd share the vodka with me and then ask for a few roubles to get more. Thanks to the illegal card game, I always had spare change, and Anikeyev often left the site of his friend's sick bed pissed out of his mind.

On one occasion Papa came to see me as Anikeyev was reeling out. Instead of spending the allotted time telling me his wartime stories for the umpteenth time, he had to drag Anikeyev out and onto a bus. The journey home took Anikeyev exactly 15 days, which was a standard sentence for the kind of disturbance he had created on the bus, including taking a swing at the arresting officer. The officer and his colleagues had their revenge at the station where they trussed Anikeyev up and took turns kicking him.

On another occasion, Anikeyev, feeling more like a lover than a fighter, went on a scouting mission to the women's wing (unlike in the NHS, there were no unisex wards in Soviet hospitals). There he broke into one of the wards and committed acts of such gross indecency that not only was he himself thrown out, but I was treated as accessory before the fact and summarily discharged. The next day the hospital administration relented and let me back in on condition that they'd never again see the degenerate in the green three-piece suit.

The rest of the time I spent reading, playing chess and cards, and, for a while, talking to Andrei Volkonsky. This harpsichordist and composer later founded the *Madrigal* ensemble, which performed medieval music in period costumes and by candlelight. I first met him on the landing of the ancient staircase leading down to the lobby. We all used the landing as a smoking area where cigarettes and stories of rape were freely exchanged. That day I had run out of fags and asked an aristocratic-looking man with glasses finely balanced on the tip of his straight nose if he could spare one.

'Do you terribly mind a Gauloise?' he asked, rolling his Rs slightly. With the natural perspicacity of youth I guessed he was referring to some foreign brand, of the kind unavailable in Russia. I said fine, I didn't mind at all, thinking the man a bit of a poser.

However, it turned out his predilection for French cigarettes had been acquired at source. A member of one of the oldest aristocratic families in Russia, he was born in Geneva whither his parents had escaped from the future they were sure wouldn't work. Having grown up there, he still preferred French to Russian in social situations, a preference common even to those of his ancestors who had lived in Russia all their lives.

Then came the Changing of the Signposts movement run by the NKVD in the twenties and thirties to finish off the Russian émigré community as a potential threat. NKVD emissaries flooded Paris, Berlin, Prague and other émigré centres with bogus stories of liberalisation, perestroika and Mother Russia ready to forgive her wayward children.

The most famous of those emissaries was Ilia Ehrenburg, the popular writer who spent the whole interbellum period in Paris. During the Khrushchev 'thaw' in the sixties he published *People, Years, Life,* the best-selling memoirs of the time. There he recalled his meetings with Aragon, Triolet, Picasso and other left-wing Left Bankers. The book was written so well that I could almost taste the pastis taken languidly at *La Rotonde.* Out of modesty, however, Ehrenburg omitted any reference to his job as NKVD talent spotter. He also left out such details as having been slapped in the face publicly by the poet André Breton, who must have seen through the whole ploy.

Volkonsky's parents were among those who didn't. They decided to repatriate, along with such luminaries as Prokofiev and Tsvetayeva. But some other luminaries, such as Generals Kutepov and Miller, didn't see the light. They had to be dealt with in other ways, described in his book by Gen. Sudoplatov, the ex-head of the NKVD 'wet affairs' department. I tactfully refrained from asking Volkonsky what happened to his parents once they had returned. But the educated guess would have been nothing benign, if the example of most other repatriates was anything to go by.

We talked mostly about music and foreign languages. (Volkonsky knew a lot about both subjects and I pretended I did.) He was recovering from a hernia operation during which, according to the disparaging reports from the patients in the ward next to the operating theatre, he had squealed like a stuck pig.

'I don't understand how I got this silly hernia,' complained the musician. 'My wardmate got his because he works at a vegetable warehouse and carries sacks of potatoes for a living. But I've never carried anything in my life except the occasional woman to the nearest bed.' 'Must have been some hefty women,' I offered. He laughed and we became inseparable friends until his discharge a week later.

I rather doubted the reports of his noisy behaviour as I refused to believe that an abdominal operation would be performed without general anaesthesia. But later I found out the hard way that many operations in Russia, including, for example, root canal work, were performed either without any narcosis whatever or with a mild local anaesthetic that didn't quite work.

Once, I remember, I was stabbed in the back with a sharpened rasp. The man wielding it and two of his friends had taken exception to my getting friendly with his girlfriend at a restaurant dance. What saved me was that the subsequent fight took place outside, the night was bitterly cold, and I was wearing several layers of heavy clothing. So the rasp didn't penetrate my left shoulder blade deeper than an inch.

I felt no pain in the heat of the battle and only realised I had been stabbed on the way home, as I leaned back against the cab's seat and felt sticky wetness. The cab was rerouted to the Sklifassovsky Institute of Traumatology, where a ham-fisted doctor stitched me up without any anaesthetic. That hurt more than the original wound, but the scar in my back still reminds me of Russia – and acts as a weather-forecasting service.

In the matter of anaesthesia, as in all others, an exception was made for Kremlin bigwigs, and an instructive story was making the rounds in Moscow at the time. A Deputy Minister of Heavy Industry was suffering from an in-grown toenail. For any poor mortal, the problem would have been solved by a 10-minute outpatient surgery. But an important comrade like that couldn't be allowed to suffer any discomfort, not to mention pain.

A decision was made to operate under general anaesthesia. Unfortunately, as the doctor administering it was either incompetent or drunk (not an infrequent occurrence in Russian operating theatres), he used an excessively high dose – or else the deputy minister's heart was too weak. Be that as it may, his heart stopped and wouldn't restart.

The surgeon was scared out of his wits, since a man of that stature dying on his table could have spelled the end of his medical career. He tried every trick in the book, attempting to restart the stubborn heart, and only succeeded with the last-ditch measure wherein he opened up the patient's chest cavity and began to massage his heart. To everybody's relief, the jump start worked. They stitched the chest up and had the deputy minister taken to his private room.

Unfortunately, the orderlies carrying the stretcher definitely were drunk. They proved that by tipping the stretcher over as they walked up the stairs. The victim fell out and, still asleep, went bump-bump-bump down the steps, breaking his leg in the process. Back to the operating theatre they went, where the surgical team mercifully hadn't yet dispersed. The head surgeon overcame the sight of a sacking notice flashing before his eyes and set the broken leg in a cast.

The next morning the bigwig woke up in his room and was perplexed to see that his chest was tightly bandaged and his right leg, encased in a heavy cast, was suspended in traction. Sticking out of the cast was his big toe – with the nail still growing defiantly in.

But even this gentleman's misfortune paled by comparison with the self-medication mishap that occurred at roughly the same time. The main character of the story was Marshal Yeremenko, one of the principal Soviet commanders at Stalingrad.

A 22-stone bear of a man, the marshal possessed an heroic capacity for food and drink. Nonetheless he regarded himself as a man of moderation and had been overheard deploring the absence of that quality in young officers.

'Today's lot ain't like we used to be,' he complained. 'I don't understand them; they have no self-restraint at all. I mean, drink your litre of vodka by all means. But then stop and catch your breath.'

One hot summer the marshal's family were sunning themselves somewhere in Georgia, and he found himself alone in his Moscow flat. To kill time he attended a banquet in honour of a visiting Mongolian general. There the marshal indulged his prodigious appetites and returned home the worse for wear. In particular, his girth had expanded five inches as if to accommodate a beach ball, and gas pressure was distending his stomach even further. Some relief was in order.

Russians tend to believe in folksy remedies. Mustard plasters and foot baths, saline inhalations, suction cups, leeches (sometimes, as in Grandpa's case, with fatal consequences) were all used routinely in my day. Enemas were popular too, and Yeremenko was a strong believer in those. Though he didn't have a proper device at home, the ingenuity of the man who had outfoxed Field-Marshal von Paulus wouldn't be defeated.

The good marshal went to the bathroom, dropped his trousers, unscrewed the head off the flexible shower hose, stuck the end into his rectum and turned the water on full blast. Physics, alas, wasn't the hero's forte, which point was driven home with utmost cruelty. The rushing stream created a pressure differential in his gas-inflated stomach and it burst like a pricked helium balloon.

The obituaries were vague on the cause of death, stating only that it had been 'sudden' and 'unexpected'. But our Boris got the story through the army grapevine and, having sworn us to secrecy, related it to the family. Papa put on the mournful expression he felt was called for and said, shaking his head, 'And for that he won the battle of

Stalingrad?'

3

Hospital doctors fought disease; GPs fought absenteeism. Russian bosses treated absenteeism sternly, as bosses everywhere tend to do when dealing with a problem of pandemic proportions.

Actually, a far worse problem is caused by a workforce that's present in body but absent in spirit, or rather because of excessive consumption of spirits. It wouldn't be an exaggeration to say that at least half of the Russian labour force are drunk on the job at any time, something CIA analysts stubbornly refuse to take into account in their economic projections.

Back in the early eighties I had an interpreting contract with Fluor, a Houston engineering firm that was designing a gas processing plant for Russia. They had asked me to assist in the discussion of the technical details of the proposed design, the result of which three-week session was supposed to be formal acceptance of their proposal.

Also party to the discussions was a group of Japanese engineers from Nippon Steel who were designing the vessels for the plant. The Japanese came with their own English-to-Russian interpreters led by an old man named Mr Makina. He had learned his Russian in a POW camp where he stayed until 1957, which experience amazingly didn't make him at all bitter towards the Russians. However, Mr Makina's Russian vocabulary was slanted towards the camp jargon, and I did my best not to laugh when he described a Soviet engineer as 'that plick'.

His knowledge of the technical vocabulary was formidable, unlike, as I'm man enough to admit, my own. Mr Makina turned up with a suitcase full of Russian and American books on gas processing. All the books were tabbed, with the critical terms highlighted in yellow. I turned up armed with the traditional Russian belief that somehow things would turn out all right on the day.

'Life is short, Mr Makina,' I once opined. 'You can't learn it all.' 'Horribre attitude,' he rebuked me indignantly. 'We're interpreters. We're paid a rot of bruddy money.'

Despite my ignorance of gas processing, things did work out. The discussion, for which the participants had broken up into several groups, went smoothly, at least as far as the Soviets were concerned. The Americans were dismayed by the Russians' incessant attempts to enlarge the scope of the contract without increasing its cost, something all Russians are conditioned to do when dealing with foreigners.

To their credit, the Americans resisted most of the outrageous demands, and their obstreperousness even drove the head of the Russian HVAC group to madness. He flipped out at a party in their hotel one night and began laying about him like McDuff, but using less deadly weapons, mostly his teeth. The next morning comrade Cherniayev, head of the general design group, turned up with a blood-stained bandage on his hand.

'My God, Pyotr Andreevich,' I said, feigning concern. 'What on earth happened to your hand?' In fact, I already knew exactly what had happened from the only Fluor engineer who had attended the party.

'There was this nail sticking out of the wall back at the hotel,' complained comrade Cherniayev. 'Shocking,' I commiserated. 'The standards of workmanship these days are appalling. And look, the nail went all the way through your hand!' I pointed at the blood stains on both sides of his bandaged hand.

'To hell with that,' explained the Russian. 'Let's get back to business. What's this here?' He pointed at a neatly drawn square in the corner of the general plan. 'That,' responded his American counterpart, 'is the waste sump.' 'I know that.' The Russian was getting impatient. 'I was asking what this dotted line is around it.'

'That's the fence around the sump,' replied the American. 'How high is it?' comrade Cherniayev wanted to know. 'Three feet, as per our regulations.' 'Well, that's not tall enough,' declared comrade Cherniayev categorically. 'Our experience says it is.' 'And I'm telling you it's not,' insisted the Russian. 'What if a worker falls over and in?'

'In our experience,' repeated the American, 'three feet is a sufficient height to prevent that from happening.' 'Yes, but what if the worker is, well, not sober?' came a perfectly natural question. The answer was just as natural, for a Westerner: 'If he's drunk, that means it's after hours, and he won't be anywhere near the plant.'

A trained observer could have discerned a great deal of anguish in the Russian's laughter. 'Don't translate this,' he said to me, one conspirator to the other, 'but he simply doesn't understand, does he?'

'No, Pyotr Andreevich, he doesn't.'

There's little anyone can do about drinking on the job in Russia, but the authorities have always tried to cut down on tardiness and absenteeism. Just before the war, for example, anyone more than 20 minutes late for work was automatically sentenced to a year in a camp – this regardless of the reason for his transgression. Missing a whole day was unthinkable, unless one was seriously ill. That lamentable condition had to be validated by a medical certificate, and writing those took up the bulk of a GP's time. That situation persisted even after Stalin's death.

For most Russian GPs it was the only thing they had time to do. Their job was to separate the sick wheat from the malingering chaff, as their superiors assessed their performance by the number of certificate requests they turned down. Of course, patients applied diametrically opposite criteria. To them a good GP was a doctor who didn't mind giving one a few days off without bitching about one's temperature being insufficiently high.

My chronic condition was a godsend in that respect, as all I had to do to get a certificate for a few days was point at my calves and complain of sharp pain. Later the same condition saved me from being conscripted.

Thus I didn't have to resort to the tricks practised by other would-be recruits, such as putting their heads between the two halves of the automatically closing doors of a Metro train to produce a concussion, injecting petrol into their arms, or swallowing hexa-nuts before the stomach X-ray. Most GPs had never heard of *polyarteritis nodosa* and happily put their illegible signatures on much needed reprieves from work or army service.

As nothing in this world is free, the payment for a reprieve was having to queue up for most of the day. Since no system of appointments existed, one simply showed up in the morning and was assigned a number in a 'live' queue. At an average of five minutes per patient, a ticket that said No. 120 was bad news and a powerful deterrent to any possible abuse of the system.

But GPs in the provinces frequently acted as the only medical help available, not merely as certificate signers. We often had to avail ourselves of the services offered by those Chekhovian characters, since for the first 10 years of my life Papa was serving his 'minus 50' banishment.

As you may remember, Papa was thus punished for having been a POW during the war, an offence so flagrant that most of the culprits who had survived German camps were upon their liberation sent to the Russian equivalents. Unless, of course, they had collaborated with the enemy, in which case they were shot. Papa got off easy, but his banishment from Moscow meant a nomadic existence in the first seven years of my life.

Much as Mama hated to stay apart from a husband of Papa's track record, she couldn't leave Moscow for longer than six months at a time, as this would have qualified as establishing residence elsewhere, putting her in default of her Moscow residence permit. All Soviet citizens had residence permits (*propiska*) stamped on their internal passports, assigning them to a specific place from which they couldn't relocate without relinquishing their old permit and having to obtain a new one. (A version of the same system still exists today, but propiska is now referred to as 'registration'.)

In my day all Soviet cities and towns were divided into categories, depending on their desirability. The category of a place determined the way it was supplied with consumer goods and food. Thus the difference between, say, Moscow and Tomsk could be a matter of life or death.

Moscow was Category 1, with Leningrad close behind. From there the classification dropped off sharply, eventually hitting the rock bottom of places like Magadan. This hierarchal structure partly explains the residential crisis still going on in Moscow, as millions of people aspire to improve their lot by moving there.

That's where residence permits come in. If one wishes to move downwards from Leningrad to Yaroslavl, or from Yaroslavl to Tomsk, or from Tomsk to Semipalatinsk, that's usually no problem. However, an upward move in the opposite direction requires either marriage to a local resident or, in my day, a direct order from the Central Committee of the Party.

This was a barrier unknown to Chekhov's Three Sisters, but perhaps anticipated by them. That's why they persevered in their desire to abandon their dreary country life and move to Moscow while the moving was good. ('Somebody ought to have given those girls three railway tickets to Moscow at the end of Act 1', quipped the poet Mandelstam.)

The decision to relinquish one's Moscow residence permit was as irreversible as the decision to lose one's virginity. Unlike the latter, however, it promised nothing but a life of unmitigated misery. That's why Mama and I would follow Papa to yet another factory settlement in the middle of nowhere, spend a few months with him and then go back to Moscow for several months to keep our residence permit alive.

The nature of Papa's work demanded his presence in Moscow a couple of times a month. Thus my pre-school years were largely spent in transit or at various railway stations, either meeting Papa or seeing him off. But the first time we travelled with him wasn't by rail but by lorry, a battered tonne-and-a-half flatbed that belonged to yet another glassworks at which Papa was serving a two-year stint.

The factory and the small settlement where the workers lived were stuck in the middle of the Briansk forest, 150 miles and two light years away from Moscow. Given the state of the roads that led there, and the condition of the vehicle that was losing pieces as we went along, the journey took two days. As it rained most of the time, the driver covered the flatbed containing Mama and me with a tarpaulin. Papa sat in the cabin, offering driving tips and making sure the proletarian driver never forgot who was boss.

The very first stop, at Maloyaroslavets, demonstrated the futility of upper-class paternalism. As Mama, Papa and I went shopping for fruit and bread, the driver Gnida, whose name means 'nit' in English, wandered off for half an hour and returned so drunk he could hardly walk. It was late afternoon, but staying the night was out of the question as the town had no hotels.

Papa and Mama dragged Nit into the driver's seat and told him to drive. Nit was laughing his head off as he put the lorry into gear without shutting his door. The rusty machine lurched forward, and Nit, still rocking with laughter, fell out into the mud. The lorry bucked like a horse and died.

'How did he manage to get so drunk so fast?' wondered Papa. 'You know how these people are,' sighed Mama as they were dragging the mirthful proletarian out of the dirt.

'So what the hell are we going to do?' Papa always preferred pragmatism to abstractions. 'You drive,' said Mama, pushing Nit's other leg onto the flatbed. 'You must be joking,' objected Papa, whose detailed and disparaging comments on Nit's driving had belied his own inability to drive. 'You're not suggesting my baby should spend the night in this lorry?' Mama pointed tragically at the three-year-old baby who was enjoying every minute of it.

Papa got behind the wheel and began learning as he went along, gradually building up his confidence to a point where he could proceed at a brisk five miles an hour. The lorry was jumping up and down in the dirt track, and as it hit a particularly large pothole Nit fell over the tailboard. The shock sobered him up a little, and he decided to follow the lorry on foot. To that end he grabbed the trailer hitch at the back and ran behind the lorry for half a mile or so, getting more and more hoarse with laughter.

Eventually we had to stop, pull off the road in the middle of an abandoned rye field, climb under the tarpaulin and grab a few hours' fitful sleep punctuated by Nit's retching. The next day we arrived, and Mama was quick to pass critical judgement on the place.

Ivot, as the settlement was called, formed a crescent around the south edge of the glassworks where Papa was Chief Engineer. There were a few private log houses for the management and several rows of workers' barracks that could have acted as the set for the film *One Day In the Life of Ivan Denisovich*. In the middle of Ivot was a tiny square, the site of a bakery and an irregularly supplied convenience shop. Around Ivot was at least 50 miles of impassable thicket in any direction.

Wolves howled by night, and slender chickens ran splashing through the puddles by day. Sometimes a hungry dog chased the chickens, and when it caught up with them feathers flew all over Ivot. Mama let me walk freely, as the moribund lorry was the only vehicle there, and everybody knew where it was at any time. The deal was that the first time I walked anywhere near the edge of the forest I'd be grounded for life. I never transgressed against that injunction as one could sometimes see wolves roaming the outskirts.

On the first day in the house we got good news and bad news. The bad news was that Nit had evidently sobered up enough during the night to have stolen the few banknotes Mama had in her handbag. That loss was irretrievable as the money had been speedily spent on a resuscitating hair of the dog. The good news was that the landlord had two daughters, one my age, the other a year older, who according to their father were so refined that no other children would play with them. Since he could see that I was a discerning young gentleman of culture, I had two natural playmates.

The good news turned out to be bad in the final analysis, as it transpired that the chief reason for the ostracism wasn't so much the girls' refinement as the contagious stage of tuberculosis from which they suffered. Everybody, except naturally us, was aware of that, and all other children had been told to give the girls a wide berth. As no one in the settlement bothered to share that information with us, within a few weeks I became a very unwell child indeed.

Before that I had taken advantage of the girls' superior knowledge of the human anatomy and their ability to relate the words I had learned from my actor friends to the organs those words designated.

'This is a minge,' intoned the elder of the worldly young ladies, raising her skirt and pointing in the relevant direction. I was impressed, thinking it looked like the join between two bread rolls stuck together. 'This is a dick,' she continued, pulling my shorts down and playing with the appendage in question. I found the sensation to be embarrassingly nice but soon learned that one had to pay for one's pleasure.

I got ill in April. The snow had just melted, rendering the dirt track that linked Ivot with Dyatkovo, the nearest town, impassable for either our lorry or an ambulance. The Ivot GP was a young woman who loathed Mama and, by association, me. She was Papa's mistress and hoped that, if we left, she could entice Papa to divorce Mama, marry her and eventually take her out of the Ivotian morass to the shining lights of Moscow.

She diagnosed an early stage of tuberculosis but refused to exceed the allowable ration of penicillin in her possession, leaving me to my feverish fate that looked to Mama worse than it was. But even to cooler heads it looked as if I had to be transported to Dyatkovo within the next few days if I was to have a sporting chance of survival. The only option was to forgo motor locomotion and use instead the horse-drawn cart that was in the charge of the local fireman.

As luck would have it, the fireman had been killed the night before by a glass blower. Having drunk two pint mugs of vodka, the worker took exception to a snide remark made by the fireman, grabbed an axe and did a Lizzie Borden. That spontaneous act left Ivot without a fireman and me without anyone who could drive the cart.

Papa had to poll the entire population until he found an old codger who reluctantly agreed to drive me to Dyatkovo, but not before he saw the colour of Papa's two bottles of vodka. Russians, in general, would often do things for a physical bottle that they wouldn't do for its monetary equivalent.

When the codger saw the two 'white heads', so called because of their aluminium tear-off caps, he recalled that as a young glass blower before the revolution he had had his own two-horse cart. He also recalled, as Papa told me many years later, the use to which he put the cart in 'the time of peace' (that is, before 1917), which was taking his mates to a Dyatkovo brothel every Friday night. There they'd drink non-stop until Wednesday and, of course, do all those things one normally does in a brothel. Come Wednesday, the manager of the glass-blowing shop would arrive, begging them to return to work, which they'd magnanimously agree to do.

'My wage was two thousand roubles a year,' he told us. 'I had a house, a cart, two horses, a dozen pigs, three cows and more chickens than I could count. Me and my wife, we travelled everywhere, Paris, Berlin, you name it. And we still had more money left over than we knew what to do with. And now…' Ignat the codger waved his hand in a characteristic Russian gesture of resignation. 'Now I have bugger-all. One pair of trousers, one pair of shoes and a cubicle in the barracks. Oh, well…,' he waved his hand again.

Mercifully he still remembered how to drive a cart and got Mama and me to a hospital in Dyatkovo without any untoward incidents. This even though he had consumed half his payment on the spot, pouring the contents of a half-litre bottle down his throat without a single swallowing spasm.

I still remember the bumpy ride and Ignat's heaving back smelling of old foot-wraps and fresh hay. He'd use the reins as a whip, yelling from time to time, 'Move, you dead stiff!' This was apparently a skill akin to driving a bike: never forgotten once properly learned. My memory of the hospital is less clear, partly because I was drifting in and out of consciousness. But they must have done something right as I recovered with nary a trace of tuberculosis in my lungs, a development not to have been taken for granted.

The conniving GP eventually got her way in the sense that Mama had to take me back to Moscow after a couple of months' convalescence, leaving the medic within striking distance of Papa. However, she failed in the sense that Papa never did divorce my mother, and the woman had to continue her languishing practice in Ivot.

My last memory of the place is happier, involving a wedding, rather than a near-funeral. I was about 16 when Papa, by now firmly ensconced in Moscow, was sent on an inspection tour of his old plant. I asked to come with him, partly for sentimental reasons and partly out of boredom. We were rewarded by an invitation to the wedding of the late Ignat's granddaughter and a young glass blower named Stepan.

It was an outdoor affair, with several hundred shabbily dressed people sitting at tables put together in a T-shape 80 yards long and 30 across. The T was set on a wide lawn at the outskirts of the forest, where all the wolves had by then been shot. The tables were laden with plentiful food heavy on pickled vegetables and salted herring, traditional chasers for vodka. Each setting featured a faceted eight-ounce glass, but no bottles were to be seen.

By then we had realised that there was an etiquette associated with the whole production, with which we were unfamiliar. Luckily we were seated next to an old woman who would have looked 80 to a Westerner but was probably in her late fifties. Having kindly taken it upon herself to guide us through the socially dangerous undercurrents, she told Papa to shut up when he expressed his dismay over the absence of bottles.

'The slower you go, the further you'll get,' she said, sharing with us the Russian folk wisdom probably traceable to the Latin *festina lente*. She was right. Within 10 minutes the quiet non-alcoholic buzz was interrupted by the sound of the Russian wedding march performed on the accordion. The accordion player then appeared on the lawn, flanked by two women in traditional village garb. They were pushing a wheelbarrow with several large jugs in it.

Half the jugs contained 'white wine', otherwise known as moonshine, the other half reeked of 'red wine'. As the accordion player segued into an easy air, the women walked along the table, filling every man's glass with white and every woman's glass with red. I got the red on account of my youth. Papa began to protest against having to drink a tumblerful of rough 50-percent spirit, but was muffled by our guide. 'Shut up,' she advised. 'If you don't shut up, they'll make you drink a penalty glass on top of this one.'

Papa did as he was told and, along with everybody else, downed his glass at the end of the toastmaster's speech, who told us to drink to the fortunate winds that had blown those two beautiful youngsters together. Everyone shouted, 'Bitter! Bitter!', the ancient Russian way of saying that the drink would taste bitter unless the newlyweds kissed. They obliged, and down went hundreds of tumblers into eagerly gaping mouths. Papa was a moderate drinker, and the experience of downing all that moonshine delivered a blow to his whole system.

Half an hour later the accordion sounded again, and the women poured another round. As the guest of honour, Papa was expected to propose the next toast, and he could think of nothing better than one of his stock Georgian pastiches that I had already learned by heart and still had to interpret for my wife Penelope 30 years later, when Papa came to visit.

'A nasty wizard turned this beautiful youth into a wolf,' began Papa in a half-hearted imitation of the throaty Georgian vowels. 'This wolf runs through the countryside, looking for a kind wizard who'd turn him back into a man. Finally he finds a wizard who tells him he'll become human again if he finds a beautiful girl and fulfils three of her wishes. He finds this girl and explains the situation to her. "Okay," she says. "Here's my first wish: make love to me like a man." The wolf was a bit surprised but did as he was told. He then asked what her second wish would be. "You know," said the girl, "make love to me again like a man."'

'The wolf complied with her wish, but not without difficulty. The third wish was the same as the other two. Hard as the wolf tried he couldn't do it, and thus remained a wolf for ever.'

'So let's drink to our handsome young men who'll never have to run like naked beasts through the woods. And to our beautiful young girls,' Papa took a bow in the direction of the blushing bride, 'who, one hopes, know how to control their beastly appetites. Best of luck to both of you.'

Papa's reward for his witty speech was a burst of applause, which he tried to use as an excuse not to down his second glass. The old woman would have none of that. 'Shut up and drink up,' she advised. 'If you don't drink your own toast, that means you have no respect for nobody here.' Papa shut up and drank up.

'What's going to happen now?' he asked, not in complete command of his tongue. 'Now we'll dance,' she said matter-of-factly, 'for an hour or so. Then there'll be another round. And then the fight will start.'

'How can you be sure there will be a fight?' After a mere pint of fortified wine, my practised tongue was steady as a rock. 'You shut up,' said our kind guide, 'when grown-ups are talking. I say there'll be a fight coz there always is a fight.'

That gave us an idea of exactly when to disappear, but Papa still danced with his erstwhile mistress, the doctor, by then a wrinkled middle-aged woman of 40. 'How about we get together after this,' he asked, all the booze obviously affecting his eyes as well. 'Can't,' she said. 'I'll be sewing up these uncultured animals all night and all day tomorrow. It's the same every time.'

I danced with our guide and asked her what we should do now. 'What you should do now,' she commanded, 'is shut up and bugger off.' So we buggered off.

I remembered the wedding two years later, when my stay at Clinic No. 24 extended over November 7, Revolution Day. All hospitals in Moscow were on red alert, ready to receive the casualties of the pseudo-revolutionary zeal liberally displayed by the Russians on this and any other festive occasion. All normal medical activities were suspended for three days, as the lift leading to the casualty department incessantly rattled up and down its rusty shaft night and day.

When the madness subsided, along with our hangovers caused by having made Tamara Petrovna 200 oranges richer, I asked Nadia what the most typical complaints had been. They turned out to be, in that order, head injuries inflicted by empty bottles; poisoning caused by drinking methanol and other chemicals, such as dyes, some of which didn't even have any alcohol in them; and injuries to heads and wrists caused by drunks falling down. Having shared this information, Nadia took our bloods and said that if the tests revealed excessive alcohol content, we'd all be summarily discharged.

Shortly after this the hospital moved to a new building designed and constructed by the Finns. It was impeccably modern, with panels of shining glass everywhere, and windows that never opened even in scorching heat. It was those claustrophobic windows that created a spot of bother when I was saying goodbye to Russian medicine and indeed all of Russia a few years later.

I was at the time 25 and unemployed, even though everyone knew there was no unemployment in Russia. I had lost my job after applying for an exit visa, which was par for the course. For it would have been naïve to expect that someone who had proclaimed a desire to disengage himself from the future that worked would still be allowed to poison students' souls with subversive lectures on Dickens and Byron. Thus I had plenty of time on my hands and thought it would be useful to milk free medical care for one last check-up. Especially since I had been told that few people could afford hospitalisation in the States.

The bearer of that datum was a lady from the Institute for US Studies, a KGB think tank. She had lived in the States for a few years and told me that the going rate for a hospital bed was $200 a day, with the treatment on top of that. Somehow she forgot to mention medical insurance, which left me feverishly adding columns of figures on a piece of paper: 'Let's see, 200 plus maybe another 100 equals 300, times 120 days on average equals – damn!!!'

Those calculations didn't diminish my resolve to leave but added an element of self-sacrifice to emigration. My fears were partly put to rest by a fellow lecturer who was also planning to leave. Yuri, who didn't know about medical insurance either but whose judgement wasn't clouded by personal interest in medicine, gave me a lesson in impartial common sense.

'Don't be an idiot,' he suggested. 'There are 240 million Americans out there, and somehow they get treatment when they need it. And their life expectancy is 20 years higher than here. You'll be all right.'

Still, there I was, incarcerated in the new building that by then had already acquired the musty smell of the old one. The windows were permanently sealed, which was fine with me as it was February, a month that doesn't normally encourage Muscovites to let some fresh air in. But Sergei, the thrombophlebitic ornithologist in the next bed, said it wasn't fine by him. Not with all those poor sparrows and pigeons starving to death outside.

By mistake we asked him what the connection was, and he explained to us heartless shits that if we could open the windows, we'd be able to feed the birdies, saving some of them from death. He had expected an emotional response to match his own but received only a few obscene comments from others and a cruel Chekhovian pastiche from me: 'In the general scheme of things, what's a few birds more or less?'

That kicked off a conversation on bestiality, featuring birds as love interests. Boria the cabbie said he had heard from a fare once that, when you screwed, say, a goose, the idea was to wring its neck at the point of no return, thus creating most satisfying contractions you know where. I contributed a reminder of the hygienic use to which Rabelais's characters put goslings, and Sergei never again spoke to any of us.

Instead he pushed his chair to the window and for hours on end watched his beloved birds freeze to death. A couple of days later, the sight proved to be more than he could bear.

After lunch that day Sergei collected the leftover bread from everybody and crumbled it. Then he picked up his chair and, before anyone could stop him, hurled it through the polished Finnish window that readily shattered into a cascade of glistening shards raining on the ground. He then proceeded to throw the bread in the general direction of the birds. The poor creatures, shaken by the violence, circled overhead shrieking hysterically.

On such occasions nurses always appeared out of nowhere, as they did then. A small detachment led by Tamara Petrovna burst in and whisked Sergei, who looked catatonic, out of our lives. On her way out, Tamara Petrovna told us that if she found out one of us flipping perverts had egged on that psycho to destroy state property, she'd personally rip the culprit's balls off. And speaking of psychos, Boot shall report to Wing 2 for psychiatric examination.

'What psychiatric examination?' I protested. 'I don't know and I don't give a shit,' replied the healthcare professional. 'The doctor says you report to Wing 2, you report to Wing 2 – even if I have to drag you there by your whatsit.'

The thought of impersonating a dog on a lead didn't appeal to me, but the idea of a brush with Soviet psychiatry appealed even less. At that time, the Soviets used shrinks as an extension of their law enforcement, specifically the branch of it that dealt with dissidents.

The way this worked was that the victim would be taken to the Serbsky Institute of Forensic Psychiatry and given an intense course of Thorazine. After that he'd become indistinguishable from legitimate madmen. He could then be presented to the outside world as proof that people who didn't believe that the future worked were all certifiable.

Alas, I had had a few brushes with the KGB. After the last one Major

Gazonov had advised me, father to son, to get out of Russia while the getting was good. So I could be seen as a dissident in some circles, and this elevated me in my own eyes above the philistine masses. Mercifully, at the time I was making a nuisance of myself the chances of getting killed for such activities were slim, and it was relatively safe to be a hero.

On balance, I think I caused more misery to Papa than to the Soviets. One morning, for example, I had to take two suitcases full of banned literature out of a friend's house because he was about to be arrested. In fact, KGB thugs were marching up the stairs just as I was lugging the cases down. I then took the subversive material to my parents' flat, hid it under the sofa and went back to the city centre.

When I returned home late at night, I found my ashen-faced parents squeamishly rummaging through the suitcases. 'What kind of rubbish is this?' asked Papa, holding up a copy of the Bible. (Classified as anti-Soviet propaganda, that book featured prominently as a sample of such material at the Museum of Border Guards.) It took me half an hour and a promise to take the cases out the next day for Papa to get his normal colour back.

A few days later he was summoned to *komitet* by Major Gazonov and asked to rein me in. For no obvious reason my ex-wife was asked to do the same thing at the same time. Both claimed truthfully that they had no influence on me, but it was Papa who got scared.

He sensed that his troubles were only starting, and subsequent events proved his antennae were in working order. The next incident he had to suffer was caused by poor coordination between the various departments of the KGB. Six months after I left the country without trouble, like, just as Major Gazonov had requested, his colleagues from another floor decided to sort me out.

The next day they showed up in force at Papa's block of flats. Since I had an undeserved reputation as a firebrand, *komitet* were taking no chances. A small detachment came to pick me up, with two men taking positions in the courtyard to cover the possible escape routes, two staying behind in the staircase, and two bursting into my parents' flat.

Mama wasn't there but Papa was, and the intrusion almost gave him a heart attack. 'We've come for Boot!' roared the officer in charge of the arresting party. 'Why... what have I... I haven't...' was all Papa could manage.

'Not you!' barked the KGBist. 'Your son!'

'Oh, well,' Papa felt relieved. 'He's not here.'

'That's all right. We'll wait.' Komitet wouldn't take no for an answer. 'Yes, you're more than welcome,' said Papa hospitably, 'but I'm afraid he has left the country. He is in, well, he is in the States now.'

The news hit the raiders with the power of a wrecking ball. Having exchanged some angry and confused whispers, they made Papa sit down and write a long explanation of why his son wasn't there and who had allowed him to leave. After that the writing was on the wall for Papa, and it said 'sack'. A man whose son was a traitor couldn't be allowed to remain in charge of 800 people. Two years later, still only 60 years old, Papa was made to retire.

That was to happen in the near, and for me happy, future. The present, however, looked grim, what with the psychiatric examination looming large. In any event, on having come out of the political closet by applying for exit, any realistic man had to be prepared for a stint in a concentration camp. But a camp was one thing and being shot full of Thorazine and losing one's marbles was another.

I thought I'd rather die than live as a vegetable. Before walking to Wing 2 I wrapped a razor blade in a piece of the Pravda. I then hid it in my shoe, doubting I'd have the strength to use it on my wrists, hoping I wouldn't have to, and wondering what that was all about.

That question was answered after my discharge a month later, when Mama mentioned casually that she had telephoned my doctor and suggested I should have my head examined. It was all for my own good, she explained, and for her own peace of mind. She had to be satisfied I wasn't a nutter, since madness was the only possible reason for someone to want to betray his motherland.

Mama had a knack for expressing herself with pathos on the subject of the Soviet state. But her patriotism didn't prevent her covering the phone with a pillow every time she mentioned anything political. That precaution, she hoped, would render the in-built listening device useless.

At that time she was laying the patriotic bit on pretty thick, and even declined Papa's offer to go to Romania for their holiday. Papa had managed to obtain two free tour packages from his ministry. Spending a holiday anywhere abroad then had the same appeal to a Russian as touring the Mediterranean in your own 200-foot yacht would have to you. Nevertheless, Mama declined and in doing so made sure I'd hear every pointed word: 'No. Absolutely not. One ought to spend holidays in one's own motherland.' It's out of this overemphasised patriotism that Mama effectively shopped me to the KGB. Even if I hadn't been high on their list of potential Thorazine recipients, a statement from my own mother could have moved me right to the top. I wonder now if that's the sort of thing implied by the song 'We always hurt the one we love'. But at that time I was happy when the whole incident blew over.

The shrink, a chubby middle-aged woman with thick sideburns and warts, talked to me for a few minutes and looked perplexed about having to examine an obviously sane man. Still, out of professional integrity she asked me a few stock questions, which I answered with aggression unleashed by fear.

'When you were a child,' she inquired, 'did you often have sexual fantasies?'

'Doctor,' I said, mocking her tone of conspiratorial confidentiality, 'I'm so happy you've asked me this because it gives me a chance to unburden myself. Throughout my childhood I wanted to have sex with my mother, kill my father and stick a needle in my eye.'

'There's no need to be idiotically flippant.' She'd have none of that levity. 'Seriously,' she insisted. 'Did you have persistent fantasies? Sexual images in your mind's eye?'

'Of course I did,' I said. 'Still do as a matter of fact.' 'How easy was it for you to bring up one of those pictures in your mind?' 'Very easy,' I replied eagerly. 'I had it hanging on my wall.'

She didn't even smile. 'In my judgement,' she said sternly, 'there's nothing wrong with you from the psychiatric point of view. You're fortunate, however, that I'm not expected to give my medical opinion on your intelligence.'

I could have kissed her sideburns.

THE RIGHT TO EMPLOYMENT

1

'THIS IS ALEXANDER L'VOVICH,' announced Maria Vasilievna, the Headmistress, in Russian. That was an unusual sound in the experimental school, where many subjects were taught in English.

'He'll be your instructor of English and American literature. This is Alexander L'vovich's first teaching assignment. So I expect cooperation from all of you, including you, Metrunin. If I hear you're giving Alexander L'vovich any grief, I'll kick you from here to Red Square. Is that understood? Metrunin, is that bloody well understood?'

Clearly Metrunin, a strapping lad of 17 who looked as if he could take three Alexander L'voviches in a fair fight, was the problem pupil. Just as clearly he didn't take Maria Vasilievna's promise as an empty threat. He sprang to his feet and responded in a clipped military fashion, 'Yes, perfectly, Maria Vasilievna!'

'Good,' relented the educator, who in her turn looked as if Metrunin wouldn't present any particular menace to her in a *mano a mano* situation. Her muscular physique, as she later told me, had withstood far sterner tests during the war when she had fought with a guerrilla unit behind the German lines.

'I could slit a sentry's throat with the best of them,' she remarked with discernible nostalgia and roared with laughter, as if recalling a funny story. I guffawed, even though the ability to kill with a knife didn't figure high on my list of feminine virtues.

'That Metrunin ain't giving you no trouble?' asked Maria Vasilievna a few weeks after my first day. 'None at all. Your warning in my first class must've helped.'

'Good. Coz when he was like 13, there was no controlling the lad. I remember once we had a new one, fresh out of university, like you, except she was a wimp, real Mama's girl. After her first class she rushes into my office and weeps, "Maria Vasilievna, a boy just said he was going to rape me!" And I say, "That wouldn't be Metrunin in

7B by any chance?" When she hears the name she begins to wail so hard she can't even say yes, so she just nods. "That one can," says I proudly, like. Then the wimp gets well hysterical and I tell her to shut up and bring Metrunin to me.

'She fetches him, and there he stands by the door, grinning from ear to ear. I come up to him and say, softly like, "What is it Liudmila Borisovna's telling me? You said you're going to rape her?" "I didn't," he says, but the snout he's got on is real uppity.

'One thing I can't stand is an uppity brat. "Oh, yeah?" I says. "You didn't, eh? So I'm supposed to believe you rather than my instructor?" "Believe who you want," he says, a 13-year-old shit! "You got what it takes to rape a woman?" I ask.

'And he grins again, you know, this cock-happy smile you all got. So I knee him in the balls, not too hard but solid. He bends over and I say, like interrogating a Kraut prisoner, "Listen to me, you little shit. You give me any more trouble and you can kiss this school good-bye. I'll expel you and put you on the blacklist, so you'll bum around for a few years and then straight to the army you go – the worst regiment they can find. And that's after I beat the crap out of you. Is that understood?" He's been okay ever since. Sort of.'

I could describe Maria Vasilievna's appearance here, but there's no need. She looked and sounded so remarkably like Tamara Petrovna, the Head Nurse, that I wondered for a while if they were related. As you've probably surmised, Maria Vasilievna hadn't picked up her unorthodox methods at a refined finishing school somewhere in Moscow. Actually, she hadn't had to rely on academic attainment for advancement. As an impeccably *nash* comrade, she was perfectly qualified to hold the post of *direktor*, the Russian for headmistress, managing director or any other top cheese.

Every outfit in Russia, from a tiny shop to a giant factory, had a *direktor*. This was invariably a Party appointment, and getting the work done was the least of a *direktor*'s responsibilities. He had his first deputy to worry about that. That underling was as a rule a real expert in the field, or in our case a top teacher.

The *direktor*'s job was detached from the actual work, and he could effortlessly float from one area to another. One year he could be, say, the *direktor* of a hospital, the next year of a theatre, the year after of a machine-tool plant. Anywhere he'd go the *direktor*'s job was to harass his underlings and to stay on the right side of the authorities.

In Maria Vasilievna's case the authorities described concentric circles around her school, with the power increasing as the proximity diminished. Her immediate superiors were the Borough Education Board and the Regional Party Committee. The next circle was formed by the Moscow Education Board, the City Party Committee and the Moscow Council. The outer circle included the USSR Education Ministry and the Education Department of the Central Committee of the Party. As gaskets between these circles she had to contend with various borough, city and all-USSR organs responsible for ideology. These were universally known by their common name: the KGB.

As a veteran of the partisan movement, Maria Vasilievna had good KGB connections. For it was that organisation that had been responsible for partisans committing the acts of terrorism that had so successfully turned the Germans against the occupied Russian population, preventing them from converting a colonial war into a liberation movement (not that they were inclined to do so anyway). She was also an unblemished Slav without a molecule of Jewish tar in the family barrel – an ironclad requirement for a *direktor*. And of course her Party credentials were unimpeachable, as they had to be for her to hold the top post.

Apart from those qualifications, she was rough around the edges and could barely keep the most foul of obscenities out of her speech even in the presence of pupils. There were no such inhibitions in the faculty room, and her command of the far reaches of the Russian vocabulary was there for all to admire. As an operational necessity she tolerated the *ne-nash* 'intels' among the instructors, but the effort involved took a lot out of her.

However, on that first day I was happy for her introduction, as it had fed me a straight line to go into the old 'good cop, bad cop' routine. The moment she left the room I sat down on the desk, emulating the favourite posture of my professor-friend Mikhailov, and addressed the class in English.

'It wasn't so long ago that I myself was at school, so I understand the way the cookie crumbles. There are what, a dozen of you here? I suspect that perhaps three of you are interested in literature, six can probably take it or leave it, and three don't care one way or the other. If things were any different, this would be a miraculous class, and personally I don't believe in miracles.

'Now I'll definitely make it interesting and, God willing, enlightening for the top three. I expect to be able to convert three of the middle six. The remaining six are unlikely to learn anything from me or anybody else. With anybody else, however, half of them wouldn't get a passing grade. With me, everybody will because, if one of you fails, I'll have to stay after work to tutor him. And frankly I have better things to do with my time. That's my part of the bargain. What I expect from you in return is to keep quiet, have a decent attendance record and generally stay out of trouble. Deal?'

The potential underachievers nodded enthusiastically, and I never had any trouble from any of them – much to the envy of other instructors. 'How do you do it?' asked Liudmila Borisovna, the would-be rape victim.

'I threaten to beat them up,' I confided. She nodded wistfully, realising that a similar threat from her wouldn't produce the same effect. I couldn't share with her my first educational coup: the introduction of a jerry-built streaming system. That sort of thing was anathema in Russia, as it is in all socialist countries, now including Britain. Back at the university we had been taught about the suffering of British children subjected to that iniquity at the time, yet even our professors found it hard to suppress envious sighs.

While I was getting on well with the pupils, the management was a different kettle of sturgeon. For teaching, and especially the teaching of the humanities, was regarded as an 'ideological' field, and one from which *ne-nash* 'intels' ideally should be barred.

As most ideals, however, this one was unattainable. For all *nash* graduates who could put two English words together got lucrative jobs with the KGB foreign service in its various guises, thus making them unavailable for teaching. *Nash* cast-offs were welcome, but they had to be diluted with a couple of competent *ne-nash* 'intels' if the pupils were to learn anything. And it was critical that they learn.

The knowledge of foreign languages, particularly English, always received a high priority in the USSR – even though only the privileged few were allowed to apply that knowledge to any discourse with native speakers. The translating and interpreting profession was thus one of the most prestigious and, quite possibly, remunerative of all, with strong practitioners often earning in a day what an engineer earned in a month. And tutors of English could make in a week the equivalent of the monthly salaries they received in their full-time jobs.

The survival of the Soviet state largely hinged on its ability, first, to present a rosy picture of itself to the West and, second, to keep close tabs on the technological advances freely described in Western journals. To achieve the first objective, thousands of the hottest linguists in Moscow manned such propaganda outlets as the *Progress* Publishing House, the *Novosti* Press Agency, *Radio Moscow*, the *Soviet Life* Magazine, the World Peace Council, the World Council of Churches and others whose name is legion.

To achieve the second objective, every research and most industrial outfits had departments of 'scientific and technological information'. These were staffed with linguists who perused Western journals and wrote abstracts of the articles that could be of interest. All in all, there were tens of thousands of linguists working in Moscow alone – and more were needed.

That's why a network of experimental schools with an emphasis on foreign languages was established in Moscow in the 50s. And that's why *ne-nash* pariahs with the gift of the foreign gab, like yours truly, had to be tolerated up to a point.

The *ne-nash* weren't rewarded as lavishly as others, but they were kept alive. Actually I wasn't doing badly in that department. My monthly salary at the school was 180 roubles (a fledgling GP earned half that amount at the time). And I doubled that by teaching literary translation at the university, tutoring, and taking translating and interpreting assignments. Thus, in the first year out of university, my income was approaching Papa's, who at the time ran an engineering company, worked suicidally long hours and had about 800 people under him.

All this explains why Maria Vasilievna and other school ideologists tolerated my obviously *ne-nash* mug and irreverent remarks. But on several occasions they hinted that I was trying their patience. The hints were accompanied by astonishingly accurate quotations from my lectures and private conversations with pupils and colleagues.

Or perhaps 'astonishing' is a wrong word because, like any Russian, I took the omnipresence of grasses, or 'tappers', for granted. One such 'tapper' was my drinking chum Igor Syrtsov who taught political translation (the art of translating political propaganda) as a painless way to idle away his time between two foreign assignments.

Syrtsov displayed all the regalia of a *nash* semi-'intel' on the rise. He wore Woolworth clothes, which unmistakeably branded him as a dandy who had been abroad; and drove a brand-new *Volga* he had purchased with the hard-currency coupons used as partial payment for Russians working abroad. Had he attempted to buy the car for roubles saved out of his teacher's salary, he would have had to wait a while – the *Volga* cost what he made in five years.

Despite his wealth, Igor was a jolly rogue and a good drinking companion. But one had to stay on one's toes in his company. He definitely had been instructed by the KGB to keep his eyes peeled and his ears unwaxed during his stopover in the educational system.

Since all the *ne-nash* teachers quickly figured him out for what he was, Igor's reports to his paymasters must have been starved of juicy stuff. All of us assiduously avoided political topics in his presence, instead steering the conversation towards booze and sex. That made Igor impatient and he'd try to turn the wheel in a more fruitful direction.

Subtlety, however, wasn't his middle name, and before long those frustrated attempts made him the laughing stock of the faculty. Undeterred, he'd redouble his efforts, delivering himself either of fire-eating patriotic remarks designed to produce an incriminating ironic response, or downright seditious statements aimed at provoking equally incriminating enthusiasm.

Thus Syrtsov was the only Russian I knew who in the course of a short conversation could utter such mutually exclusive statements as 'say what you will, but the Soviet Union is the most just society on earth' and 'wouldn't it be a great idea to drop a nuclear bomb on the Kremlin?' 'I'll bow to the wisdom you picked up while travelling,' was my answer to the former, and 'What a monstrous thought! All that gorgeous Italian architecture!' to the latter.

After a while Igor gave up on me, and we often shared a bottle between or after classes. Occasionally we were joined by Volodia, the young rosy-cheeked lieutenant who taught military matters, and Tania Proskurova. She was a lewd 15-stone PE instructor whose beefy appearance belied her occupation and who fancied Syrtsov's dark pock-marked looks to a point where she was unable to conceal it even in front of pupils.

As an officer, Volodia received a higher salary than any of us – not a bad deal for a village boy for whom the only other available career would have consigned him to manual labour. Now, after three years at officers' school, this 21-year-old was making what an engineer couldn't always earn after 20 years of spotless work. Apart from the odd evening duty in the Moscow Military District and perhaps 12 hours a week he had to teach goose-stepping at the school, he had nothing to do. As all worthy men, Volodia devoted his leisure time to wine, women and song – but very easy on the song.

That passion got him into trouble, as he once told me. The backdrop to the confession was provided by his tiny cubicle of an office decorated with portraits of Lenin and Suvorov, the iconic eighteenth-century general. Displayed in between the two portraits was the slogan 'Train hard, fight easy', chauvinistically attributed to Suvorov.

'Listen,' he began in a half-whisper. 'You're a man of culture. So maybe you can help me with this little problem I've got. Advice is all I need,' he hastened to add, as if sensing I feared he was going to ask for money.

'You see, I've caught this gono… gono… a dose of clap is what I mean.' Instinctively I wiped my hands with a handkerchief under the table, hoping Volodia wouldn't notice. 'So I don't know what to do.'

Advice was cheap: 'I don't see that you have much of a choice,' I said. 'You can't go to a state polyclinic because they'd report it to your CO and he'd have you for breakfast. So you have to scrape 100 roubles together and go to a private quack. I may be able to help you find one, my mother knows many doctors.'

Volodia was disappointed that a university-educated man of culture could be so dense. 'I know all that, for Christ's sake. That's not the problem, finding the money or a quack.'

'So what's the problem then?' 'Well, you see, I have a date with my captain's wife tonight, he's out of town.' 'So? Miss it, do her another time.' 'Easy for you to say.' Volodia clearly believed that an 'intel' couldn't understand a working man's problem.

'The captain will be back tomorrow, and then who knows when he'll go out of town again. Do you reckon I'll give it to her if I only do her once?'

'Of course you will.' I felt duty-bound to enlighten the defender of the realm in matters medical. 'She'll then give it to him. And if he hasn't done it with anyone else, he'll force her to own up. After that, it's court martial for you, mate.' I still hadn't abandoned ill-judged attempts to adapt chameleonically to my interlocutor's lingo.

'Yeah,' acknowledged lieutenant Volodia wistfully. 'Suppose you're right. Don't you think I know you're right?' He was sounding agitated to a point of being incoherent. Finally, he made a characteristically Russian slapping gesture with his right hand.

'Ah, same dick,' he said ['makes no difference', as translated from colloquial Russian]. 'I'm gonna do her anyway. She's got, you know,' he held his hands with curved fingers in front of his chest. 'Arthritis?' I suggested helpfully. He laughed.

Soon after that Volodia was transferred to another school, and I never found out just how far his easy-going attitude had got him. But every time I think of him, I am reminded of a story that was making the rounds in Moscow at the time. This man gets his medicine from a chemist, pays and walks towards the exit. 'Wait, young man,' calls the chemist after him. 'You asked for potassium chloride, and I gave you potassium cyanide by mistake.' 'Ah, same dick!' The young man's inflection and accompanying gesture would have been exactly like Volodia's. 'That may be so,' agrees the healthcare professional. 'But you owe me three kopecks more.'

Syrtsov too exhibited this same-dickness of an attitude, but only in his more relaxed moments. As he did one day, when he suggested we pop over to the collective farm where our pupils had been sent to harvest carrots. There was nothing uncommon about that event. Every year at harvest time thousands of Moscow 'intels' were sent to collective farms to help out the short-handed peasants – and to redeem their hoity-toity sins through the goodness of physical labour.

'We have forty percent of our population employed in agriculture,' my professor-friend Mikhailov said once, 'but that's not enough to cope with the effects of bad weather, a constant plight ever since nineteen-seventeen. The Americans have three and a half percent working in agriculture, and they're feeding half the world. Just goes to show how much better the climate is in the States.'

For a *ne-nash* it was a matter of honour to wiggle out of such unpaid forays into alien fields, but few ever managed. My cousin Alec always did – with a characteristic lack of finesse. He'd flatly refuse to go, and when told he was obligated to do so by law, he'd dart to the solicitors' office across the street and obtain a statement that there was no such law on the books. That made the *nash* higher-ups hate him with a passion, as they always hated anyone who quoted their own laws back at them.

The *nash* knew viscerally that all those casuistic turns of legal phrase were there for show; the will of the authorities was all that mattered. Police novels of that period often featured cops who, with the author's tacit approval, expressed distaste for the 'legalists' demanding to see a warrant when arrested or searched. This contempt for legality cuts to the core of the Russian soul, which is why it has survived all those perestroikas, democracies, free markets and what not.

The Russians are averse to any disciplined form that might contain their fluid content, which is why all those democracies and free markets can never succeed there. As all infantile people, they believe themselves to be deeper and more spiritual than anyone else and loathe any formal inhibitions, legal or otherwise, of their self-expression. (Unless, of course, these are imposed by a no-holds-barred tyranny.) That's why, for example, though all Russians hail Pushkin as the greatest thing since sliced Dante, the poet's classicist form and cut-glass Mozartian cadences had no followers.

According to my professor-friend Mikhailov, this disdain for form even penetrated the Russians' gene pool, having produced the ill-defined, amorphous facial features so different, say, from the chiselled Germanic profile. 'Just look at our faces – well, perhaps not mine,' Mikhailov once said, smiling sardonically with his thin, tight lips. 'Many of our people, even those from good families, have this lack of straight lines in their faces. It's as if, having drawn a sketch of their features, God then went over it, smudging every line with his thumb.'

Yuri Ossipovich Mikhailov was spot-on in his observation, as he was in his assessment of his own physique. Most Russians with well-defined faces like his either emigrated or were murdered when the future began to work. That made him look slightly foreign, which to the unsophisticated masses had to mean Jewish. Thus I knew many ethnically pure Russian 'intels' who found themselves on the receiving end of anti-Semitic slurs and assaults. In fact, whenever things got a bit rowdy at a boozer, and drunks began to air their frank views on the Jews, Yuri Ossipovich would inch his way to the door.

'What have you got to be afraid of?' I asked once. 'You're as Russian as they get, passport and all.'

'That may well be,' agreed Mikhailov. 'But it's not your passport that gets punched, it's your mug.'

Alec and I are related through my mother, and I inherited some of the same bloody-minded intransigence. But in my case it's leavened with the Boots' survival instinct. That's why, whenever asked if I was going to show up next Saturday and go to a collective farm, I always responded with fulsome enthusiasm: 'But of course! I wouldn't miss it for the world.' Then I'd develop a mysterious illness and skip the trip.

That time I hadn't even been asked to go, as it was Tania who had been appointed to represent the faculty as the general overseer. Syrtsov hadn't been asked either, which is why his suggestion came as a surprise.

'Why on earth would you want to go?' I asked with genuine bemusement. 'Coz I want to nail that bitch Tania, that's why,' explained Igor. 'Christ, can't you find a better place? I mean there'll be forty pupils there, sleeping in the same house.'

'You're stupid, you know that?' To Syrtsov that was a sufficient explanation. 'They'll be in the same house, but they won't be in the same room. You'll be in the same room, and you're welcome to a piece of her too.' 'Yes, I know she's got plenty to go about, but I think I'll pass.'

But then Syrtsov keyed in that magic combination that opens the heart of any Russian. 'All the booze is on me,' he said. I still played hard to get, replying with unshakeable resolve: 'To hell with booze. I'm not going.'

The next morning, as we were driving to the farm in his beige *Volga*, I asked Igor why he wanted me along anyway. 'To allay suspicion, old man,' he explained. 'If it's just the two of us in the same room, tongues will wag. With you along, it's three Soviet teachers shepherding the flock in the spirit of unpaid communist labour.' That made sense.

He, I and a shopping bag full of vodka and tinned food got to the collective farm at about noon and found the house empty: everyone was out in the field, pulling carrots out of the ground. That gave us a head start and, by the time Tania marched the pupils back home, we were feeling no pain.

The pupils winked at us with precocious understanding: while they had never before seen us actually drunk, they had seen us hung-over on most mornings. In fact, Metrunin once had taken pity on me when watching me struggle with the gastrointestinal equivalent of the Great October Revolution rolling through my guts.

'Shall I get you some beer, Alexander L'vovich?' he volunteered. I threw the ethics of my profession to the wind and grabbed the lifeline. 'Please, Metrunin. Here's some money. But keep your mouth shut, eh?' 'Like the grave, Alexander L'vovich,' the 17-year-old promised, running to the off-licence across the street.

Still, having pupils witness a teacher in a state of recently produced inebriation represented too steep a downfall. Conscientiously we tried hard not to slur words as we sent the youngsters to their bunks shortly after dinner.

The house was divided into one large room and a broom cupboard. The room had bunk beds, and that's where the pupils were to sleep. The broom cupboard had a mattress on the floor and served as the sleeping quarters for Tania flanked on either side by Syrtsov and me.

It was autumn, and the house was unheated, which meant that propriety was observed, with not a stitch of clothing removed. There were, however, a few stitches undone, as Igor and Tania embarked on a heavy foreplay session. The former was displaying the skills he had acquired on his foreign journeys, and the latter was responding with vociferous vigour.

The current joke was that a Russian man's idea of foreplay was to give the girl five roubles, while his idea of afterplay was to take the money away from her by force, with her driven to ecstasy both times. Belying that *ne-nash* perception, Igor was clearly familiar with the geography of erogenous zones, and had a deft touch. Proof of that was Tania's thunderous response, interspersed with her performing the function she had been assigned and trying to keep the pupils in the adjacent room quiet.

'Oh yes,' she'd moan. 'Yes! Yes!! Yes!!! Oh-oh-oh – Hey, shut up you over there! Yeah, baby, yeah, there, there... It's twenty-three hundred hours!!! I said no noise!!! Ah..ah...a-a-arhggg. There, yes a bit higher... Yes!!! Yes!!! Hey, didn't you hear what I said? I'll report you all to the headmistress!!! Now, baby, now... yes... yes...'

Throughout that surreal monologue I was doing my best to pretend I was asleep, keeping my eyes almost shut. The pretence was thin, considering that the mattress was small, and their intertwining limbs and the occasional breast or thigh were being flung over my chest all the time.

After half an hour of that futile thespian effort, the lovers' ardour ebbed. Syrtsov reached over Tania's flattened, rapidly cooling breasts and tapped me on the shoulder. 'Hey, old man, sorry about the disturbance. Hey, I know you're awake. Listen, would you fancy some?'

I insisted on my pretence and began to snore demonstratively. The stifled giggling in the adjacent room was acting as a strong deterrent.

2

We woke up early next afternoon the worse for wear, with Syrtsov looking even more fragile than me. Tania and the pupils had gone off to the field, and neither of us particularly wanted to see them that day. Syrtsov went over his depleted stock of vodka and announced that the three of us had drunk two litres (Tania had demurely agreed to pull her massive weight). That simple calculation made us even more hungover than before, but the fact that we still had a litre and a half left brought a flicker of hope.

To clear the cobwebs we had a greasy breakfast-cum-lunch, and then went for an obligatory walk in the woods. 'I love nature,' announced Syrtsov. 'You can piss wherever you want.' He proceeded to illustrate his point graphically. It was getting late and it was time to head back.

The collective farm was located 150 miles of potholed track south of Moscow, and even at 20 miles per hour our insides were getting jarred more than we could endure. Having stopped a few times to relieve ourselves through various orifices, we realised we weren't going to make it that night. It was time to stop, which was easier said than done.

There weren't – still aren't – any motels on any other than a couple of major roads. The only option available was to emulate wandering pilgrims of the past, knock on the door of a log hut somewhere in a village, beg refuge for the sake of Christ, and share with our hospitable host the modest repast God had sent us.

That, minus the unfashionable ecclesiastical references, was precisely what we did when the creaking *Volga* carried us into an unprepossessing village in the middle of nowhere. The creature who opened the door to our knock appeared sexless in its shapeless rags and the ubiquitous felt boots that still stink up the Russian countryside as they did centuries ago.

Its voice, however, identified it as a man. 'I'd be happy to, boys,' he said in the broad vowels one never heard where we came from. 'But I don't have no food in the house. You'll be better off there,' he pointed at a sturdier-looking hut at the edge of the village. 'Coz you're cultured city boys, and that's Pantelei Stepanovich's house. He's a teacher, a university geezer. His wife too, they both teach at our school. They're bored with us coz we don't read nothing. They'll be happy to take you in.'

His crystal ball turned out to be in perfect order. The intellectual Pantelei Stepanovich, a red-nosed 50-year-old wearing a three-piece pinstripe suit with the trouser legs tucked into his felt boots, was more than happy to take us in. He was ecstatic, and so was his wife, a mousy little woman with bifocal glasses and a heavy scarf permanently wrapped around her scrawny neck. When we came in, she pumped up the kerosene lantern that cast a murky light over the house.

'Come in, come in, colleagues. No, no, the pleasure is all mine. You can't imagine being stuck here in the sticks, surrounded by these uncultured savages, starved of intelligent conversation. Why, not one of them has read Pasternak. The idiocy of rural life, as Marx said. Sit down, colleagues, sit down. Natasha! Serve everything we've got in the house. Now what's that?'

The question referred to the two half-litres Syrtsov had pulled out of his shopping bag with the flair of a conjurer. 'Oh, I say! Government issue!' This term was used by Russian country dwellers to distinguish the vodka they could only occasionally buy in the state shops from the moonshine they drank normally. The exuberance of Pantelei Stepanovich's reaction went a long way towards explaining the colour and indeed the texture of his nose.

Natasha served everything they had in the house, which was assorted pickles to chase the vodka, home-baked brown bread, potatoes and meat patties fried in lard. Developed over history, that food was specifically designed to soak up the national drink.

After she served the meal, Pantelei Stepanovich patted her rump and dismissively waved his hand in the direction of the kitchen. 'You stay there,' he said. Natasha smiled at her husband lovingly, walked out, and that was the last we saw of her that evening. Feminism hadn't yet arrived in Russia, still hasn't and, the good bet is, never will.

We 'sucked in' our first 'dose', and it was time to sing for our supper. 'So how about that Nixon détente, eh?' All the pent-up inquisitiveness that our host had had to suppress in his cultural wasteland broke through the dam, and it was a long night. Inevitably, locally distilled moonshine saw the light of day as the blackness outside was just turning grey.

Later that afternoon we managed to reach the outer ring road around Moscow. Entering it from the slip road, the first thing we saw was a giant white-on-red poster saying, 'Ahead towards the victory of communism!' 'What do they mean "ahead"?' rasped Syrtsov. 'It's a circular road, for Christ's sake!' He squinted at me to check for any sign of agreement, but even in my fragile state I knew not to offer any.

A painful realisation slowly sank in that we had to cross half the city on the way home. When we got to the outskirts, Syrtsov, who badly needed a pick-me-up, knew that in his present condition he was ill-fit for city driving. We stopped at a workmen's caff.

The speciality of the place was *pelmeni*, Siberian dumplings bearing some familial resemblance to wontons, their Chinese antecedents. The commercial variety weren't bad, if a bit heavy on the pastry and light on the meat. Many Russians, including me, always kept a few boxes in the freezer.

All one had to do was dump them in boiling water and wait until they floated up to the surface. Then one scooped them out and ate them with vinegar, mustard, butter or soured cream. The choice of the condiment spoke volumes for one's moral character, as only vinegar and mustard fit the après-vodka use to which worthy Russians put that delicacy.

The place we selected for our restorative pit stop didn't serve booze, and there was a large sign on the wall saying that consumption of alcohol on the premises was illegal. But the appearance and demeanour of most patrons suggested that the management, in the bulky shape of a fiftyish woman who also acted as the cook, didn't insist on obeying the strict letter of the law. At least not where spirits were concerned.

Syrtsov had our last remaining half-litre (which he had wisely held back the night before) in his coat pocket, and when we ordered (three servings of *pelmeni* each, six roubles for the lot) he winked, 'And two empty glasses, darling.' The woman smiled in that gentle, understanding way so characteristic of her sex and nimbly pocketed the corkage fee of one rouble I slipped into her hand.

The steaming delicacy arrived, Syrtsov deftly twisted the silvery foil top off the half-litre, poured two tumblers under the table and hid the almost empty bottle behind a table leg. We drank, tipping our heads back, and – as an amazing serendipity life is so replete with – at least ten other patrons performed the same procedure in well-orchestrated unison. The day was the sixteenth of the month, which meant payday to most Russians, and so everybody was flush – at least until the seventeenth.

Poets of the past, from Pushkin on, wrote odes to monarchs and hymns to the plump female form (that is, when they weren't busy writing nasty epigrams about the former and scabrous obscenities about the latter). Soviet poets who had their predecessors' mantle wrapped around their shoulders wrote either panegyrics to Lenin and the achievements of Soviet agriculture, or scathing attacks on American imperialists and German *revanchists*.

That left them no time to write about the first and sixteenth of every month, when toilers for the future that worked received their pay envelopes. (Business was transacted strictly on a cash-and-carry basis, and there were no banks, cheques or credit cards).

And yet the whole 250-million population of that great land, minus some children under seven, a few wimps here and there and perhaps those poor bastards whose livers had already been shot, lived for those magic numbers. The unsung first and sixteenth.

These were the days – the only days – when one enjoyed fiscal freedom. When one could afford to drink a whole bottle of vodka – or two! – and wallow joyously in one's own vomit. When one didn't have to drink floor varnish or 'Boris Fyodorych' (an endearment the Russians used to describe BF glue, whose initials they jocularly deciphered as a common combination of name and patronymic). When one could have fun tossing rocks through windows, fighting painlessly, bellowing songs with only one possible rhyme for 'luck', harassing passers-by and then falling asleep across the pavement. These were the only days one was free.

They also had a great deal of significance for most Muscovites of the *ne-nash* persuasion. For these were the days when one didn't venture outside unless absolutely necessary. When one avoided dark streets and areas that had a bad reputation. When one crossed the street from the side where a group of young men could be seen on the pavement a hundred yards ahead. And when those few who had cars took extra caution not to send a reeling comrade to that great boozer in the sky.

Having fortified himself, Syrtsov could drive reasonably straight, negotiating with some élan the slalom course in which veering pedestrians with bulging eyes and dripping mouths acted as flags. Our excursion was over.

The next day I walked into my classroom, where I had to deliver a lecture on the great American writer Theodore Dreiser. If you wish to contest the first adjective of that designation, I'd like to remind you that in every Soviet school or university curriculum 'great', when used to describe a Western writer, officially meant 'left-wing, and the further to the left, the greater'. Dreiser was a paid up member of the American Communist Party, and thus as great as great could be. Ditto Upton Sinclair.

The great British writer, as any literate Soviet could have told you, was James Aldridge, and please don't tell me you've never heard of him. He was more than great – he was regarded as the greatest English writer in Russia, the only land where his books were published in large circulations and where he spent much of his time.

Old GBS was great. The author of *Mrs Warren's Profession* visited Russia in 1931. At the time, the country was getting a lousy press in some, admittedly few, Western papers on account of its penchant for murderous peccadilloes. Shaw would have none of that: 'It is a real comfort to me, an old man,' he declared in a speech, 'to be able to step into my grave with the knowledge that the civilisation of the world will be saved. It is here in Russia that I've actually been convinced that the new Communist system is capable of leading mankind out of its present crisis, and saving it from anarchy and ruin.'

H.G. Wells was great because he had met Lenin and described him as 'the dreamer in the Kremlin', thus proving that our founding father's ruse had worked to perfection.

Of the older writers, Swift was great because he exposed the inherent corruption of imperialist Britain with its impotent parliaments and omnipotent monarchs. Dickens was great because he uncovered the brutality of the British class system at the time of the Industrial Revolution, which was a revolution in name only, not at all like ours. Galsworthy was great because he emphasised the indolent, bloodsucking nature of the British upper classes. Mark Twain was great because he was the only American who had ever spoken out against racism. James Baldwin was great because he was black and thus a member of the oppressed. Graham Greene was so great that he may even have collaborated with his good friend Kim Philby.

John Reed could have been great had he not placed an undue emphasis on Trotsky in *Ten Days That Shook the World*. Hemingway was great because he had supported the right side in Spain. George Orwell had been on his way to greatness, and actually had fought on the right side in Spain, before he sank into oblivion by writing such demonstrably ungreat books as *Animal Farm* and *1984*.

In other words, Orwell was a 'reactionary writer', which term was reserved for any Western man of letters who wasn't great. In fact, Orwell was so reactionary he wasn't even mentioned in the Twentieth Century Eng. Lit. curriculum. Neither was Waugh or Chesterton, Joyce or Eliot.

What made my work palatable was that the curriculum was loose, unlike in Russian literature, for example. Most entries were presented as recommendations rather than dictates. For instance, it was recommended that seven periods be devoted to Shakespeare and nine to Dreiser, which unusually vacillating wording gave me a loophole to try to enlighten my students in the ways of true greatness.

Also, no textbooks on English and American literature approved by the Ministry of Education were in existence, and it was thus left to the instructor what he chose to teach about his subject. The notes the students took in class replaced both literary criticism (nonexistent) and the actual books (unavailable, at least *en masse*).

This lack of support made my life difficult, as I had to spend a lot of time telling my pupils what the books were about. But it also made life easier, as I enjoyed the kind of freedom of which Raisa Pavlovna, the Russian literature teacher, couldn't even dream. (For that reason, and also because as a foreign language instructor I earned an extra 15 percent, she hated me.) Thus, for example, I devoted a whole term to Shakespeare and even organised an outing to the theatre next door, where a blond

Russian was doing a rather histrionic Hamlet.

As for Dreiser, I had decided to reduce the number of periods to one, and was feverishly trying to recall *An American Tragedy* as I walked into the classroom. The students rose to their feet, as they did in Russia, and I waved them down. They knew that the recommended number of periods on Dreiser was nine. So it was a matter of some delicacy to explain to them – without making overtly seditious remarks that could spell the end of my career, or worse – why they were getting an abridged version.

'Theodore Dreiser,' I began, 'was a great writer because he was a member of the American Communist Party, which he belatedly joined in the year of his death but with whose cause he had wholeheartedly sympathised all his life. That by itself was enough to make him, or for that matter anyone else, great – and it did.'

So far there was nothing in their notebooks to present incriminating evidence, as irony and facial expressions are hard to describe when one takes longhand notes. 'That's why, if I were to teach the history of the Communist Party USA, which I'd dearly love to do, I'd devote a great deal of time to the study of this great man.

'Unfortunately, however, I'm here to teach you literature, which subject, theoretically speaking, is supposed to have something to do with artistic value. It's in this area that, regrettably, Comrade Dreiser's greatness is revealed with less clarity than in his life. In fact, he could have said about his art and life the same thing that Oscar Wilde once said about his. Now what was that, Bolokhonsky?'

The question was addressed to one of my few pedagogic successes, a brilliant *ne-nash* boy who tended to imitate my accent and mannerisms. He'd be over fifty now; I wonder how he has managed to survive in Russia.

He delivered, as always. 'I put my genius into my life but only my talent into my work.' 'Correct,' I acknowledged. 'Except that the difference between Dreiser and Wilde was that the former, as a communist, had a true genius for life but, alas, very little literary talent; while with the latter it was more or less the other way around.

'One can understand how his struggle for the liberation of mankind would distract Theodore Dreiser from any serious attempt to work on his art. God knows we need communists more than we need artists.

'But once again, since it's art and not exclusively communism that you're here to learn, I am going to tell you in the next twenty minutes all you need to know to pass your end-of-term exam should you draw Dreiser as your subject. So write this down: Theodore Dreiser was born in...'

The lecture ended the moment the buzzer rang for the break. I sat down, fighting hangover. Another day, another rouble.

3

I thought I had been devilishly clever in managing to plant the seeds of scepticism via extra-verbal means. But the balloon was bound to go up sooner or later, for thanks to Maria Vasilievna's knack for 'ideological' work there were snitching 'tappers' in every class. Young though they were, the snitches were excellent at detecting subversion even when it was only conveyed by inflection.

Reports on my unorthodox way of teaching Anglophone literature must have been piling up on Maria Vasilievna's desk from the first days of my fledgling career. The kopeck probably had dropped after the first week, and it's a tribute to her methodical nature that she took her time collating the evidence to crush me under its cumulative weight.

Late in May she summoned me to her office and pointed towards a comfortable leather armchair standing in the shade of a potted palm tree. 'Alexander L'vovich,' she began, speaking in an officious tone, 'it has been brought to my attention that you are exerting a corrupting influence on our pupils.'

'Maria Vasilievna!' My voice was full of righteous indignation. 'Me? Corrupting influence? What do you mean?'

From that moment on the direktor began to sound like the authors of the American Declaration of Independence listing their grievances against King George. 'First, there was your ugly behaviour at the viewing of *The Liberation*. You were laughing your head off throughout. Just what exactly was it that you found so funny?'

Mea culpa, I thought. *The Liberation* was a monstrously long, quasi-factual film about the glorious Red Army liberating first Russia and then all of Eastern Europe from the Nazis. I and another *ne-nash* instructor had had to take a group of pupils to view it as part of their – and our – extracurricular ideological activities.

Now to take them there was one thing, but to behave with the dignity and solemnity befitting a 'fighter on the ideological front' was quite another. Because, as far as propaganda went, the film made Dr Goebbels's output look like the epitome of subtlety, and we laughed all the way through. One scene in particular cracked me up.

A Waffen SS unit was making a last stand at a zoo somewhere in Germany. Soviet tanks were driving towards the elephant enclosure from where the entrenched baddies were dousing them with a steady barrage. There were a few close-ups of animals being hit, always by the beastly Germans. The director's aim must have been to create the emotional impact of the rabbit-shooting scene in Renoir's The Rules of the Game, but his effect was spoiled by non-stop intercutting with massively staged battle scenes.

Though the air was thick with flying lead, a young Soviet tank commander opened the hatch to yell at a panicking antelope to run for cover. As a result of that nobly naïve gesture (so characteristic of Russian soldiers entering Germany, and reflecting the spiritual catharsis only the combination of Russia and communism can produce in the souls of men), the youngster caught a bullet right in the middle of his forehead and died with his eyes wide-open in that naively noble way of his.

A few frames later there was a shot of a sergeant with a cute monkey on his shoulder. Both had their arms bandaged. Marshal Konev (whose favourite way of clearing a mine field was to march some *ne-nash* soldiers over it) was passing by with his staff.

'What the hell is going on?' he demanded in a stern military voice. Though obviously scared of the great demiurge, the sergeant still said his piece. 'Well, it's wounded, you know, Comrade Marshal, so I... sort of... reckon, I mean it's a living creature too, ain't it, so we shared the same bandage pack, he and I...'

Konev laughed and patted the kind-hearted NCO on his good shoulder. 'That's okay! Take the monkey to hospital. Tell them Marshal Konev said it was fine.'

Not to laugh at that point would have taken the stone heart of the Atlantes supporting the balconies in the building next door. Especially if one knew that there hadn't been a single unraped woman in the path of the advancing Soviet troops, who – after getting their collective jollies – would often feel that cutting a victim to shreds with their bayonets would constitute satisfying afterplay.

'Why do you find it funny to see Russian soldiers die?' Maria Vasilievna asked. 'Nobody died. We weren't watching a real battle,' I tried to explain. 'It was a film, a work of art as it were, and it should be judged on its own merits, regardless of the subject-matter.'

'Art for art's sake, eh?' Maria Vasilievna had heard about it and knew it was wrong. 'Well, let me tell you something. We don't want that shit in our country. Art, socialist realist art, is truth. It reflects our life, not your half-arsed hoity-toity ideas. My husband, he has a PhD in Marxist philosophy, I'll have you know. Nobody's smarter than him. He didn't find nothing in The Liberation to laugh at. In fact, he cried. Because he's a real Russian. He don't laugh at Russian blood being spilled.'

There was nothing I could say to that, so I said precisely that – nothing. Maria Vasilievna, on the other hand, wasn't quite finished. 'And what is it I hear about you taking the piss out of progressive writers?' 'Whom specifically?' 'Don't you whom-specifically me, matey. Dreiser for one, that's whom specifically.' She was quite good at imitating the way I spoke.

'I did nothing of the sort!' I had to protest. 'On the contrary, I emphasised his membership in the Communist Party USA as the crowning achievement of his career.'

'The only achievement, is how you put it.' Maria Vasilievna consulted her notes. 'And then you took the piss out of him, coz you said as a writer he was a big fat zero and we only study him coz he was a communist.'

'But you yourself said that art for art's sake means nothing, Maria Vasilievna. However, being a communist surely means an awful lot. So I wasn't taking the piss at all, I was extolling his virtues.'

'Think you're smarter than anyone else, don't you? Your type always does. And then you give our children pornographic literature to read.' 'Me, pornographic literature? That's ridiculous!' 'It's not ridiculous when the parents' committee, Party members all, complain about it. Here.'

She produced a copy of John Braine's *Room at the Top* with bookmarks identifying the dirty bits. 'Did you or did you not recommend that our children read this filth?'

I had her there. 'It's not I who recommended it,' was my triumphant retort. 'The Ministry of Education recommended it.' I took a copy of the curriculum out of my briefcase and showed her the bottom of Page 14 where it said "John Braine and the Angry Young Men, exposing the moral decay of post-war Britain – 2 periods." 'It says two periods, and I gave it two periods.'

Maria Vasilievna was aghast. 'So you follow the curriculum blindly, is that what you do? You're an adult, you have to make your own decisions.' 'But Maria Vasilievna,' by now I knew I had lost, 'I'm a young teacher. I can't take it upon myself to decide not to follow the curriculum approved by the Ministry of Education.'

'That's what I'm here for. That's what our Party cell is here for. You could've come to us and asked for advice. But no-o-o-o. We're too lowly for you. We're not hoity-toity enough for you. We're too Russian for you.' Actually, I had understood the veiled anti-Semitic slur the first time and didn't need several repeat performances. But this time I had a rush of blood to the head.

'That's right!' I said, blowing my cool. 'I don't need advice from the likes of you! Look for someone else to take this crap from you lot! You can keep your advice for the next sucker! Better still, shove it! I quit!'

That rather infantile outburst acted like a boost for a dying engine: the conversation suddenly became civilised and the tone returned to normal. 'Are you sure that's exactly what you want to do, Sasha?' Maria Vasilievna was now sounding downright maternal. 'Because if it is, I can stop the full-scale investigation the parents have instigated. And there may be no need to inform the organs of State Security.'

I, in turn, sounded almost filial. 'Well, I think that's the best thing to do, don't you?' 'Yes, I think so. Just write me a letter saying you ask to be dismissed of your own volition and I'll see you get paid for the whole summer. We'll post-date it 1 September, how bout that?' 'Generous.' I headed for the door.

'You know, Alexander L'vovich, Sasha, I'm glad we had this little chat. I'm sorry things haven't worked out.'

In common with bureaucrats the world over, Maria Vasilievna visibly relaxed once the problem was off her hands. 'I think you have a lot of fine qualities. And I enjoyed our tipples together. You're a cultured lad, you know. Not unlike my husband.'

'Thank you, Maria Vasilievna.' The fight was over, so there was no point in further hostilities. I walked out, unemployed for the first time.

When my blood pressure had gone back to normal, I realised that things weren't so bad after all. I'd get paid for a three-month holiday. After that I could easily support myself with freelance work, which is what I was planning to do anyway.

But I couldn't draw unemployment benefits, for there was no such thing in Russia. When socialism becomes truly and ultimately victorious, social services aren't on the agenda because they no longer serve a useful purpose. That's why every Russian child had to learn the phrase 'He who does not work, neither shall he eat', even though few were aware of its Pauline provenance.

Fortunately, in my case work didn't have to mean full-time employment, as a good linguist was in no danger of starving. The loss of 180 roubles a month wasn't such a big deal to someone who could earn 30 roubles a day tutoring and perhaps even more translating. The problem was what to do with my summer, and even that problem was partly solved by an invitation from Mama's cousin Victor.

4

Victor lived in Alma-Ata, then the capital of Kazakhstan, where he managed the opera and ballet theatre. In the cloistered environment of that republic, this position gave him an Allah-like status, for he could always use free boxes or front-row seats as tools to advance his social standing in the community.

What worked against him was the immutable fact of his ethnicity, for Russian infidels could never be completely trusted. On the other hand, his wife, a soloist in his ballet, was a Tartar, which almost put Victor back in the good books of the ethnic establishment.

On 16 June, around noon, I got on the Metro train going to the airport. Generally, it was a good idea to avoid public transportation on the first and sixteenth of every month, but taxis were expensive, and I felt that my unemployed status had to impose at least some frugality.

Once we had cleared the city centre, the train almost emptied and there were only two passengers anywhere near me. Both looked as if they had overshot their stops. One was an army colonel in full regalia who was sitting up so stiffly that I thought he had tetanus.

Upon closer examination, I realised he was quite terminally drunk. Obviously, the magic numbers of first and sixteenth of every month had the same significance for defenders of the motherland as they did for the rest of us.

The colonel's much decorated chest began to heave and, with an automatic reaction that comes naturally to Russians, I checked to make sure he didn't have the range to hit me with his puke. Then the colonel's vitrified eyes began to reflect sheer desperation.

He knew that his last stand against emesis was coming to an end and that he had lost. But as an academy-educated officer of staff rank, he couldn't just upchuck all over the floor of a Metro train. It wasn't quite the done thing. With the ingenuity so typical of Russian fighting men, the good colonel found a solution. He took off his peaked cap with a patent-leather visor, held it in front of him like a bucket and promptly filled it with vomit.

The other passenger was a well-dressed drunk holding a brown paper bag full of caviar. As there was no plastic wrapper inside, the moist delicacy had made the bottom of the bag soggy. Soon a large hole appeared, and black flakes began to fall out onto the man's hands, trousers and the floor. Realising he was in no state to do anything about the tragic loss, the middle-aged dandy was licking his fingers with his long, whitish tongue. Tears were dripping down his ravaged face. The train stopped; I got off.

It was not without some trepidation that I walked to my plane. Most of the travelling I had done in Russia had been by train; and I had never developed a knack for flying. Also, I was familiar with Aeroflot's safety record. In fact, my favourite party trick was singing 'Tu-po-lev liner is a wonderful machine' to the tune of Chopin's funeral march.

I sat down and leaned against the back of my seat. The back immediately collapsed into the lap of the passenger behind me and wouldn't come up for the rest of the flight. As I was a bit tense, I didn't notice until we were ready for take-off that most other passengers were Kazakhs. In addition to a full complement of gold teeth, they were all wearing sheepskin coats and Astrakhan hats.

Now June is a rather hot month even in Moscow, and we were flying south. I was wearing light trousers, an open-collared shirt and a jacket flung over my shoulder. 'Those savages,' I thought. 'They don't even know how to dress.' But once we gained altitude, I realised it was I who didn't know.

The plane wasn't heated and, as it climbed, the temperature plunged (mind you, it was still preferable to the other way around). When it had dropped below freezing, I could no longer stay in my seat. Ignoring the contemptuous comments of my fellow passengers, I got up and began to perform a combination of jitterbug and St Vitus's dance in the aisle.

Joining me there was another Russian traveller who didn't even have a jacket with him. The dance became a *pas-de-deux*, but it was poorly choreographed. As the pilot was indulging his frustrated ambition as aerobatics performer, we kept bumping into each other – much to the amusement of the stewardesses who were keeping themselves warm by sitting in a circle around an electric stove.

When I walked down the Alma-Ata tarmac three and a half hours later, sub-zero became sub-tropical. On top of my ordeal, the contrast made me so weak that I could barely respond to Victor's bear hugs.

After a short drive through a run-down modern city, he took me straight to his flat. His wife had prepared a feast along Tartar and Kazakh lines, with a mountain of lamb pilaf arriving when everybody was already too full. Victor was amusing me with the latest jokes, a lot of which, for his wife's benefit, dealt with the Tartars.

'You know how we say, "An uninvited guest is worse than a Tartar?" I nodded. 'Well, seems the Tartar community petitioned the Supreme Soviet to ban this proverb, as it's offensive to them. The Supreme Soviet agreed after a long deliberation, and decreed that from now on the proverb should read "An uninvited guest is *better* than a Tartar." ' We all laughed, though his wife sounded less hearty than we did.

The next day I became the guest of honour at the first shoot I was invited to in my life. The host was Babayev, chief of Alma-Ata police; the only guest other than Victor and me was the Second Secretary of the Alma-Ata Party Committee.

Not only was that the first shoot of my life, but I had never before found myself in such august company. The auspiciousness of the occasion made me uncharacteristically taciturn as we wandered aimlessly through the woods, never finding a bird to shoot and steering an unwavering course towards Babayev's hunting lodge. To slake my ethnographic curiosity, I had been promised a traditional Kazakh meal once we got there.

The lodge turned out to be a giant bungalow farmhouse sitting on several acres of land surrounded by a high brick wall with barbed wire on top. The cacophony of bleating we had been able to hear long before we reached the lodge was coming from a barn behind the house.

We were greeted by three lovely Kazakh women wearing the traditional garb of brightly embroidered quilted gowns with sashes. 'This is my wife... this is my niece... this is my sister...,' Babayev introduced the ladies. 'They are all his wives,' whispered Victor. 'You can't imagine what a civilised person has to put up with, living among these... people.'

We went in and found ourselves in a dining room that looked different from any such area I had ever seen. The furniture was on the minimalist side, consisting of a large rug surrounded by a dozen embroidered cushions strewn about with studied carelessness. The rugs on the walls were decorated with the martial accoutrements of steppe nomads: daggers, lariats, shotguns and horsewhips. The portraits of Lenin and Dzerzhinsky looked out of place among all that paraphernalia.

Since Victor had instructed me to do as everybody did, I reclined on the cushions, which turned out to be quite comfortable. That is if one didn't mind the numbness in the arm propping up one's head.

The ritual started with the niece-wife lugging in a case of vodka and placing it solemnly by my side. 'They do it so that the guest of honour knows there's plenty of vodka and he doesn't have to hold back,' whispered Victor. No nibbles were anywhere in evidence, and I feared that the local custom called for the fiery liquid to be consumed on an empty stomach. The fear turned out to be slanderously unfounded, as the sister-wife carried in a flat porcelain dish about two feet in diameter.

Having expected some exotic local delicacies, I was surprised – even now I can't say 'pleasantly' – to see that the dish was full of caramel sweets interspersed with large lumps of sugar. The Russians, of course, always chase vodka with pickled or salted nibbles. The very thought of putting a lump of sugar into his mouth was repellent to any drinking Muscovite.

Still, 'when in Kazakhstan, do as the Kazakhs do'. I courageously chased my first glass with a sweet and even managed to suppress a gurning wince. Soon it transpired that, while Victor and I were drinking *allegro*, the two Kazakhs preferred a spirited *prestissimo*. This divergence of tempi became the subject of the early conversation.

Soon the bleating that had been providing a steady obbligato to our quartet grew nearer. The door was flung open, and the wife-wife, followed by the other two, dragged in a dishevelled sheep. From memory, the beast looked perhaps twice the size of the neatly shorn creatures I had seen in photographs of Wales.

The shaggy sheep, as if anticipating the function it was going to perform at our dinner, was fighting every step of the way. The wife-wife, assisted by the sister-wife, propelled the sheep towards me and shoved its head into my face. I looked at Victor, hoping that the local custom didn't call for the guest of honour to French-kiss the animal.

'She's waiting for your approval,' whispered Victor. That was painless enough, and I nodded as if approving a bottle of wine at a restaurant. The three wives immediately dragged the sheep outside. Desperate squealing two minutes later announced the beginning of the cooking ritual.

In an hour or so, one wife after another began to carry in steaming dishes, each representing a different way of cooking lamb. I can testify that the Kazakhs had practised nose-to-tail cooking long before it became popular at smart restaurants. I was particularly impressed with the sheep's eyes staring at me with reproach out of the first dish. Even apart from that, it transpired that the Kazakhs' nutritional ideas were quite different from mine.

'A real man,' explained Babayev, as he and the other Kazakh exchanged glances suggesting that my claim to that title had already been undermined by my wimpish drinking, 'eats about five kilos of lamb at a meal like this.'

Hungry and half-drunk as I was, the thought of consuming 11 pounds of meat in one sitting evoked a vivid image of a burst balloon. But I decided to do my level best.

Five pounds later I was full to the gunwales, and Babayev had to inquire solicitously if my Spartan eating was perhaps caused by some secret illness. As far as he was concerned, there was no better remedy for any dysfunction than more lamb.

At the risk of appearing rude I had to decline his further hospitality, and the evening soon petered out. The host belched and bid us a good journey home. The wives didn't come out to say good-bye.

5

When I returned to Moscow, I had to pay my last debt to the school. The deal I had struck with Maria Vasilievna involved an extensive briefing session with a successor deemed to be a safer bet than me.

Upon close examination, however, Dima Bindin sowed seeds of doubt in my mind. He was a tall man with the kind of bulging eyes Russian women find irresistible. The clothes he wore made him even more so, as they betrayed intimate familiarity with visitors from the land of Marks & Sparks. He spoke, incredibly fast, in a mixture of 90 percent Russian, 10 percent English favoured by *fartsovshchiki*, young men who pestered tourists in the streets with offers to barter their sisters and other local bric-a-brac for blue jeans and chewing gum.

The thought crossed my mind that perhaps my pupils were in for a letdown. For it was obvious that Dima hadn't devoted a great deal of his life to the study of English literature and related subjects. I said as much, not in so many words but in the circumspect way of an unmitigated 'intel'.

'Don't talk bollocks (*nye pizdi*),' responded Dima with the easy cordiality of a salesman. 'It'll be a piece of piss. I'll read a few prefaces here and there, study your notes…'

It was my turn to get in a word edgewise. 'Well, yes, you see, there are no notes…' 'You talking bollocks? What d'you mean no notes? How can you lecture without notes?' 'Well, if one reads a lot, books themselves, you know, and some criticism, one just talks to the pupils. It's more immediate that way, more personal…'

'Listen, you're talking bollocks.' By now I had realised that such anatomical references were Dima Bindin's preferred way of shaping a thought. 'You're probably trying to throw a spanner into my works. But that's fine. I think we can still be friends.'

'I'm sure.' I wasn't at all sure. Anyway, I had done what I could. It was time to get on with my freelance survival scheme.

For the next couple of months I lived the life of a linguistic mercenary, tutoring here, interpreting there, and devoting more time to the evening seminar I taught at the university. Suddenly, out of the blue, I got a phone call from Maria Vasilievna. She sounded as if she had at last managed to track down her prodigal son.

'Sasha, darling! How are you keeping?' 'Fine. And you?' I was, perhaps understandably, a bit monosyllabic. 'Oh, wonderful! Well, maybe not so wonderful.' 'I'm sorry to hear that.' I wasn't at all sorry.

'You see, we have a spot of trouble with Dmitry Borisovich. You know, Bindin. He is… well…' She was finding it difficult to get words out.

Some help was in order. 'Incompetent?' I suggested helpfully. 'Well, he is that, but this, as we say, is half the trouble. No, the fact is, he is' 'Never there?' was my alternative offer. 'Well, not any more. Because, you see, he is, well, don't laugh, he's in prison.'

'In prison?' Now that sounded interesting. 'What on earth for?' 'You know how it is. He'd go to a shop in the city centre and buy a dozen jumpers, thirty roubles each. Then he'd go to the Kiev Station and flog them to demobilised soldiers in transit – for sixty each. Got a year for speculation.'

'Well, well,' I hoped I wasn't sounding too triumphant with my *Schadenfreude*. 'Looks like that position is jinxed. First you had to suffer an anti-Soviet pornographer, now this.'

'Yes, I know. But you know what I was thinking? Mind you, I've looked around, and frankly those who can, really can, lecture on English Lit. in English aren't thick on the ground. So you know what I reckon? I think maybe you and I can patch up our differences, you know. Maybe you could come back.'

'Maria Vasilievna! I am honoured! But you know what we Russians say? Only the grave will cure a hunchback. I haven't changed my views on how this subject is to be taught. Neither, I'm sure, have you. So what's the point?'

'Sasha, come on. We used to be friends. Okay, maybe I wasn't… maybe I was wrong. Come back and do it your way – within reason. But for Christ's sake, take your finger out and get over here at the double! We are two months behind the curriculum! You know what they'll do to me at the Ministry? They'll do me in every hole! Tell you what, do twenty periods a week, and I'll pay you for twenty-four. Bet it's the best offer you've had today.' The ignominy of defeat had made Maria revert to her usual jargon.

It was time to be magnanimous. 'Very well, Maria Vasilievna. I'll come back. But no extracurricular work, no indoctrination meetings, no junkets to farms. Nothing but straight twenty a week. Right?'

'Right, right, you bastard. I knew I could count on you.'

She couldn't, as it turned out. A year later, prodded by Major Gazonov's suggestion that going West was my only alternative to being shipped East, I applied for an emigration visa. Poor Maria Vasilievna had to fire me a second time. But first she was officially reprimanded by the Party Committee for having failed to raise the standards of ideological work to a point where young instructors wouldn't flee 'like rats abandoning a sinking ship'. That was how Maria Vasilievna described my action in her farewell speech.

'So the ship is sinking, is it? You said it, not me.' Having nothing to lose had emboldened me. 'Did you think of what your treachery was going to do to my career?' She actually meant what she said.

'Of course, Maria Vasilievna. That's all I was thinking about. I could've thought of my parents, my son, my fiancée, my friends, none of whom I may ever see again. But all I thought about was your career.' She said something about our whole accursed race, but by then I had got to a point where I didn't care.

At that time I wasn't the only threat to Maria Vasilievna's standing in the KGB-inspired community. More and more pupils were also applying for exit visas with their parents, and in some quarters this could only be seen as an ideological failure on the Headmistress's part. To counter that unwelcome development, Maria Vasilievna was getting ready to take desperate measures. This she proved when a particularly bright boy announced that he and his family would be emigrating within a week. The Headmistress immediately called an all-school meeting, with the unspoken agenda of showing that she was not only a loyal but also selfless person.

'Petia,' she said solemnly, half-embracing the boy, 'you can stay in the Soviet Union, you know. If you wish, I can adopt you.' Petia's answer invalidated everything he had been taught for 10 years. 'I'm no Pavlik Morozov,' he said. 'I won't betray my parents.'

Meanwhile, here I was, at a loose end again, yet feeling strangely relaxed. That blissful state, which lasted until I left a year later, stood me in good stead when the next elections rolled along. At the time the ruling coalition of the Communist Party and the Communist Party usually scored landslides in the neighbourhood of 99 percent of the electorate. The remaining one percent were the vermin who'd rather not vote at all than vote for the only available candidate.

I had been in that meagre percentile ever since I had reached the voting age of 16. But until now I had relied on guile, avoiding downright confrontations with the 'activists'. That term was used to describe the canvassers whose responsibility was to ensure a 100-percent turnout in their area. To that end they had a list of every resident aged 16 and older. If by 2 p.m. some still hadn't voted, the 'activists' would wander from flat to flat, cajoling, issuing stern reminders and occasionally threatening punitive measures.

At two on the dot the doorbell rang. I opened the door to let three 'activists' into my parents' flat where I was living out my time in Russia. At first they were politeness itself. 'We couldn't help noticing that you haven't cast your vote yet, citizen, to do your civic duty.' Thus spake the leader of the pack, a craggy man in his forties wearing a blue serge suit with a pen and three pencils in the breast pocket.

'I question the word "duty",' I replied in the practised manner of a seasoned debater. 'It's your duty under Soviet law to cast your vote.' The leader sounded impatient.

'But not at all, my dear fellow.' If ever a Soviet citizen put on the Russian equivalent of the Old Etonian accent, I was doing it now. 'According to our constitution, it's our right – not our duty. And I'm choosing not to exercise this right.'

The leader was in no mood for semantic jousting. 'Listen, citizen, you're talking bollocks.' The echo of Dima Bindin reverberated through the flat. 'Just never mind the bollocks, get your finger out and vote. Who d'you think you are? If you don't vote, we're gonna call your place of employment and inform them that you're an anti-Soviet prat.'

'Be my guest,' I was all calmness. 'And I'll thank you not to use in my house the language of the gutter in which you grew up.' 'Yeah, yeah. We'll talk to you in a different way elsewhere.' Now he sounded unpleasant. 'So where do you work?'

I laughed into his face. 'You don't expect me to assist you, do you? Seek and ye shall find. And now, if you'll excuse me...'

As the frontal assault wasn't working, another member of the raiding party, a woman wearing horn-rimmed glasses and thick stockings with seams noticeably off-centre, decided to add a feminine touch. 'Listen, citizen. I'm sorry if we're sounding impatient. But you see, we can't go home until everyone has voted. Take pity on us, we've got families too. I have a ten-year-old at home, he's waiting for his Mama to serve lunch.'

'Then you shouldn't have accepted this job.' Charity still hadn't made inroads into my heart.

'You don't seem to understand.' The third member of the flying squad was a working-class lad in his twenties, perhaps a year or two older than I was. 'We phoned the Regional Party Committee an hour ago and told them we had a hundred-percent turnout.'

'So you lied to the Regional Committee?' Waxing indignant, I was capitalising each word. 'Now that's not good. Downright subversive I'd say.'

'Please,' pleaded the woman. 'Do you want us to go down on our knees?' 'I certainly don't want my home to provide the stage for a cheap spectacle like that,' I replied firmly. The conversation was going nowhere, and it took Papa to break the deadlock.

He winked at the party and said, 'Come on, comrades, I haven't voted yet either. Let's go, comrades, everything will be fine.'

And so it was. Papa simply filled out a voting slip in my name and cast an unauthorised proxy vote. Yet another canvassing station could report with communist pride that the chickens had come to roost.

'Good thing they didn't attempt to find out where I worked,' I said to Papa afterwards. 'Would've buggered up their full employment law.'

THE RIGHT TO ASSEMBLY

1

BY THE TIME I COMPLETED MY FIRST YEAR OF UNIVERSITY, I was doing well academically, but I already knew that my career would never climb out of a nosedive.

There were two requirements for success, and the university powers-that-be had communicated them to me in so many words. First, one must do well academically; second, one must be a *nash*. The big cheeses were sometimes prepared to compromise on the first. Never on the second.

That meant that the long walks through the Alexander Garden of my childhood had immunised me against success. Mama had been too effective in imbuing me with *ne-nash* attitudes and ethics.

With her usual uncompromising rigour she had taught me never to tell a lie, never to humiliate another person if I could help it, never to look out for Number One before anybody else, never to commit a dishonourable act, never to mistake betrayal for expediency or expediency for the truth.

'Never' is of course too absolutist a concept for our relativist world. I have sinned against all her commandments, but perhaps not so much as I would have done had I not been indoctrinated in that vein. Above all, my every pore was impregnated with Mama's awareness of the polarity between good and evil, and – like a priest snogging a parishioner in the vestry – each time I sinned I knew the transgression for what it was and suffered remorse.

There is only so much remorse a man can bear, but I became quite good at it. For in the Russia of my childhood every one of Mama's injunctions, if rigidly observed, could have paved an eight-lane motorway to perdition.

Lies, in particular, were spewed at us from every direction. And not only were we supposed to grin and bear it, which would have been possible, but we were also under orders to repeat them with fire-eating fervour. That wasn't feasible, at least not for a dedicated *ne-nash*.

Take the West, for example. Our newspapers screamed non-stop about the appalling living conditions there, homeless workers roaming the streets in search of a crust of bread, negroes dangling from every tree, crime that made citizens live their lives under lock and key. Evidence for all that was produced or, in its absence, concocted, while no conflicting reports ever reached our ears.

We weren't allowed to travel to the West and see for ourselves. A travel permit was a reward akin to the medal of Hero of Socialist Labour, and only the most trusted comrades qualified. When such trusted comrades returned from their voyages, they weren't allowed to point out a single positive aspect of Western life. Or, rather, there was one: roads.

At some point the Propaganda Department of the CPSU Central Committee decided that the populace was getting too sophisticated to be fooled by clearly unbalanced reports. Thereafter returning travellers were instructed to extol Western and particularly American roads, comparing them favourably with ours. So one *nash* tourist after another would intersperse dangling negroes and starving masses with the crisscrossing highways of the West. Somehow that attempt at even-handedness made their accounts sound even more mendacious.

A different account came from Mama's friend, a singer in the Red Army Choir. British visitors admired their singing, admitting wistfully that the Royal Marines weren't as gifted vocally. Of course, the Red Army Choir has as much to do with the Red Army as the Democratic Republic of Congo has to do with either democracy or republicanism. They are all classically trained professional singers whose job is to practise their art clad in the monkey suits of Soviet PR. In my day the choir, along with Moiseyev's dancers, carried to the decadent West the folksy vigour of Soviet men and women joyously frolicking for the motherland.

Nikolai Nikolayevich Kuznetsov's velvety baritone and perfect biographic credentials got him into the choir when it was first formed, carrying him all over the world. At first he was only allowed to go on tours of socialist countries, later he earned an upgrade to capitalist lands ('capcountries' in Soviet jargon). The first capcountry he toured was France. The tour lasted three months, and Kuznetsov came back a changed man.

In common with many singers, he didn't have a far-reaching intellect, so he didn't even attempt to comment on the socioeconomic fabric of French society. What had blown his mind was the abundance of cheap consumer goods, and he had used his hard-currency allowance to bring back 27 cases stuffed with products of decadent capitalism.

We were invited to a fashion show in his flat and spent four hours watching him, his wife and maiden daughter parade blouses, suits, skirts, trousers, shoes, dresses, swimsuits ('a bit naughty, wouldn't you say?'), hats and shirts. I was bored. Mama was quietly envious.

From that day, Nikolai Nikolayevich used his experience of Western consumerism, to the exclusion of other topics, as both a conversation starter and finisher. In response to an innocuous statement, such as, 'A fine day, isn't it, Uncle Kolia?' (at age 12 I already knew not to try anything more involved with him), he'd put on a conspiratorial face and hiss: 'Fine day, eh? Who cares about the weather? One rouble for two litres of orange juice! Twenty roubles for a suit! Five hundred roubles for a car!'

'So are things better out there than over here then?' That question never failed to restore Nikolai Nikolayevich's sanity. 'Of course they aren't. You see, we have socialism! It's just that… well, two roubles for a shirt! Three roubles for a pair of shoes! Fifty kopecks for a chicken!'

Comparing such accounts with those printed in the papers, even a 12-year-old was bound to smell a rat. With the passage of years the rat became smellier.

In general, the West has always occupied a particular place in the Russian psyche. The first schism between the Westernisers and Russophiles occurred roughly at the time Russia was baptised 1,000 years ago. And it has been a dominant feature of Russian society since Peter I decided to westernise the country by force or, as he put it, to chop a window into Europe.

Sooner or later, violent action was bound to produce an equally violent reaction, so battles between Westernisers and Slavophiles began to rage with renewed intensity and, in a modified form, have been raging ever since. The former exaggerated the virtues of the West as grossly as the latter overemphasised its vices.

The first famous Westerniser was the philosopher Chaadayev, while

Dostoyevsky and Solzhenitsyn are the Slavophiles best known in the West. According to them, only Russian peasants have virtue – a view not universally shared by anyone with first-hand experience of that social stratum.

Characteristically, Russian literature – whether produced by Slavophiles or Westernisers – includes not a single positive portrayal of a Westerner, at least none that I can recall. For example, the great German generals Bennigsen and Stein emerge as pedantic bunglers from Tolstoy's pages, and even Napoleon comes across as a military nincompoop.

In my day, the echoes of that battle could still be heard, but bolshevism had distorted the echo into a discordant noise. Many of the *ne-nash* were Westernisers who saw the West as the saviour of the world. They automatically assumed that every Westerner was a sage, profound, encyclopaedically educated man who had taken full advantage of liberty to become a carrier of condensed wisdom and virtue.

The *nash* were, still are and always will be, West-haters to a man. Even when they acknowledged that people in the West lived better, they tended to ascribe their prosperity to moral decay, as contrasted to the spiritual vigour of the Russians. Since they were militant atheists, they refused to accept the foundations of Western liberties. Those they hated with a passion, even though they didn't mind getting their hands on the goods the liberties produced.

Perched somewhere in between these two extremes were the truly bright people who in Russia are as rare as everywhere else. I was fortunate to have been exposed to some of them as a young man, and to have one as a close friend and mentor. His name was Yuri Ossipovich Mikhailov. He taught English grammar at our university, which meant I spent a lot of time in his company.

Our six hours of practical English every day were broken into phonetics, vocabulary and grammar, and as we went along the weight of grammar increased. All in all, in an average day we spent more hours mastering the language than our Russian-studying colleagues at Oxford or Cambridge would spend in a week.

At the same time, we were taught no English history or, practically, literature. Our typical third-year students could express themselves in fluent and idiomatic English but would have been unable to place the name of the Venerable Bede, didn't know what Henry VIII was famous for, had no idea what Thomas More died of, and wouldn't have read any Shakespeare in anything other than Russian translations, if that.

By contrast, a visiting third-year student who read Russian at Oxford would often know the work of even obscure Russian writers – but would be hard-pressed to say 'my name is Nigel' in Russian. Neither would he have spent much time on the courses that completed our curriculum: History of the Communist Party, Dialectical Materialism, Historical Materialism, Marxist Political Economics, Scientific Communism and Marxist Aesthetics. These were compulsory for all students, regardless of their specialisation.

Another compulsory course was military studies, conducted under the auspices of the Military Chair that reported directly to the Defence Ministry. In our English department this course was broken into two parts: general military training taught by Major Myndin and military translation taught by Lieutenant-Colonel Gerasimov.

Major Myndin was a short, bow-legged man who always wore his uniform and was cast in the traditional sergeant-major mould. Lieutenant-Colonel Gerasimov wore well-cut suits, spoke better English than most of our professors and taught us how to interrogate captured English and American soldiers.

Of the two, Myndin was better value. I still remember his opening lecture: 'You look at me,' he began, 'thinking that I'm pushing fifty, that I've got kidney stones, that my wife has left me, that I am short. Yes, I am weak. But I still have enough strength left in me to break any one of you in half!' It went downhill from there.

I never missed his classes because he provided endless food for party talk. 'What material is the Kalshnikov assault rifle made of?' he'd ask. 'Steel, Comrade Major!' a student would reply eagerly. 'That's correct, as per regulations,' the major would nod. 'And what material is the bayonet for the Kalshnikov assault rifle made of?' 'Steel, Comrade Major!' The student would feel he was on a winner there, but not for long. 'That is incorrect. The regulations say, "the bayonet is made of the same material as the rifle." '

Alas, the subsequent generations of students were to be deprived of Major Myndin's sagacity. A few years later he attempted to put his stock threat into practice, struck a student and was fired, only to be replaced with a perfectly anodyne officer.

As an ex-spy, Gerasimov was more polished and had a certain haughty air about him. He avoided most other instructors, except Mikhailov, the only Russian-born professor whose English was better than his.

Not all our instructors were Russian-born. Quite a few were old American communists and YCL members who, under Eleanor Roosevelt's spiritual guidance, had emigrated to Russia in the thirties. There were also a few Englishmen likewise inspired by the Webbs and G.B. Shaw (who somehow never got around to taking such a step themselves).

On arrival, by way of introduction to the future that worked, they were all sent to hard-labour camps for espionage. Most didn't survive the introduction, but those who did settled down upon release in English-language faculties around Moscow, and in such organisations as *Radio Moscow, Progress* Publishing House and *Novosti* Press Agency.

One ex-Englishman provided the sole exception by becoming a taxi driver and something of a celebrity in Moscow. Once several of us got into his cab and, as we often did when discussing sensitive subjects, spoke to one another in English. Suddenly the driver, who by then looked no different from his Russian colleagues, addressed us in an English that was a great deal more authentic than ours. 'Why not?' he shrugged in response to our obvious question. 'I like driving, the money's good and there's no hassle.'

One could see many expats in the *Illuzion* cinema that every Thursday showed English-language films from the thirties, many of which the expats remembered. There wasn't a dry seat in the audience and they all waxed nostalgic. Yet they remained dedicated communists, perhaps the only specimens of that breed left in Moscow. I knew some of them, and was friendly with one, Norma Schikman, who taught at the same college as my ex-wife.

Norma did her tenner in one of the worst camps. There she met another American, Alexander Dolgun, who later mentioned her in his book *An American in the GULAG*. They fell in love, but at the time I knew Norma she was well beyond the age of consent. An unreconstructed communist, she described her misfortune with the Russian proverb 'when you chop wood, chips will fly', which was seldom used in that context by the people who themselves had been among the chips. By that time her whole family had left for the States, but Norma concealed her desperate loneliness behind her chirpy demeanour.

When she found out I too was planning to emigrate to America she was aghast: 'Why on earth would you want to do a horrid thing like that?' 'Freedom, Norma,' I said. 'You know, liberty, the rule of law, things like that.' 'Freedom to do what?' 'Oh, I don't know. Read whatever I want, see whatever I want, travel wherever I want, things of that nature.'

'If you only knew how silly you are,' said Norma, who had last seen America when *Brother, Can You Spare a Dime?* was climbing up the charts. 'Don't you understand they'll work you so hard there, you'll have neither the time nor the energy to do any of those things?' Amazingly, her views on my emigration weren't so different from Mikhailov's, though he would never have expressed them in such a platitudinous way.

When I first met him, Yuri Ossipovich Mikhailov was 38 years old, 20 years my senior. He had moved to Moscow from Rostov only five years previously, which anyone who heard his refined Russian accent refused to believe. His English was amazingly good too, for a man who had never, in his formative years, had a conversation with a native speaker. His accent was mid-Atlantic but he could swing either way with ease, slanting his vocabulary accordingly. He even looked English: tall, lean and aquiline-nosed.

At that time, I was extremely impressed with his mastery of the language. But what impressed me even more was his erudition, which was that of an Anglophone don and a Russian intellectual rolled into one – a combination I've never encountered since.

He deigned to expose that side of his personality to me only later, when he became my research advisor and, eventually, friend. All I saw at the time was a brilliant, if obviously reluctant, instructor of grammar. Mikhailov used every solecism with which an unfortunate student would abuse the language of Swift as a starting point for scathing sarcasm, levelled at the culprit in particular and all of us in general.

'I understand,' he'd say, 'that you are not, nor can be, expected to understand the core philosophical, historical and psycholinguistic principles that lie at the foundations of English grammar. If this were a real university, in the mediaeval mould, you would be.

'But since this is nothing but a dog school where you are being paper-trained to acquire purely mechanical mastery of practical skills, I expect you to learn the difference between the Past Indefinite and Present Perfect by rote and never – I mean never – again confuse them in my presence.'

Every one of us thought that his criticism was aimed at our classmates but not us ourselves. We'd all squint at our neighbours to see if they were writhing under the impact of Yuri Ossipovich's disdain.

In due course, I asked him to supervise my extra-curricular work in literature, and he agreed – provided I let him choose the subject and the angle of approaching it. What resulted was an ever-growing work comparing the Angry Young Men, notably Braine, with the French 'critical realists', notably Maupassant. The work eventually snowballed to the size of a doctoral thesis, and, more important, provided a pretext for our long chats on every subject under the sun. He did most of the talking. I was sponging up every word.

More and more often, those chats shifted from our university halls to the BASIN, our acronym for the Boozer Across the Street from the Institute. Yuri Ossipovich drank in the compulsive, suicidal way Russians tend to drink, but that didn't affect his conversation, which sounded unlike anything I had ever heard. That both of us detested the state we had to live under went without saying, but he contemptuously tossed aside infantile dissent.

'Our brave dissidents, Sasha,' he'd say, 'don't realise that the only difference between communists and anticommunists is that of a mathematical sign. Plus, you're one; minus, you're the other. They should remember de Maistre's words, *"Nous ne voulons pas la contrerévolution, mais le contraire de la Révolution."* Not counterrevolution, but the contrary of a revolution. Positive, not negative.'

I made a mental note to find out who that de Maistre was, as Mikhailov continued. 'Unless you form a positive philosophy of life, Sasha, communism will remain your frame of reference, and you don't need it. But find out for yourself. You've already read some philosophy and theology. That's good, and by all means you should continue. But we live in a political age, so you must learn your Englishmen, plus

Tocqueville. Anti-communism alone is not going to do it.'

Mikhailov didn't know that a few years earlier the word 'anti-communist' had been given an unwitting kiss of death by a U.S. senator from a Southern state. That gentleman, Strom Thurmond if memory serves, once said at a drinks party that Eisenhower was a communist. His interlocutor replied that quite the opposite, Ike was an anti-communist. 'I don't care,' the senator said, 'what kind of communist he is.'

Indeed one must agree with Mikhailov that, mathematically speaking, an anti-communist is nothing but a communist with the opposite sign. Remove, as it happened to millions of our compatriots 15 years later, communism as a point of moral reference and you create a vacuum crying out to be filled.

It was from Yuri Ossipovich Mikhailov that I first learned about Burke and Hobbes, Locke and Canning – in addition to de Maistre and Tocqueville. He had their books at home and, even though they represented an irreplaceable treasure, would lend them to me, knowing that I'd always return them – if only for the pleasure of another tipsy conversation with him.

Eventually, we shifted our sessions to his home, a tiny room in a communal flat. I'd bring vodka, he'd cook simple meals that always looked better than they tasted ('Form, Sasha, is more important than substance. It lasts longer.') It was in that room that I met his friend, the poet Arseniy Tarkovsky. His less gifted son was becoming a cinematic guru at the time, thus vindicating Lenin's pronouncement that 'of all arts, film is the most important'.

Once when Yuri Ossipovich went out to the kitchen, Tarkovsky chased his third 'dose' with a limp pickle and asked me if Yuri had ever shown me his poems. 'I didn't even know he wrote any,' I confessed. 'Oh, you must read them. His talent makes us all look like pygmies.' Coming from the man widely regarded in our circles as heir to Mandelstam, that was a powerful statement indeed.

When Yuri Ossipovich came back with a plate of fried potatoes, I mentioned his verse. 'You've been talking again, Arseniy,' he reproached. 'Sasha doesn't need another decadent poet in his life. Anyway I'd never dare recite my feeble scribbles in front of you.'

He never did let me in on that side of his life, even as he refused to talk of the five years he had spent in a concentration camp as a young man. 'Concentration camps, Sasha,' he'd tell me, 'have not only replaced our prisons. They are replacing our conscience and our history. They've become an intellectual cop-out.'

Neither did I know much about his private life. I only saw that he was alone, indeed lonely. And even though I knew that girls found his nervous physique attractive, I never saw him in the company of women. He was consumed by his private pain and refused to go public with it. Instead he drank himself to death and smoked two packs of raw Russian cigarettes a day – this despite suffering from tuberculosis as a memento of his camp days.

'You have a very unattractive quality, Sasha,' he'd say in that apologetic way he always used when scolding me. 'You pour scorn on those who are less clever or enlightened than you are. That wastes the ultimate advantage enlightenment provides, charity.'

'You're a fine one to talk, Yura.' When drunk I'd occasionally slip into a less formal mode of address. 'The way you incinerate us students with your sarcastic contempt.'

'Oh, there's a big difference there, Sasha. I despise soulless people, not those who are less intellectual than I am. You see, I believe in the immortal soul, but – and this is my sin – I don't think it's given to everybody. In fact, whenever I hear arguments on creation versus evolution, I want to tell the debating parties they're both right. Some were indeed created by God and endowed with immortal souls. Others, most I'd say, are essentially animals who've evolved from the ape. Amazingly, this conciliatory stance never fails to get me in trouble with both sides.'

I wondered to what extent he was being facetious. 'But intellect, Sasha,' he'd continue, 'is only one manifestation of the soul, and not the most significant one. There are others, and in your infantile dismissiveness you can overlook them in other people and, inevitably, ignore them in yourself.'

He poured scorn on Slavophile attacks upon the spiritual impoverishment of the West. 'Here in Russia,' he'd chuckle, 'we have so little food for the body that we willy-nilly overdose on food for the mind. If we had fresher beef and more cars, most of us would chuck all that nonsense faster than you can say philistine.' Within a year, observing the microcosm of the acquisitive Russian community in America, I realised how prescient he had been. And now all of Russia is going that way.

Mikhailov liked to compare the Russians and the English, unhampered by the absence of any first-hand knowledge of the latter. 'We pride ourselves on our emotionality,' he'd say. 'The mistake we make is confusing sentiment with sentimentality and emotional depth with emotional incontinence. The English, on the other hand, make the mistake of confusing emotional restraint with emotional impotence.'

When I announced to him that I was leaving for good, he took it hard. 'What you're searching for, you won't find in the West, Sasha.' He killed one cigarette and lit another.

'Freedom is not without, it's within us, and that's where you should look for it. Liberty is not a *sine qua non* of freedom; it's closer to being its antagonist than ally. Please don't go where they equate civilisation with fluffy loo paper, and prosperity with quality of life.'

'But Yuri Ossipovich,' I'd object. 'I'm going to the West of Burke and Tocqueville, not the West of Henry Ford and J.B. Rockefeller.'

'That West is no longer there, Sasha.' Mikhailov had never been west of Moscow, but his intuitive understanding was worth more than the experience of a million banal lives. 'Learn humility, forget vanity. Didn't Christ teach to render unto Caesar that which is Caesar's?'

'Believe me, if all they wanted was that which is Caesar's, I'd spend the rest of my life in Moscow. But it's also God's thing they want, and that I can't accept. Nor can I get up and salute all the lies we're supposed to take at face value.'

'You're supposed to do nothing of the sort. I mean, do you believe the reality of Hamlet talking to his father's ghost? Do you take it at face value? Of course not. But you accept that make-believe works intrinsically on its own terms, those set by its creator.'

'What you're saying is that we live in two worlds. One is real life; the other a construct, a play in which we all have assigned roles.'

'Precisely. And the two worlds lie on separate, never intersecting planes. It's more Lobachevski than Euclid.'

'My problem, Yuri Ossipovich, is that I no longer can play those schizophrenic little games. I'm well and truly fed up.'

'Well, God be with you,' said the man whose dry, sad face has been haunting me ever since. He then kissed me on the forehead, an act devoid in Russian men's eyes of any naughty subtext.

Actually, in Mikhailov's case I did wonder occasionally why he was never seen with women. For in some barely perceptible ways his general profile fit the group that the homophobic Russians call 'the blue ones'.

2

Homosexuality was in Russia then roughly where it had been in England before the war. Practised almost exclusively by the artistic intelligentsia, it still hadn't trickled down to the other orders of humanity, at least not overtly.

The Soviet Criminal Code contained an article proscribing deviant behaviour, and every few years it would be enforced, with ensuing trials widely publicised. The pianist Schtarkman and the operetta performer Shishkin were among the best-known culprits. Each had done a few years for what even in a permissive West hadn't yet been described as merely an 'alternative lifestyle'.

In the Moscow police the job of combating homosexuality was given to a retired KGB colonel Vilenko. He had started his professional life in a Ukrainian village and his view of the vice under his aegis contrasted sharply with that of his Plato-quoting charges.

He'd summon yet another artist or musician to his office and try to talk sense into him. 'Look at yourself,' he'd admonish. 'Just bloody look at yourself! You've lost all semblance of humanity! You act like a bloody animal! And why, you wanker? Why!?! You don't have to do this shit. You're a handsome man, you could find yourself a pretty girl, no problem...' The man on the receiving end of that tirade would raise his chin, cross his legs and defiantly throw his long silk scarf around his neck.

My own brush with deviant sexual practices came in the untidy shape of Misha, an old friend from the Tverskoy Boulevard chess community. He'd come there every day, even though he wasn't much of a chess player. His interest lay in the 'bell-ringing' barracking that for many there took precedence over actual playing. Misha was good at that. His banter was lighter on obscenity and heavier on wit than most players', and eventually we started going out for a cup of coffee and a chinwag.

Misha's late grandfather had been Stalin's token President of the

USSR. Even though his wife had done a stint in a camp, Grandpa had been allowed to die in his own bed. He had therefore been able to bequeath to his two grandsons a lavishly appointed flat just north of the boulevard.

That flat became a frequent site of card-playing all-nighters, as Misha was a crack preference player. A bit of a hustler, he used the boulevard as a source of 'fish', as we called them. Under his tutelage I quickly raised my game to his standards, and we started hustling together, a practice we continued for years.

Our typical stratagem was to catch a boat to the sanatorium located on the banks of the Kliazma. On those occasions Misha would shave off his colourless stubble and put on a less outlandish shirt. We'd go directly to the river beach where shivering holiday makers would be pretending to bask at the Black Sea. As on a real beach, a lot of preference was played.

Misha, who at 27 looked ten years older, would search for a well-heeled mark. I, looking younger than my 17, would stay some distance from him, pretending we didn't know each other. After a few minutes of looking nonchalant and bored, Misha would zero in on his mark, for some reason often an army general. He'd then accost the 'fish', using his ready charm to ingratiate himself. The conversation would eventually gravitate towards cards, and the general would be skilfully goaded into admitting that a relaxed game would be a nice way to idle away an hour or two. Too bad there were only two of them. (Preference is a three-handed game.)

'Oh, that shouldn't be a problem. We're only going to have a friendly game, so anyone would do.' Misha would make a good show of looking around and then point at me. 'Why, maybe even that boy could play.' Waving away the good general's objection that I looked way too young, Misha would ask in his usual camp way, 'Ever played preference, you naughty boy?'

I'd acknowledge modestly that indeed my Papa had taught me the rules of the game, and I could now play almost as well as him. But, alas, I didn't have enough lunch money on me to cover a bet of more than 10 kopecks a point. Even though that was ten times the amount of the usual ante, the grown-ups would generously allow me to join in. However, the general would still be unsure that he wanted to clean out a child.

Such an outcome was never on the cards, as it were. For the general would be a social player who'd play for fun and take silly risks with his princely salary. Facing him would be two automatons, skilled, merciless and impervious to emotional impulses. The disparity of class was so huge that usually we didn't even have to cheat. After a relaxed afternoon the general would feel happy in spite of having lost a tidy sum, and we'd be on our way, still pretending to be strangers.

When we first met, I was about 13. Though at that innocent age I couldn't figure out what was so strange about Misha, there was no denying that he was odd. Later I realised he was as queer as a four-rouble note and marvelled at his restraint in not having made a pass at me when I had been at my most nubile.

Inexplicably, that restraint went right out the window shortly before my permanent departure, when I was 25, divorced, and firmly set in my sexual ways. Nevertheless, Misha began courting me in style, and his propositions grew progressively more graphic, not to say pornographic.

Since we were old friends, I couldn't just tell him to piss off, so we had long talks on matters Grecian. Before long those began to sound like university debates. He'd be profusely quoting assorted Greek philosophers; I'd counter with Exodus, Leviticus and Romans, threatening him with the fate of the good citizens of Sodom. Misha had more experience with the topic and won every theoretical debate, but without winning the practical prize he coveted. Eventually he abandoned classical references and began to appeal to my sense of adventure.

'How do you know if you haven't tried?' 'I haven't tried eating shit either, but somehow I know I wouldn't like it.' 'Wrong analogy, Sasha. You owe it to yourself to broaden your emotional horizons.' 'Misha, so far I don't feel I've adequately explored the avenues open to me naturally. When I'm ready to switch, you'll be the first to know. Anyway, I wouldn't be able to get it up for a man.' 'Don't worry, we'd get it up for you,' he promised.

To get rid of him I finally gave him the phone number of a happily married friend who I said was wavering. Misha started phoning my colleague Zhenia every day and, when he got his wife, she'd call out: 'Zhe-e-e-nia! Some woman for you!'

In Yuri Ossipovich's case I didn't know and, frankly, didn't care: the man was too important to me to be reduced to such an inadequate pigeonhole. We'll never meet again in this world, and if we meet in the next I hope he doesn't ask me which of us was right on the issue of emigration.

'It's a tough one, Yuri Ossipovich,' I'd have to admit. 'You were right that the West wasn't the proper place to look for what we needed. But then neither is Russia, and one might as well live in congenial circumstances while suffering a life of spiritual futility.'

3

In the middle of my second year at the university, affecting ennui and pretending I really thought 19 was a mature enough age, I got married and moved into a tiny one-bedroom flat with my wife and her mother.

I was desperately in love, especially since my wife didn't even remotely resemble the girls I normally hung out with. She had been raised in an old professorial family, and only fell for me because I was good at hiding the rougher edges of my personality. Still, pretence could only go so far, and once I suffered a lapse.

Shortly after we met, we were walking in the rain and I inadvertently stepped into a deep puddle. Ice-cold water rushed into my shoe, and I uttered the kind of obscenity that would have made even Major Myndin blush. Olga was aghast. But since that was my only lapse against the background of non-stop chattering about poetry and philosophy, I got away with it.

We'd walk the frozen boulevards of Moscow that looked touching in the winter, when heavy snowfall would cover the cracks in the lopsided yellow-and-white houses once inhabited by minor nobility. In a way, we'd rediscover our native city together, for love makes one see things in a different light. Once, I remember, we took a short cut from Merzliakovsky Lane to Suvorov Boulevard. Olga pointed at the bronze statue of Gogol in the middle of a tiny garden. The great writer was sitting in an armchair surrounded by his characters.

'Have you seen it before?' she asked. 'Once or twice. I always wondered what it was doing here, tucked away like this.'

'Have a closer look.' Olga led me to the statue. We approached Gogol from the left, and the writer's profile grinned at us in the sarcastic way one would have expected from the great satirist who all his life was desperate to portray a good Russian. Then we slowly moved to the other side, and Gogol's right profile reflected deep sadness, probably caused by his inability to find a good Russian to portray.

'This is wonderful,' I exclaimed, for once abandoning my usual nihilist wisecracks. 'I've never realised it was so... wonderful.'

'Different, isn't it? It's by Andreev, who I think is great. And you know what? When we were little, this statue occupied that glorious plinth at the top of Gogol Boulevard. You know, where the new statue sits now.'

I nodded. The new statue, bearing the inscription "From the government of the USSR", had Gogol look at the world with the smug expression one so often saw on the faces of official, socialist-realist hacks. The old statue was clearly behind the times.

Our endless walks punctuated by kisses on park benches eventually led to love, but they didn't necessarily have to lead to marriage at such an early age. By then, though, I was desperate to get out of my communal flat and away from Mama's prying. So get married we did, and I moved into the flat in Leninsky Prospect – only to discover that my mother-in-law's meddling was even worse.

Every country has its mother-in-law jokes, but Russia has more than its fair share, possibly because so many Russian men have to live with their in-laws. One springs to mind: 'Papa, why is Granny running around in zigzags? 'To you she's Granny, to me she's mother-in-law. Quick, give me some more ammo.' The less said about my first wife's mother, the better; especially since she is now dead and, you know, *nil nisi bonum* and all that.

There, I've used a Latin phrase again, albeit one that everyone uses, and this means that perhaps Ivan Ivanovich Lavrov, our Latin professor, did a better job on me than we both thought at the time. For two years he tortured me with conjugations and declensions, Virgil and Horace, Caesar and Cicero. I'd curse under my breath, recalling with gratitude the Caliph Umar who burnt the Alexandria Library, thus depriving Ivan Ivanovich of yet more instruments of torture.

Prof. Lavrov was a decrepit man of about 80, the last of a dying breed. Though senile, he had retained enough sense to drool at the girls in our class and threaten me with a failed exam. It was his ageing libido that distracted him from acting on this threat, for on the day of the final examination all the girls wore particularly short and low-cut dresses. They'd lean forward all the time and cross their legs when contemplating their answers.

When Lavrov shuffled into the room, the best-endowed girl shoved a huge bouquet into his arms and brushed her breast against his arm. We all roared, '*Ave, Magister!!!*', scaring the old man out of his wits. But he recovered, dropped a tear and eventually passed us all, including me. 'I wouldn't wish to spoil the impression of an otherwise excellent group of youngsters,' was how he explained his unexpected generosity.

His Latin wisdom prevents me from talking about my first mother-in-law, but not about our next-door neighbour, Vera Ivanovna. Vera Ivanovna was a more cultivated version of my childhood nanny. She displayed in abundance that common sense with which sturdy Russian women compensate for their men's drinking.

Vera Ivanovna came from the family of a successful merchant in Samara. Before the advent of the future that worked she had graduated from a gymnasium, a secondary school for girls. If her example is anything to go by, it educated its students better than the Moscow University of my day. And I had ample opportunity to discover the scope of Vera Ivanovna's knowledge. For we became friends, and, spurred on by the jet-black tea she brewed, often chatted through the night.

Soon after the future went to work, she fell in love with a dashing cavalry officer, Rafael Khmelnitsky. He was aide-de-camp to Voroshilov, the Commissar of the First Horse Army commanded by Budyonny. Marriage ensued, or rather the Bolshevik equivalent thereof: socialist cohabitation without the capitalist vows. Together, they followed the First Horse on its protracted raids. Young Rafael hacked heads off with his trusted sabre, regrettably twice saving Voroshilov's life. Young Vera cooked and made love.

'A good man he was,' she confided in me. 'Had a big arse, that's important in a man.' 'Why, Vera Ivanovna, is the arse so important?' 'It's like when you pickle cabbage, you put it under weight. A man needs a big arse to put one under weight. You, Sasha, need to grow yours.' Since then I've followed her advice willy-nilly, but without any noticeable improvement in my sex life.

After the Civil War had ended, Voroshilov moved to Moscow and hitched his wagon to the rising star, Stalin. Of course, his trusted aide-de-camp came along, and Vera Ivanovna was thus transformed into a

Kremlin Lady.

When Voroshilov became one of the first five marshals, her husband was promoted Lieutenant-General, or whatever that rank was then called. Luckily for him – and for Vera Ivanovna – Voroshilov then became one of the two marshals to survive the purges. He actually sat with his friend Budyonny in judgement at the tribunal sentencing the other three to death.

Vera Ivanovna attended every Kremlin ball and knew every dignitary, including Stalin, personally. Voroshilov used to court her surreptitiously, his friendship with her husband not providing an adequate obstacle, as it never does for the passionate Russians. Vera Ivanovna was vague on the outcome of that courtship and I didn't press for an answer.

Then came the time to teach the Finns dialectical materialism the hard way, and Gen. Khmelnitsky saw action in command of the crack Proletarian Division. As 20 years earlier, Vera Ivanovna followed him to the front. There he'd duck snipers' bullets, and she'd cook and make love. For that heroism Vera Ivanovna received an Order of the Red Banner, quite possibly one of the first half-dozen women so rewarded.

When the big war broke out, Gen. Khmelnitsky was appointed to command a shock corps, which was a corps in name only as it exceeded the strength of most armies. This time she stayed at home, which must have jinxed her husband who got injured so badly that he had to convalesce for the rest of the war. Vera Ivanovna looked after him.

They kept an open house, lavishly entertaining the Kremlin bigwigs and their artistic hangers-on. Among their frequent visitors were the sculptor Merkurov, famous for his busts of Lenin and Stalin, and the playwright Kirshon, whose plays set Stalin's pronouncements in dialogue. Kirshon's son eventually married Vera Ivanovna's daughter. She also had a son, a dashing naval officer.

That idyll came to a harsh end when Stalin finally got fed up with his in-laws, the family of his late wife Nadezhda Alliluyeva. As one does, he had them all either imprisoned or shot. No Russian man who has lived with his in-laws would find it in his heart to blame the monster for that particular crime. But, going a bit further than even the most ferocious mother-in-law haters would have countenanced, Stalin then set off the customary chain reaction by putting away all his in-laws' friends.

Vera Ivanovna, along with many other Kremlin Ladies, such as the wives of Molotov, Kalinin, Andreyev and Poskryobyshev, was among those friends. She faced a hastily assembled tribunal whose members called her an old slag and sentenced her to eight years in a concentration camp. No questions asked, no answers required.

Compared to the camps in the Arctic North, Vera Ivanovna's camp was, according to her, a resort. The inmates did light agricultural work, slept in heated barracks and had more or less enough food. In spite of those luxurious conditions, in the time Vera Ivanovna spent in that tiny molecule of the gigantic penitentiary body, more than 10,000 inmates died. On that and other similar evidence, one is tempted to think that Prof. Rummel's count (in his book *Lethal Politics*) of 61 million deaths perpetrated by the future that worked is, if anything, too modest.

Vera Ivanovna's robust Volga stock pulled her through, and she emerged healthier psychologically, if not physically. She returned to her old flat, only to find that her ailing husband was now sharing it with his new wife whom he had married the bourgeois way, paperwork and all.

One look at Vera Ivanovna, and he left his new wife for the old one. The official wife made it difficult for them, claiming that while she was the general's real spouse, Vera Ivanovna was nothing but an ex-mistress, a camp whore and an unreformed enemy of the people to boot.

As neither the general nor his patron Voroshilov still possessed the clout they had once had, it was touch and go for a while. Only the interference of Gorkin, the general's old comrade, and at the time the Supreme Prosecutor of the USSR, swung the battle Vera Ivanovna's way. But not before the impostor got the general's stately apartment.

The reunited couple moved into a modest flat in Leninsky Prospect, where Vera Ivanovna's husband soon died. A few years later my marriage took me to the flat next door. Voroshilov visited his friend's widow once every couple of months until his own death, and every time I espied his limousine rolling into the courtyard, I'd give Vera Ivanovna a piece of my youthfully indignant mind.

'But Sasha,' she'd pour tea into my glass nestling in its ornate silver holder, 'of course I know he's a mass murderer worse than Himmler. But you only know him as a monster, whereas I remember him as a young man astride that black steed. With those shoulder straps and a Mauser on his thigh he was the most dashing thing on a horse I've ever seen. Next to my husband, of course,' she'd add mischievously.

While I waxed indignant about concentration camps and their victims, Vera Ivanovna, in her quiet housekeeping way, talked less but did more. Countless former inmates, broken and often half-crazy old women from out of town, drifted through her flat. They knew they'd always find a warm bed and a hot meal there.

Vera Ivanovna turned no one away. We were often joined in our nocturnal chats by an Estonian 'bourgeois nationalist' (who had dared obtain a higher education before her country's 'liberation'), a Georgian 'exploiter of the toiling masses' (whose parents used to make a living by any other than menial jobs) or a 'Nazi spy' (an aristocratic lady who had been sentenced to death for having treacherously survived the siege of Leningrad, which just sentence had been at a moment of liberal weakness commuted to 10 years' hard labour).

All those women fluently used the camp jargon, which hadn't yet penetrated common usage then as it has now. These days even the tsar Putin, speaking *ex cathedra*, doesn't mind using such language when, for instance, saying that Chechen terrorists have nowhere to hide, not even in the lavatory.

'We'd waste'em even in the shithouse,' promised the current custodian of the future that works. In private the good colonel expresses himself with even greater freedom. Once, when a celebrated musician spilled some red wine on his jacket at a Kremlin party, Putin pushed him aside with both hands. 'Some fucking virtuoso you are,' he hissed.

The old victims of Putin's *alma mater* used such language the way they breathed, which was hardly surprising. What amazed me was their lack of bitterness. They exuded quiet forgiveness and, much as I despise folk wisdom, the thought crossed my mind that maybe the old Russian proverb 'don't ever turn prison down' had some meaning after all.

Once I found her crying, something totally out of character. 'Vera Ivanovna, what's the matter?' 'Well,' she sobbed. 'You know next week I am going to see my family, what's left of it, in Samara, Kuibyshev, whatever the hell they call it now. So I rang them to ask if there was anything they wanted me to get for them in Moscow. I thought they'd ask for, you know, records or books, or maybe some clothes, but you know what they wanted?'

She took a sip of water and so was able to continue. 'They asked for... some... sausage... and a dozen or two... eggs! Eggs! You know... Sasha... when I was young... you know, in peace time... [I knew that older people, even those of the basically communist persuasion, used that term to describe the time before the future began to work] ...In peace time, they used to say... when Samara province had a good harvest... it could feed all of Russia... and the rest of the grain in the country... could all be exported. And now... eggs, Sasha. Eggs and some sausage.'

She wiped her eyes with the back of her hand and went to play with her grandson Klim, so named in honour of Voroshilov.

4

The building we lived in was a couple of miles away from the campus of Patrice Lumumba University, where Third World students studied for advanced degrees in terrorism, subversion and related subjects. One of their ablest Latin American alumni would later become famous as Carlos the Jackal. But most students were African, which gave the young men on our block something to do on those wet Friday nights.

The Russians hadn't had any experience of black people until the 1957 International Youth Festival, the massive propaganda exercise following which the Patrice Lumumba was founded. All of a sudden many negroes appeared in the streets of Moscow, and the shock proved more than Muscovites could bear.

The term 'blackarses' now had to do extra service to include not just Georgians and Armenians, but people who actually were black. Within months, the same racial stereotypes as in the old American South became standard fare around Moscow. Negroes smell. They have oversized penises they like to stick into willing blondes. They rape the unwilling ones. They secretly practise cannibalism. They – well, you get the picture.

Russians wouldn't be Russians if at some point they hadn't begun to act on such stereotypes, particularly since the police tacitly approved. In fact, the well-oiled KGB rumour mill quickly went into high gear promoting racial hatred. One suspects their motivation was the same as that of the Tsar's secret police that had produced the infamous *Protocols of the Elders of Zion*. Anything was welcome that could act as a distraction and relief valve.

Before long the more precocious boys at our school began to show around photos of muscular negroes coupling with meaty white girls, presumably Russian. In fact, the first time I ever saw a graphic depiction of a sex act was when my classmate Edik showed me a few shots that were so out of focus one could barely tell what was going on. Edik, though indignant about the miscegenation, drooled over the pictures nonetheless.

By the time I got married and moved into the building in Leninsky Prospect, interracial relations in Moscow had crystallised into a pattern not dissimilar to that of Alabama in the second half of the nineteenth century. Whenever a black man walked with a Russian girl in broad daylight, both would be cursed and sometimes spat at, a scene I witnessed many times smack in the centre of Moscow. If they dared to walk together after dark, the man would be beaten within an inch of his life and sometimes beyond that point.

Such incidents were hardly ever investigated. The cops would simply shrug with the same 'well, what d'you expect' nonchalance exhibited everywhere by policemen asked to investigate a crime they consider trivial. 'Wrong place at the wrong time,' they'd say, as if the incident had been *force majeure* with no human agency involved.

Our courtyard had a playground that acted as arena for vigorous five-a-sides every weekend. I liked to play football in those days, and the lads accepted me even though I was a Johnny-come-lately and an 'intel' to boot. But they appreciated the way I dribbled and passed the ball around, so before long we became friendly, as far as it went.

Once after a late afternoon game, the best player there, a tall rosy-cheeked lad, asked me what I was doing that evening. He looked conspiratorial, which put me on guard.

'I'm not sure. Why?' I didn't want to commit myself to a friendship beyond the natural camaraderie of fellow ball-kickers.

'Well, we're all off to the Lumumba tonight. Thought maybe you'd like to come along.' 'What on earth for?' I was genuinely perplexed as I knew there was nothing around that campus of any interest whatsoever.

'Well, you know. The usual sort of thing. We'll have a couple of drinks, bash a few darkies, have a good time. You're welcome to join in, coz you're a regular bloke.'

Actually, I wasn't that regular a bloke and so I remembered an arrangement my wife was supposed to have made for that very night. Just out of curiosity, though, I asked if they did that sort of thing often.

'Oh, once or twice a week,' answered my football friend. 'Maybe you'll be able to make it next time. We don't want too many blackarses around here, you know.' 'Love to.' I smiled in a cowardly fashion and went home.

After that I stopped playing football there and avoided going out at all when a game was in progress. Whenever they did bump into me in the courtyard, the boys would look away. I had let the side down.

Then came a particularly snowy winter during which two black students disappeared. What was left of them was found when the snow melted in April. They had been beaten to death.

The next day several hundred African students staged a demonstration of protest in Red Square. Such events were never publicised as the papers had more important things to worry about, such as the non-stop lynchings in the United States. But it's impossible to keep a rally in the centre of Moscow under wraps. Before long rumours began to circulate, and the KGB felt they had to set the record straight by countering with rumours of their own.

'Have you heard of that darkie rally in Red Square?' asked our neighbour, the car mechanic Semyon who also occasionally played football in the courtyard. 'Vaguely,' I said. 'Well, you know what it was all about?' 'I haven't a clue.'

Semyon became agitated. 'Seems like the blackarses were protesting against the absence of whorehouses in Moscow. They were demanding a hard-currency brothel staffed with Russian blondes. Just for themselves.' The KGB knew what they were doing, I thought. One ought to welcome competence, whichever form it took.

These days papers in the West are amazed at the rate of racial murders in Russia (dozens if not hundreds every year). Many Russians are also indignant about such incidents. But they are never surprised.

5

There was another older woman who was a good friend at that time: Galina Fyodorovna Vatrushina, the professor who had taken over from

Mikhailov as our grammar instructor. Tall and ramrod straight, in the manner of upper-class English women who sometimes look as if they suffer from a rectal condition, Galina Fyodorovna's was a forbidding presence. She seldom smiled and used humour sparingly, though she was capable of it.

In her own way she was as enigmatic as Mikhailov. One felt there was some mystery lurking behind her unrelenting blue-stocking demeanour.

Her command of English wasn't as formidable as Mikhailov's, and perhaps not even as good as mine was at the time. But she was by far the best teacher of grammar I had ever had. Unlike Mikhailov, for whom teaching grammar was a chore, she loved her subject, a condition that proved to be contagious. One just didn't feel like being obstreperous in her classes, and we got on very well.

Eventually, I did a couple of papers on structural grammar under her auspices, and we became friends, without ever crossing the barrier of formality that, in Galina Fyodorovna's view, always had to separate a professor from a student. After a year of having tea at her place, I was sworn to secrecy and told the story behind her loneliness.

When she herself was a student, in the late thirties, she lived with her parents, a professor of philosophy and his wife, a doctor. Families of that type tended to raise their children, especially daughters, in an austere vein, and Galina Fyodorovna had been until her twenties innocent about the seedy side of life.

Her home life couldn't have been more different from mine. Whereas Papa vouchsafed to me, when I was about 16, the contraceptive benefits of terminating an act of love in the orifice free of reproductive organs, at age 22 Galina Fyodorovna wasn't entirely sure where babies came from. Her innocence might have contributed to the fervour pitch of her first love – and didn't do much to protect her against its disastrous outcome.

She met a young man who was the answer to her maidenly dreams. Though not handsome, he had a pleasant, intensely cerebral face that reflected an elevated spirituality. At a time when reading banned literature was tantamount to a suicide attempt, he gave her books by Mandelstam, Rozanov, Berdiayev. They often went to concerts, listening with bated breath to the genius that poured through the fingers of Sofronitsky or Yudina.

And then there were long walks along the moonlit embankment of the Moskva, the first touch of hands and the first chaste kiss. The boy was introduced to the parents who welcomed him as their own son and... Just how trite do you wish me to get with these clichés before you realise that this was the kind of soppy love that made Barbara Cartland cry all the way to the bank? But don't despair, gentle reader, as old Barbara might say: we are in Russia now, and things aren't going to remain treacly for long.

Tragedy struck a fortnight before their wedding. One fine night Galina Fyodorovna's parents were both arrested and charged with whatever *ne-nash* people were charged with in those days to conceal the real indictment: being *ne-nash*. For that crime the Vatrushins were sentenced to a tenner each, and both died in Kolyma within the first year.

The principal witness for the prosecution at their trial was Galina Fyodorovna's fiancé. He turned out to be an NKVD officer assigned to spy on the Vatrushins, and had used Galina Fyodorovna as a conduit to her parents. Afterwards the man, who had apparently fallen in love with her for real, begged forgiveness on his knees. Galina Fyodorovna just gazed into space. She never as much as went to the cinema with another man again.

When we met, she exuded rectitude, a quality much rarer in Russia than intellect, which she also possessed. For some inexplicable reason, she was well thought of at the university, and no one was unduly surprised when she was appointed chairman of the State Examination Board.

State examinations were different from our regular exam sessions at the end of every term. Given pre-graduation at the end of the fifth year, they were always attended by representatives of the Ministry of Higher Education. In a way, while regular exams checked the students' knowledge, the state examinations were used to assess the overall academic standards at the university. The faculty felt, with some justification, that it was they, rather than their students, who were being judged.

Clearly, a rotten apple or two couldn't be allowed to spoil the reputation of the university in front of representatives of the Ministry of Higher Education. Thus our state exams were traditionally rigged every year, just as every race at the Moscow Hippodrome was.

Cheating, in general, isn't frowned upon in Russian institutions of higher learning as much as in their Western counterparts. While there were three cases of plagiarism at Oxford in all of the last century, there were thousands at our university every year. 'When you rip off one article,' explained Mikhailov, 'that's plagiarism. Two is a compilation. And three is a dissertation.'

Among undergraduates, cheating was more widespread than drunkenness, which is saying a lot. For many a student, crib sheets entirely replaced knowledge, and the virtuosity displayed in concealing them was astounding.

Girls would write whole theses on their thighs and would demurely pull their skirts over their knees when the examiner looked their way. Boys would tuck books into their trousers. Girls would conceal cribs in their bras and knickers. Boys would climb through the window the night before and paste pages torn out of textbooks onto the undersides of the desks. Both would shamelessly copy whole sections from books in their essays.

In a classic clash between shell and armour, some professors, known as 'bitches', were as good at detecting cribs as the students were at hiding them. So exams were occasionally failed. When that happened, the underachiever had to resit the same exam. Three failures in the same examination session meant summary expulsion. All that was standard operating procedure, and everyone knew that failures were inevitable – but not at the state exams.

These were always oral, with questions written on numbered cards lying face down on the examiner's desk. When it was one's turn, one flipped a card, read out the question and then answered it to the best of one's abilities. Since nobody knew what the blindly drawn card would have in store, one had to know a fair amount not to be thrown off track by an unexpected question.

To avoid such an embarrassment, our junior instructors who ran the nitty-gritty of the state exams would mark the reverse sides of the cards with the skill of a riverboat gambler. That way we all knew which card we'd 'randomly' select and had to prepare only one topic, which wasn't hard even for the intellectually challenged.

We found out about that arrangement about a week before the state exams, and most students cheered. But I and a couple of others said we wanted no part in it, proving we still hadn't been drawn into the *nash* collective. However, the *nash* students pointed out that by refusing to play the game we'd introduce an element of luck, break the prearranged rotation and bugger it up for everybody. Not to be spoilsports, we agreed to pick up the assigned cards under the stipulation that we wouldn't know in advance what was in them.

The exams turned out to be a great success. There wasn't a single failure, and the inspectors congratulated Galina Fyodorovna on a job well done. I wondered how she could reconcile her unbending rectitude with the swindle that had had even the relativist me up in arms. In a couple of days I got my answer.

Galina Fyodorovna rang me at home at some ungodly hour, something I don't think she had ever done before. 'I want you to come to my place immediately,' she said in a preemptive tone she never used when talking to her favourites.

When Galina Fyodorovna wanted you to come to her place immediately, you got on the bus straight away. She lived only a mile away from me, and I was at her place in 20 minutes.

'Is it true?' she asked in response to my greetings. 'Is what true, Galina Fyodorovna?' Somehow people always knew when I was dissembling. 'Don't dissemble, Sasha!' she barked. 'The scam. With exams. Is it true?'

'Galina Fyodorovna,' I mumbled. 'You mean you didn't know?' 'If you think that I could have anything to do with this... pornography, I ought to throw you out of my house. Did you take part in it?' 'Only under duress, Galina Fyodorovna,' I confessed and explained to her exactly what I had done.

'Pity,' she said sadly. 'I thought you were different.' 'But I am, Galina Fyodorovna.' Somehow it was important that she shouldn't think ill of me. 'Only by degree,' she ruled, and that was the last time I saw her outside the university. And she never sat on any examination boards again.

6

My other friends were closer to my own age, and most of them were artists of one kind or another. Quite a few were conservatory students who were embarking on international careers. That meant they had to play competitions all over the world.

The Soviets treated international competitions of any kind, be it sports or music, more seriously than they deserved. The idea was that competitive success would strike a blow for the achievements of bolshevism. So it did, but counterblows came from revelations of the questionable sexual identity of some Soviet female athletes, or else doubts about the age eligibility of some Soviet musicians. For example, the violinist Boris Gutnikov, who won the Second Tchaikovsky Competition, was a balding conservatory professor at the time. But my musician friends were definitely eligible for international competitions, as they were all under 30 at the time.

Many of the youngsters setting off for Leeds, Brussels or Montreal would receive pep talks from the Culture Minister Furtseva herself. It was widely rumoured in Moscow that she was, or at least used to be, Khrushchev's mistress. If true, their union might well have been based on a shared love of art. Khrushchev displayed that love publicly in a series of major speeches, and privately every time he attended an exhibition opening.

He held a dim view of modernism, something I can't fault him for. But his mode of expression tended to be a bit crude, especially when he was in his cups. 'What kind of a fuck-your-mother is that?' he asked when Furtseva was leading him through the famous Manezh exhibition of Russian modern art, the first such event in recent Soviet history. The expression Khrushchev used was his favourite, as it is with most Russians, who rely on it to convey fine shades of meaning and emotion.

'This, Nikita Sergeevich,' replied the wounded modernist, 'is not a fuck-your-mother. It's a work of art.'

'It means sod-all, it is sod-all, and if you go on painting this kind of fuck-your-mother, you'll be sucking dick [go penniless, in colloquial Russian] for the rest of your life. You have no place in the Soviet Union.'

'Oh, yes I do,' objected the suicidal artist, 'and I am even going to join the Party.' 'We won't take you, we don't want pederasts like you,' replied the leader of all progressive mankind. [The word 'pederast' is used as a general desemanticised term of opprobrium in Russian.]

'That's not up to you to decide. The decision will be made by my local Party cell.'

'Bloody hell,' laughed Nikita. 'That's my kind of talk!' He slapped the painter on the back, shook his hand and later told Furtseva to make sure the wanker never got another exhibition in his life.

Furtseva's own pep talk to the youngsters who were about to carry the banner of Soviet musical achievement abroad always started with a masculine bang of fist on the desk. 'I want the top three prizes,' she'd demand. Then she'd soften up and coo, 'Just bugger those Americans up the arse for me, boys.'

Once, when three young pianists were setting off to play a competition in England where the Brahms/Handel was a compulsory piece, she asked them, 'Boys, why would they choose that piece in England, of all places? Why Handel I mean? Brahms I understand, he was after all an English composer…'

My best friend among musicians studied with a conservatory professor who believed that the meaning of music ought to be communicated not only with tones but also with body gyrations. 'I want to see it all on your darling little snout, lovey,' he'd intone in his camp way. My friend would thus be encouraged in his natural tendency to practise what I called the Marcel Marceau school of piano playing.

We were inseparable for a while, and talked about music endlessly. 'Music,' he once explained to me, 'isn't sounds. It's what's behind the sounds.' 'True,' I agreed. 'But that something ought to be expressed through sounds, not a wholehearted attempt to copulate with the piano.'

'Why don't you talk about something you know?' Valeriy angrily swallowed his 'dose'.

Soon afterwards my friend played at a major competition in Paris that he was favoured to win. However, he forgot a portion of the Rachmaninov Second Concerto in the final, lost the orchestra, and as a result could only manage third prize. 'Rach Two is one hell of a piece to play after a night of shagging and boozing,' he complained later.

Nonetheless the emotional French audiences were spellbound, showering him with praise, flowers and expensive gifts. Then he returned to Russia, and harsh reality set in.

Actually, the reality of Russian audiences wasn't harsh at all. At that time people in the West were already beginning to regard classical music as merely another form of entertainment. They were increasingly reluctant to make the effort of concentration required at a classical concert, instead letting their minds wander towards the après-concert supper.

No such problem with the Russians. Entering the foyer of the Grand Hall in Moscow one could already sense that music was serious business. The men would wipe the usual smirks off their faces and talk in half-whispers as they formed a beeline to the bar serving beer and sandwiches with caviar or sturgeon. The women's faces would be solemn as they busily peeled off and checked the numerous outer layers of their clothing, replacing their snow boots with the high-heeled shoes they brought with them in shopping bags.

And then the men and the women would converge in the great hall and hang on to every note with bated breath, leaning forward on the edge of their seats, faces tense, eyes riveted to the platform. Whether they knew musical theory better than their Western counterparts is doubtful: musical notation, for example, wasn't taught at Soviet schools. But what the audience had learned, or else imbibed with their mothers' milk, was the gut feeling that music was serious, important, vital.

When they listened, their physical existence was on hold. Music was life or death. So they never missed a single note as it bounced off the glorious chandeliers of the Grand Hall, spreading its reverberations over the two amphitheatre tiers, with every seat occupied and hundreds of people sitting on the steps between the aisles.

No, Valeriy and other youngsters who had already played abroad and had a basis for comparison, didn't have any problems with Russian audiences. It was the bosses of the musical establishment who made life difficult.

All performers in the Soviet Union were handled by *Goskontzert*, the state organisation that decided where and what they should play. No matter how big a star a musician was, he had to put in his time playing at inauspicious locations. These included small towns where pianos could be badly out of tune, or even collective farms where pianos would often be missing half the keys.

As a matter of fact, Valeriy was once sent to play at a farm that didn't have a piano at all. 'So have you cancelled the recital?' he asked innocently when given the good news on his arrival. 'Not at all,' answered the farm chairman. 'We thought maybe you wouldn't mind playing the accordion. I mean, it has black and white keys too.'

'Great!' beamed Valeriy, anticipating the mileage he'd get out of this adventure at Moscow parties. As he had never touched an accordion in his life, he requested half an hour's practice time before kick-off, and the recital was a great success. Valeriy stamped his feet on the floor as he played, imitating squat dancing and driving the audience to ecstasy.

Immediately following his Paris near-triumph, Valeriy was assigned to tour Kazakhstan with a chamber orchestra. He had to accept the assignment stoically, even though he had a premonition it would end in disaster.

The musicians were loaded onto two coaches and sent on their way. The empty road meandered from one little town to the next through the wastelands of that republic where, apart from some pockets in the capital city, music wasn't a high priority. A hundred miles out of one town and two hundred from their next gig, the party stopped for lunch at a roadside restaurant.

'What's good today?' asked the artistic director in the affably familiar way of a Moscow boulevardier. 'Try the mutton stew,' suggested the manager. 'It's all we've got anyway. But it's nice and fresh.'

Mutton stew it was, but the freshness claim turned out to owe more to salesmanship than to veracity. This the party found out half an hour later, and the coaches had to come to an abrupt halt in the middle of the steppe. 'Men to the right, women to the left,' the conductor screamed, which battle cry was heeded by the squatting orchestra. Thus relieved, the party could go on, only to have to stop in another twenty minutes, their need even direr than before.

After half a dozen more stops they managed to reach their concert hall with minutes to spare before the start. The hall, as its *direktor* proudly declared, had just been built. Actually, it wasn't quite finished, as the lavatories still hadn't been installed, which oversight the *direktor* promised to correct before their next visit. That, the dehydrated conductor had to explain, didn't solve the immediate problem, which was urgency itself.

As the public began to slow-clap, demanding their fun, the support staff hastily found half a dozen aluminium buckets and set them up a few yards backstage, so that the musicians didn't have far to dash in case of emergency. Throughout their subsequent rendition of the Mozart A-Major Piano Concerto, K488, one musician after another would put his instrument down and rush backstage.

The arrangement was eerily reminiscent of the Haydn 'Farewell' Symphony, but with two salient differences. First, having used the buckets, the musicians would then come back. Second, and more important, the hall acoustics were such that the public could hear every sound made backstage even more clearly than the actual music. I would have paid good money for a recording of that historic performance, but for once Valeriy had been too distracted to switch on his trusted tape recorder.

When he found out I was planning to emigrate, he stopped seeing me, fearing with some justification that any association with an outcast could damage his international career. Then we lost track of each other for 20 years, meeting again in London where he was playing a recital at Wigmore Hall.

We went to my place for dinner after he had earned his keep by attacking the piano with a sensual display. The key features were coital hip gyrations and orgasmic gasps worthy of Harry Reems, the star of *Deep Throat*. (That, against all odds, didn't prevent him from playing quite beautifully).

'Music, you see,' explained Valeriy over roast pigeon at my place, 'isn't sounds. It's what's behind the sounds. It's a whole complex of psycho-motor activity.' Though that explanation showed a remarkable consistency of opinion over time, my reply effectively ended our friendship. 'Let's just hope the piano doesn't get pregnant,' I said, 'and you won't have to pay child support for a baby grand.'

Back in Moscow we both belonged to a narrow club-like circle of friends. The venue in which we gathered almost every night was the large flat Valeriy was leasing from Manechka Margulis. The landlady, a shrivelled woman of 85, lived in the back room and was exceptionally good value. After a spot of vodka, babushka's ruin, she'd tell us that she was actually 22, although admittedly looking somewhat older. On the other hand, our girlfriends only pretended to be in their twenties and were in fact much older than her.

When our parties included a bit of sex, we always made sure Manechka had been safely tucked in before the fun started. But the sounds still must have penetrated her sleeping brain. One night we were shocked to hear her make orgasmic noises in her sleep.

Shortly before she died, I noticed her rummaging through an old chest and looking fondly at yellowish documents from her younger days. Most of them belonged to her late husband, Prof. Margulis, who before the war had been an international authority on the treatment of tertiary syphilis.

All of a sudden she showed me an old note scribbled on Kremlin letterhead. I gasped when I saw that the note was signed by Nadezhda Krupskaya, Lenin's wife. 'Dear Prof. Margulis,' went the note, 'on Volodia's behalf, I would like to thank you once again for everything you have done for him and me. Yours respectfully, Nadezhda Krupskaya.'

The note was sheer dynamite, as it was the only document I am aware of that confirmed the persistent rumours that Lenin was a syphilitic. Circumstantial evidence that note might have been, but evidence none the less. The thought crossed my mind that perhaps I should slip it in my pocket when I left Russia. But then I imagined the possible consequences of a border check discovering the note in my possession and chased the thought away.

The permanent members of our unofficial club also included my old colleague from the Ferro-Concrete Institute Grisha Gorin, whose poetry was maturing by the day; Misha Polsky whose unpublished short stories showed a precocious talent and a strong influence of Bulgakov; Sasha Ritsky who didn't have any artistic aptitude but was a gifted procurer of food, drink, girls and concert tickets; and another poet, the eventual snitch Volodia Kramer who, in addition to writing Gumilev-style poetry, spoke English as well as I did.

It was our ability to speak almost native-quality American English that produced the best prank of my Moscow days. The idea came out of nowhere, one lazy August afternoon after Misha and I had just finished our assignments at the Moscow Film Festival, where he had interpreted films from French and I from English.

During the assignment we had been invited to have our meals with the Festival guests at the Rossiya Hotel. That was the only time in my life that I rubbed shoulders with such A-listers as Monica Vitti and Jean Marais. The head waiter spoke some English, enough to call Monica Vitti 'baby', as in 'Baby, how come you're asking for mustard when no one else is?' or 'Baby, can't you see I'm busy?' The spoilt film star, unaccustomed to such treatment, complained to everyone willing to listen, which group didn't include the restaurant *direktor*.

Interpreting at the festival was a real bonanza, and not just because the pay was good. The assignment gave us the chance to see films we otherwise wouldn't have seen. For watching foreign films was a privilege as rare as wearing real clothes or eating palatable food. Such films could only be seen at 'closed' viewings to which by and large only privileged comrades had access.

When the fortunate ones got to see the odd film, they brought their Russian experience into the cinema, and their take was different from Western audiences'. Just before the festival, I remember, a *nash* chap I knew had gone to see *The French Connection*. The experience left a lasting impression.

I wasn't in the West when the film was released, but one can venture a guess that the reviewers must have singled out the car chase scene, or Hackman's performance, or perhaps the gritty colour and choppy cutting volume. None of those had impressed Sergei, but he was nothing short of shaken when telling me about one scene.

'Listen to this,' he enthused, 'this bloke's driving a Lincoln with a million dollars' worth of heroin hidden under the panels. He drives it to a vacant lot where a dozen gun-toting gangsters are expecting delivery. And he's alone and unarmed! So they get the smack out of the car, test it and then – pay the bloke the full amount!

'Just imagine the same thing happening here! They'd take the drugs, then shake his hand and say, "Thanks mate, see you around, off you go." And the bloke would say, "But what about my money?" The gangsters would stop smiling then. "What bloody money? Get the hell out of here while you're still in one piece!" True or not?'

I had to agree that his take on Russian business ethics was spot-on. Then, when I went on to interpret several American films at the festival, and caught a few glimpses of a life so different from ours, I knew how he felt.

Now the job was finished, and Misha and I sauntered down Tverskoy Boulevard, lazily trying to decide what to do with the rest of the summer. The conversation didn't follow any particular pattern, and eventually we stumbled upon the subject of being able to pass for a Frenchman (he) or an American (I).

At that point Misha recalled a funny story. He knew a lad, he said, who read English and French at the Moscow District Pedagogical Institute, which was the lowest of the low in our field. We often made jokes at the expense of those underachieving ignoramuses, which elevated us in our own eyes.

That chap Kazakov, recalled Misha, once wanted to impress a girl with his international connections, when in reality he had none. So he asked Misha to play the role of a bogus Frenchman for an evening, and Misha thought that would be a fun thing to do. The session went like a dream. Meeting a real Westerner so impressed the girl that they both had her before the end of the evening, thus promoting international friendship.

'Listen, how good is his English?' I asked. 'The usual Moscow District standard, I suppose. Why?' answered Polsky with the snobbery common to students of better universities everywhere.

'Why don't we pull the same kind of trick on him? That would be turning the tables neatly, wouldn't it?' Misha thought it was the best idea he had heard all day, borrowed a two-kopeck piece from me and phoned Kazakov immediately.

'I have this problem,' he said. 'An American chap, a friend of a friend, is passing through Moscow. I'm seeing him tonight, but he doesn't speak a word of either Russian or French, and my English is nowhere. Any chance you could come over and give us a hand?'

Asking a student of English if he wanted to meet an American was a bit like asking an unemployed actor if he'd like to meet a famous director. But Kazakov, the phoney that he was, made a show of checking his schedule and barely finding a spare hour that very evening.

The fish had bitten, and I rushed home to prepare. I put on a blue button-down shirt Mama had made for me that at a pinch could pass for a Brooks Brothers product, slipped into my pocket a pack of contraband Kents with one cigarette remaining, and picked up an American friend's business card identifying me as Ian Taylor, International Sales Representative.

It all went beautifully. Desperately trying to look nonchalant, Kazakov accepted the card and began to interpret, badly, the conversation between Misha and me. I lit up the remaining Kent, held out the pack to the mark, pretending I didn't realise it was empty, and was genuinely sorry for the lad who was left panting for the rare treat.

My English was easily good enough to pass muster in that company, and halfway through the evening Kazakov began to write down all those cool English idioms I was using. 'Ian,' he'd ask earnestly, 'did you say "bugger me sideways" or "bugger me sideway"?'

The difficult part was not to burst out laughing, especially when Misha would say things like 'Kazakov, ask him if he's a homosexual.' 'Really, Misha, what kind of question is that? Americans don't answer questions like that.' 'This one will. Go on, ask.'

'Arr you gomosexual, Ian?' 'No, but what makes you ask, you handsome devil you?' Kazakov translated my reply as best he could, and Misha explained, 'It's just that our papers say that all Americans are pederasts.'

It was a pun since, as you remember, besides its original meaning 'pederast' is used in Russian as a general term of abuse, not much stronger than the English 'bastard'. Straining not to let on that I understood Russian, I turned so crimson that later Misha said he feared I'd have a stroke.

I survived; Kazakov left; and we began to plan the next session, this time at Valeriy's flat. In his capacity as director of the show, Misha assigned the roles.

Kramer, who actually looked Western, was to play another American, a wealthy industrialist. I was to act as a rowdy American drunk, which was type-casting if you ever saw it. Valeriy, whose house was full of Western trinkets he had acquired in Paris, was cast as a black marketeer looking to buy a consignment of American chewing gum. My Russian girlfriend Natasha was, with a singular lack of imagination, assigned to play my Russian girlfriend Natasha. Ritsky, who alone among us had a car, was to be our driver.

Kazakov showed up on the dot. Ten minutes later Kramer and I made our entry, with Kramer ceremoniously presenting to Valeriy the Remington shaver he had borrowed from the recipient half an hour earlier. At the sight of that princely gift, Kazakov's eyes lit up, he threw manners to the wind and asked 'Richard' if he happened to have another shaver he could spare. Or anything else along the same lines. Kramer expressed his regrets so profusely that even Kazakov felt uncomfortable. The evening was off to a flying start.

Russians commonly believe that foreigners can't hold liquor and, conforming to that stereotype, I pretended to be rat-arsed after two shots of vodka. I even slapped Kazakov around for the sake of verisimilitude. He took his punishment meekly, not daring to strike back at a representative of the decadent West.

Eventually the conversation veered towards political matters, and Kazakov, who was getting legless, said a few disloyal things about the future that worked. However, he sobered up somewhat when I began to recruit him for the CIA, again catering to the common notion that all foreign visitors were somehow employed by that outfit. Kazakov didn't give me a definite yes but neither did he give me an unequivocal no, which gave Natasha the cue she had been waiting for.

She took Kazakov out into the kitchen and said, 'Mitia, not every person is what he or she appears to be on the surface. I, for example, am an officer in the KGB, and I must say I feel disappointed with some of the statements you've seen fit to utter this evening.'

In fact, some of the statements Kazakov had seen fit to utter that evening would have qualified him for at least a fiver in a camp. And his benevolent hesitation when being recruited by a CIA agent was a clear-cut violation of Article 1 of the Criminal Code, High Treason, worth at least a tenner, possibly even capital punishment.

Kazakov's hazel eyes turned even more bovine than God had originally made them. He slumped in his chair, while Natalie pressed on: 'You realise of course that I could destroy your life at this point. The only reason I'm not going to do that – yet – is that I find you attractive as a man.'

Like a drowning man clutching at a straw, Kazakov reached for her breast, ready to do anything it took to get into her good books. But Natasha pushed his hand away. 'Not now please, not while I'm working. And speaking of work, there's one thing you can do for me.' Kazakov's face showed willingness to jump out of the window, if that would make the whole wretched incident go away.

'You see, comrade' said Natalie, all business now. 'We've been keeping track of this gang of degenerates for a long time, but so far we've been unable to nail them. I want you – darling – to start sending me written reports of their activities every day. I shall ring you up soon to arrange for a drop.'

Kazakov agreed to cooperate, but claimed he didn't have a phone. 'Don't lie to me, dear,' smiled Natalie in that sexy way of hers. 'You know I can find out in ten minutes flat.'

A few minutes later Kazakov left, his walk unsteady, his cheeks deadly green. We waited an hour, and then Natalie dialled his number. 'You see, darling,' she cooed the moment he answered the phone, 'it didn't take long.' She hung up without waiting for a reply.

By that time we were all running the risk of laughter-induced hernia, but the vote on any subsequent activities was split. I was in favour of collecting a few of his written reports on our subversiveness. Misha was dead-set against it as he feared that Kazakov could just be stupid enough to top himself. Finally Misha prevailed and the meeting was adjourned.

When Misha got home at three in the morning, he found his mother and grandmother, neither of whom was in the habit of staying up late, sitting on the sofa next to the phone, looking grim. 'My God, what happened?' Misha was genuinely concerned.

'What happened is that your friend Kazakov has been ringing all night. He sounds incoherent and keeps muttering that you're all in mortal danger. He said to ring him no matter how late you got in.' 'Oh, pay no attention to him,' laughed Misha. 'He's simply drunk, that's all.'

He dialled the number, and Kazakov answered on the first ring. 'Misha,' he announced with the pathos so characteristic of his ilk, 'the sword of Damocles is hanging over our heads. I have been coerced into the employ of the KGB…'

Misha didn't let him finish. 'Oh, you mean Natalie is up to her old tricks again? Ian and I don't know what to do with that girl. Every time she's had a few, she pretends to be a KGB recruiter. Can't take her anywhere.' Kazakov was thus saved by the bell, having proved there was a *ne-nash* strain to his character somewhere.

There were a few other meetings, and finally Kazakov asked if Richard and Ian would terribly mind attending a friendly dinner with the other students in his class. They had all chipped in to provide a repast worthy of our refined American palates. We didn't mind in the least, and the whole gang went along for the ride. This time we decided to record the meeting for posterity, and Valeriy slipped into his briefcase the miniature tape recorder he had bought in Paris.

Ritsky drove us there in his creaky *Pobeda*, and a great time was had by all. The good boys and girls of the Moscow District Institute gave us *pelmeni* and vodka, with Mitia wagging a finger at me: 'No vodka for you, Ian. Not after vot you deed lust time.'

By way of cultural exchange Kramer and I sang *We Shall Overcome* and *Down By the Riverside*. Our hosts responded by putting a lit candle on the table and delivering a sugary rendition of Pasternak's *A Candle Burning on the Desk*. As the evening got in full swing and the atmosphere relaxed, Kramer and I took advantage of the God-like status foreigners enjoyed in Russia by getting friendly with the two prettiest girls. In short, it was a lovely evening in every respect.

Eventually, however, it was time to say good-bye to our hospitable hosts and to go into the finale we had rehearsed beforehand. We all walked to Ritsky's *Pobeda*, everybody but the two pseudo-Americans got in, and I shook Kazakov's hand.

'I'd like to thank you for a most delightful time,' I said in the purest Russian to be heard east of Kiev. Kazakov's jaw dropped and he turned to Kramer as the last resort. He was in for another shock.

'I too would like to thank you from the bottom of my heart.' A Russian Dr Higgins would have placed Kramer's diction somewhere between Gorky and Herzen Streets. 'And do convey our gratitude to your female classmates.'

We jumped into the car and Ritsky floored the accelerator, blowing exhaust fumes at the frozen group in our wake. All the characters looked as if they were re-enacting the celebrated silent scene from Gogol's *Inspector General*.

When we got back to Valeriy's flat, Polsky immediately dialled the scene of our conquest. Kazakov picked up the phone and, without any preamble, went into an obscene, if forgivable, litany. 'You wanker, you dickhead, you shit-eating…'

'Hey, hold on a second,' interrupted Polsky indignantly, puffing up his well-padded cheeks. 'Why are you abusing me just because my American friends felt called upon to learn a few Russian phrases as a courtesy to their hosts?'

Kazakov would have none of that: 'You wanker, you dickhead, you shit-eating…' At that point Kramer took over the phone. 'Listen, Dmitry,' he said in English. 'But that's exactly what happened. Just like Mike said, Ian here and I had been rehearsing those phrases for a week before the party. So,' he switched back into Russian, 'who are calling a wanker, you worm?'

He hung up and we spent the rest of the night listening to the recording of the party, which was surprisingly good quality, and drinking in a most un-American way. Valeriy still has the tape but, now that he's angry with me, I'll probably never hear it again.

A week later I bumped into Kazakov in the street and we had the friendly chat of two actors in a successful play that had just closed. The chat was conducted in Russian, and Kazakov said he just couldn't get used to my speaking in that language. He admitted the prank had been masterly and only wanted to ask one question:

'Those cool American expressions you were using? Ones I kept writing down? Were they for real or did you make them up?' 'The real McCoy, old man.' I felt he was in need of reassurance. 'Completely on the level. Wear them in good health.'

7

Another member of that narrow circle was Zhenia Kapman, a top student at our German-language department. That took some doing as Zhenia was blind from birth. He lived with his girlfriend Valia whose heart was bigger than her body, which was saying a lot. She looked after Zhenia without ever complaining and was effusive about his amorous stamina which, according to her, wasn't so much hampered as enhanced by his disability.

A jazz fanatic to the point of madness, Zhenia never turned down a request for his party trick: humming an accurate reproduction of a whole Dixieland band. He was also an excellent harmonica player, which talent he had parlayed into profitable moonlighting with Mosfilm.

Every other film produced by that state monopoly was about the war. Most of those featured the obligatory German soldier playing the harmonica when not busy torturing Soviet babies. And most of those performances were dubbed by Zhenia, who had an inexhaustible repertoire of Nazi songs.

He often rehearsed them in the men's lavatory on our third floor, much to the displeasure of one of the German-language professors. As that old lady had escaped from Nazi Germany in the nick of time, she was loath to hear *Horst Wessel* played over and over again. But though she found Zhenia's renditions to be physically painful, she could do nothing to stop him as she couldn't go into the men's loo. That's why, knowing we were friends, she'd often ask me to act as her agent. 'Please tell that *dummkopf*,' she'd plead, 'that if he doesn't stop immediately I'll report him to the dean.'

Zhenia had developed his own way of dealing with blindness. Though he wore dark glasses, he hardly ever used his long white cane, relying instead on his infallible senses to keep him from bumping into obstacles. Actually, those senses weren't as infallible as all that. He once fell off an underground platform, and was only pulled out seconds before the train arrived.

Being in perpetual denial, Zhenia would say things like, 'I haven't seen Misha for three days,' or 'Whose red *Volga* is that, parked outside?' At the same time he wasn't averse to milking his disability for all it was worth, saying things that sighted people wouldn't have got away with – and eliciting similar remarks in return.

'I'm going to have a career in the KGB after I get my degree,' he once confided in me. 'People think they can say anything in my presence, just because I'm blind. Well, I'll show those bastards…' To Zhenia 'bastards' included all sighted people with, we hoped, the possible exception of his close friends.

Once two of the 'bastards' justified Zhenia's low opinion of the sighted majority. During the Six-Day War, he burst into his favourite hang-out, the *Molodiozhnoye* jazz club, screaming, 'Hooray! Hooray! Our tanks are approaching Gaza!' As the Soviet Union had been supporting the Arabs, two of the Soviet patriots present took exception to the pronoun 'our' and the general spirit of jubilation. They dragged Zhenia out into the courtyard and beat him up savagely, no doubt feeling that every haymaker they landed on a defenceless blind man was striking a blow for the future that worked.

Zhenia was a slim man of about 5'5" whose pockmarked face was of indeterminate age and ethnicity, a condition I've often observed among blind people. In his late twenties at the time, he could have passed for 50. And, though Jewish on both sides of his family, Zhenia could easily claim to be anything else. As I once found out, he often parlayed that ability into material gain, not only his own but also his friends'.

It was yet another bitterly cold winter and Muscovites were all wearing fur hats with earflaps down, fluffy scarves wrapped around their faces and layers of clothing under their heavy overcoats. That made us look like a nation of brown bears, but even those four-legged animals would have found it hard to negotiate the sheet ice covering every pavement – while dodging icicles falling down from the roofs.

Some of those projectiles were two feet long and ten inches in diameter, which made them good to avoid.

As everything else in Russia, winter clothing, especially fur hats, was in short supply. Thus those hats acted as status symbols, ranging from patrician mink for 150 roubles to plebeian rabbit for 12. No one who was anyone would have stooped below nutria. I myself never rose above a succession of rock-bottom rabbits, as I was so absent-minded that every winter I'd leave at least one hat behind on a bus. Finding a replacement was never easy and I often had to brave Moscow frosts wearing an inadequate cloth cap worn over a heavy scarf protecting my ears from an otherwise guaranteed frostbite.

It was during one of those cold spells that Zhenia asked me what kind of fur hat I had. 'None actually,' I admitted ruefully. 'How come?' 'Lost it. You know how I am.' 'Now that was a stupid thing to do.' Zhenia liked to state the bleeding obvious.

'You'll end up like Van Gogh, missing an ear. But not to worry. If you have twelve roubles on you, we can go to any fur shop and buy you one. You're size fifty-nine, aren't you, big-headed bastard that you are?'

I laughed with the bitterness that only a fellow Russian would have understood. 'You a tooth fairy, or a magician? How are you going to pull a rabbit hat out of a shop when not a single counter in the city displays one?'

'Sasha, Sasha, Sasha,' reproached Zhenia. 'You have no faith in your friends. I've done this a million times. Come on. Let's go.'

Not knowing what to expect, I led Kapman to the fur shop in Stoleshnikov Lane and pointed him towards a pretty salesgirl with smudged mascara disfiguring her baby-blues. 'One twelve-rouble rabbit hat, please. Size fifty-nine,' said my friend nonchalantly.

Kapman was fortunate not to be able to see the contemptuous smile that made the girl's face look rather less pretty. 'Which planet are you from, comrade?' she asked rudely. 'Can't you see... oops, I mean, don't you know that we hardly ever have those things?'

'But you are a fur shop?' asked Kapman who liked to dot all the t's and cross all the i's. 'Yes we are.' 'You are a fur shop and yet you have no fur hats.'

The girl's voice effortlessly went from ennui to irritation. 'That's right, comrade. We're a fur shop and yet we have no fur hats. Will there be anything else?'

By contrast, Zhenia's voice was deadpan. 'I'd like to see the manager please.' 'A whole lot of good that will do you. Well, all right. Pal Palych!?!' shouted the girl who by then had had enough of us.

Pal Palych, a bald fiftyish man whose face looked liked a blob of butter propped up on top of a giant jumper-clad ball, appeared instantly, no doubt smelling trouble. 'What can I do for you, comrade?' Talking to a blind man, he was making an effort to sound polite.

'One twelve-rouble rabbit hat, please. Size fifty-nine,' repeated Zhenia affably, turning his whole body in the direction of the manager's high-pitched voice. 'Sorry, comrade. Didn't get our supply this month. Try us in April. Or in May.'

'You sure you don't have just one, somewhere?' Zhenia was still calm and collected. 'Sorry,' repeated the manager as he turned to go back to his office.

'Right,' said Zhenia, taking a step back. Suddenly a horrible convulsion distorted his face, white foam appeared in the corners of his mouth, his whole body began to shudder like a *Pobeda* that wouldn't start, his fingers curled each at its own angle, and he screamed louder than I'd ever heard anyone scream indoors: 'Thieves!!! Robbers!!! Jewboys!!! One thief on top of another!!! Nothing but blood-sucking thieving Yids!!!'

That last accusation was rich coming from someone named Kapman, but then his audience didn't know Zhenia's surname. He then went into a shamanistic dance, ending up on the floor, frothing at the mouth and jerking his limbs in uncoordinated directions.

'Christ killers!!!' he bellowed, showing a well-tuned psychological insight. 'D'you know who I am?!? I burnt in my tank in the battle of Rzhev! I lost my eyes protecting kikes like you!!! Should've let Hitler finish the job!!! Bloody Yids!!!' Zhenia was actually born in the year of that historic battle, but his face, as I've mentioned before, was ageless.

His audience were stunned, and so was I. The manager and his employee, neither of whom looked Jewish, carefully helped Kapman to his feet, as if handling a precious statue. 'Please, comrade, please,' implored Pal Palych, 'everything will be all right. You'll be fine, just please calm down…'

Calm down Zhenia did, instantly. 'Right,' he said as if nothing had happened. 'One twelve-rouble rabbit hat, please. Size fifty-nine.'

'Well, you see, comrade,' the manager sounded nervous and contrite, 'we really, really don't have any today. Wait,' he begged hastily as Zhenia produced a grimace that looked even more awful than the one before.

'Just come tomorrow. I promise we'll sort it out, comrade. As God is my witness,' he added in a most un-Soviet way.

Throughout this whole scene I felt like fading into the wallpaper, thinking that losing my ears to frostbite would have been the easier option. But the manager was as good as his word. The next day I stopped by the shop and walked out wearing my new hat. Everyone in the store was polite to the point of servility, asking after my friend's health.

A fortnight later I lost my fur-lined gloves, a loss almost as irreplaceable – and potentially as perilous – as the loss of a hat.

'How come your hands are so cold?' asked Kapman as we greeted each other at the university. 'Lost my gloves,' I answered unthinkingly before I could stop myself.

'Buy yourself another pair,' suggested Zhenia. 'I can help, as you well know.' I assured my friend that no help was necessary. I'd wear my father's spare gloves.

'As you wish,' frowned Kapman. As far as he was concerned, the sighted were an ungrateful bunch.

8

And then there was Kostia, my last friend in Russia. He came from a family of minor nobility, made famous by his nineteenth-century ancestor. Though the ancestor was a hero of 1812, it wasn't his valour that made his name known to every Russian.

For Kostia's ancestor later became chief of Nicholas I's secret police. In that capacity he exchanged lively letters with Pushkin, telling him in an avuncular fashion to toe the line – or else. Pushkin, though a rebel, replied in the fawning tone one adopts automatically when discoursing with the chief of the Russian secret police. The correspondence was conducted in French, the official language of the time.

However, when he needed to, Pushkin could easily switch into Russian. That he did, for example, when writing that most lyrical

Russian poem, *I Remember That Wondrous Moment, You Appeared Before My Eyes*. Dedicated to his neighbour Anna Kern, the poem was standard fare for all school children.

Good as the poem was, a couple of months later Pushkin scaled the real heights of the Russian language by writing to his friend Sobolevsky: 'Scatterbrain! I have received your letter and you write nothing about the 2000 roubles I owe you, but write instead about Mme Kern whom last night, by the mercy of God, I fucked.' As a young man, I often wondered how the same object could inspire such different sentiments within such a short time. When I grew older I stopped wondering.

Kostia's name was a sure ice breaker. But as he approached the end of his course at the Institute of Foreign Languages, he eschewed the social benefits the name conferred by adopting his mother's maiden name, which was less pregnant with historical associations. It was a smart move. Even though aristocratic names were coming back into fashion, they still weren't universally acceptable to the men who ran such sought-after outfits as *Radio Moscow* or *Novosti* Press Agency.

Unlike my artistic friends whose drinking would have been regarded as heavy only by Western standards, Kostia drank for real, much in the manner of my erstwhile pal Anikeyev, my current friend Mikhailov and other true Russians.

Whenever Westerners comment on the root of that particular vice, they invariably bring up the harshness of Russian winters, the overall bleakness of Russian life and other incidentals. Such explanations miss the point entirely. They don't account, say, for someone like Khrushchev who, even in mid-summer and in the splendour of the Kremlin, always started his days with a tumblerful of vodka, tossed back in one go and followed by a bowl of rich borscht with marrow bones. (This breakfast idea somehow still hasn't caught on internationally.)

The Russians drink not for material but for spiritual reasons. Environment has nothing to do with their intake, and Feuerbach, with all his materialism, can go boil an egg as far as they're concerned. For many of them dipsomania is the sum total of their lives. For someone like Kostia, it wasn't, of course. He drank to alleviate the acute pain every *ne-nash* Russian feels when he realises that he is at irreconcilable odds with his own people.

Being an 'intel', Kostia had to rationalise boozing every night he got pissed, which is to say every night. 'Booze,' he'd say, pointing at a bottle of *Moskovskaya*, 'is our religion surrogate, our Holy Spirit.'

He'd 'suck in' his next glass (it was *infra dig* to drink a glass of vodka; one always 'sucked in a glass') and continue, 'Hell, it's more than a surrogate. It is our religion, something we worship but ultimately don't understand.'

An educated man, Kostia would support his point with historical references. His favourite was that, when in 988 the Grand Duke Vladimir was considering the choice of a monotheistic creed for his mostly pagan subjects, Islam was the front runner. What enabled the Greek Orthodox missionaries to snatch it at the wire was the Islamic injunction against alcohol. That would have been an intolerable hardship for the budding nation, declared the Grand Duke ('Drinking is the joy of Rus').

It's not that St Vladimir was a pisshead himself (he was, but that was beside the point). He simply realised that, without sharing mead with his cohort every day, he could never ensure their lasting loyalty and – extrapolating to the nation at large – the love of his subjects. Thus the primacy of booze over God became a uniquely Russian trait, which is regrettably ignored by every theological treatise I've read.

Even though he was in the habit of publicly raping captured enemy princesses, the Kievan ruler was justly canonised for this seminal contribution to religion. That's why even London boasts a statue to Vladimir, erected by the Ukrainian community to 'the ruler of the Ukraine'. (In reality, the Ukraine came into existence several centuries after that Scandinavian prince ruled Kievan Rus. Vladimir was as much the ruler of the Ukraine as Alaric was the Chancellor of Germany.)

Kostia cherished the tragic aspect of his boozing heritage, accentuating it as best he could. In a manner so characteristic of the young *ne-nash* who take their Turgenev seriously, he was at that time tragically in love with a medical student. The girl was well known, carnally, to everybody who was anybody in Moscow.

'No one understands Sveta,' he'd complain. 'Everybody just sleeps with her without exploring the crevices of her soul. But they are more interesting than even the crevices of her body. A whore she may be, but she's the Whore of Babylon, she's a Mary Magdalene, she is…'

'She's nuts, is what she is,' I'd object with my characteristic lack of sensitivity. 'You seem to forget that baby…' In point of fact, Kostia never did, and it was that incident that eventually made him part company with Sveta.

Once, during a visit to a morgue, a frequent foray in her chosen field, Sveta felt a sudden rush of sorrow over the corpse of a year-old baby. The darling corpse just lay there, waiting quietly its turn to move under the pathologist's knife. Before any such fate could befall the poor creature, Sveta picked the corpse up off the slab, put it under her coat, smuggled it out of the morgue and took it home.

There she went straight to bed and spent the night holding the baby to her breast, hoping that the warmth of her body would revive the child in a sort of perverse answer to Pygmalion. But resurrection failed to happen.

The next morning she woke up, smelled the formaldehyde and proved that she still had some vestige of sanity left by surreptitiously depositing the corpse into a garbage skip outside her house. Her mistake was to tell everybody she knew about that cathartic experience, with the immediate consequence that most of her friends began to give her a wide berth. Kostia too began to steer clear, which however didn't diminish his drunken effluvia one bit.

Without having reliable research data at my disposal, I can't say with certainty that mental disorders are more widespread in Russia than anywhere else. But they certainly appear to be: one sees obvious madmen everywhere one goes. Recent research bears this out: according to Russia's official statistics, 3.8 million Russians require constant psychiatric hospitalisation, while 14 million (10 percent of the population) need regular psychiatric help.

Not wishing to act as an amateur diagnostician, I won't even attempt to analyse the nature of this seeming pandemic of psychosis in Russia. However, one suspects the curve is skewed upwards by an inordinate incidence of drink-induced *delirium tremens*, that much feared 'white fever' of every Russian's nightmares. Be that as it may, a rambling 'psycho' was a permanent fixture of the Russian urban scene, and we all unfailingly followed Mikhailov's advice to me: 'When you see a madman, step aside.'

The occasion on which he delivered himself of that homespun wisdom was remarkable. There was another professor at our university who taught the art of literary translation and who was the only one of his colleagues Mikhailov could stomach.

The subject Prof. Lopatin taught enjoyed a status that it perhaps wouldn't have had in the West. Since throughout history many great Russian writers often haven't been allowed to publish their own work, they've had to keep body and soul together by translating someone else's. That has brought to bear on the art of translation the kind of talent that in the West wouldn't usually stoop to such a lowly task.

Pasternak, for instance, translated Shakespeare, Mandelstam Dante, Bunin Longfellow, and so forth. Their magnificent efforts have been formalised into a practicable theory of translation, which has enabled even lesser artists to score notable successes in that second-hand genre.

At our university it was taught as an academic subject and, when he was sober, Lopatin was perhaps the best instructor we had, if not the best translator. That distinction belonged to the handsome Armenian woman who had just produced a remarkably good *Alice in Wonderland* in which she had transformed Mock Turtle into 'Imitation Seal' to accommodate the vagaries of the Russian tongue. Lopatin fancied this Rubenesque colleague something rotten. Borrowing Gogol's phrase, he'd describe her to his students as 'a lady pleasant in every respect'. However, the lady didn't want to know, partly, one suspects, on account of Lopatin's drinking.

Unlike Mikhailov, who was merely a drunk, Lopatin was an alcoholic. That, in Yuri Ossipovitch's experience, made a hell of a big difference. 'A drunk, Sasha, drinks when he wants to. An alcoholic drinks even when he doesn't want to.'

A neat point, I thought, but academic since both groups drank non-stop anyway. The real difference, again an empirical observation only, lies in the amplitude of alcohol intake.

In order to figure out the psychological profiles of his blue-collar co-workers, the writer Benny Yerofeev described plotting amounts of alcohol consumed within a unit of time onto a graph with two axes. If someone had constructed such a Cartesian graph for Mikhailov or me, the resulting relief would have appeared as a slightly jagged horizon whose general elevation would have indicated rather serious drinkers.

In Lopatin's case, the graph would have resembled Himalayan peaks and troughs. That is a dead give-away of an alcoholic cautiously treading the level ground of sobriety most of the time and then suddenly soaring to an apex of a bender.

Unlike Mikhailov, who in his youth had done a mere fiver, 'child's time' in GULAG parlance, Lopatin had done a man-sized tenner and a half for 'espionage' (talking to an Englishman in the street). When I knew him he was a 'last-legger', camp jargon for someone who doesn't have much time left to live.

Those of us who attended his seminars knew a bender was coming when he'd start to bring a half-finished bottle of vodka into the classroom. From experience we knew that in another day or two his brilliance would give way to petulance, then to incoherence, and then he'd drop out of sight for a couple of weeks.

In his more incoherent moments, he'd pull a dirty rag out of the bottle right in front of the students, take a deep swig and offer the vodka around, seldom finding any takers. Then he'd openly make passes at the girls in the class, his taste running towards the heavier blondes (possibly because he was rejected by his dark-haired colleague). If gossip was to be trusted, those overtures were often received more favourably.

One day I had skipped the first two lectures and was running up the stairs past the faculty room, hoping that my late arrival would pass unnoticed. Suddenly I saw the back of a stark-naked man standing in the doorway. The back was stooped, densely covered with curly black hair and rather unappetising, but the aesthetic aspects of the apparition came to me only later. At that moment I was so startled by the sight that my thoughts resembled a kaleidoscopic chaos.

My first guess was that yet again someone had got caught shagging on the faculty-room table. But then I realised it was 11 o'clock in the morning, when the room wouldn't have offered the intimacy of a later time. My next thought was that there was a medical examination being conducted among our professors. But that thought was just as stupid, for no medic would have asked our faculty to strip in public.

The man turned, and I saw Lopatin's piercing eyes with the whites clearly visible both above and below the irises. He was muttering, 'Please... look... no microphones... you see... can't you see... I'm not wired... I'm no spy... please... let me go... please.' He was holding his hands up, making no attempt to cover up his dark-brown genitals.

It was then that Mikhailov emerged from the faculty room, grabbed my arm protectively and made his pronouncement about stepping aside when seeing a madman. He then dragged me away over my protestations that the man needed help.

We got drunker than usual that night. 'No one can help a last-legger, Sasha. That was the first thing we learned in the camps,' explained Mikhailov. 'When the *nash* really work a man over, there are no pieces left to pick up.'

Psychosis being so widespread in Russia, it became not only a popular charge levied against dissidents, but also a classic ruse of 'chemistry': malingering with the intent of avoiding arrest or conscription.

An artist friend of mine, for example, managed to stay out of both kinds of trouble by having learned the clinical picture of most psychiatric disorders so well that he regularly fooled even the sceptical Soviet shrinks. He'd check into an institution once a year or so (the only man I knew who did so of his own accord) to be re-certified. Thus he successfully avoided censure for his sizeable black-market dealings in icons, which he bought cheap, restored skilfully and then sold dear.

His stories about fellow inmates could fill a book provisionally titled *The Interesting People I Met in the Loony Bin*, but that's his book to write, not mine. One story, however, was so extraordinary that I have to tell it, stealing his thunder and risking his wrath.

He met a soft-spoken blue-collar chap named Fedia who was so quiet that he had been placed in the same ward as my friend. 'What are you in for?' was the typical conversation starter in the Serbsky Institute. Fedia's reply to that question impressed even my friend who thought he'd heard everything.

'I'm from Tula, see,' began Fedia. 'I work at a rifle factory there.' The second sentence was redundant as Tula is the centre of the small-arms industry, and Fedia's self-description could have come from almost anyone living there.

My friend braced himself for a dull afternoon, as Fedia continued. 'You know how you can have dreams? Like going to the moon or doing Sophia Loren between her tits? Well, my dream was to rob a bank.' Things were beginning to sound interesting.

'So I sit back and give it a think. First thing you need to rob a bank is a gun, right? Well, I didn't have no gun. It's like a shoemaker whose kids have no shoes. Assembling rifles every day. And no gun. So I start nicking parts out of the factory, screw by screw. I'm an assembly man, right? I know what it takes. After a couple of months I snatch enough to put a simple repeater together. And then I nick some ammo, no problem there.

'So I'm like ready, right? Am I, hell. You don't go to rob a bank with an untested weapon. What if it fails on you? So I draw a target on a piece of paper, walk to this forest not far from us, pin the target to an oak tree, take aim and bang! Bull's eye!

'I walk back home, thinking I'm ready to give it a go. And then I say to myself, hold on Fedia. It's one thing to hit a piece of paper, another to hit a man so he stays hit. Stopping power, right? How do I know my gun has it?

'So back to the forest I go, looking for a mushroom picker. It was October, right? The place was crawling with them. Sure enough, this cute little girl in an apron bends down to cut a cep stalk. I take aim between her plaits, bang! She's down.

'So back home I go, and I say to myself, hold on Fedia. You hit a sta... stationary target, right? But when you rob a bank, someone's got to be moving. Can you hit him? Back to the forest I go, right?

'Then there's another mushroom picker, walking fast. I take aim, lead him a bit, bang! Down he drops. I get back and I think, hold on Fedia. That was just one moving target. But what if you need to hit several one after another? Back to the forest I go...'

To cut a long story short, Fedia had killed 17 people before he felt he was adequately prepared for the big mission. Alas, the Interior troops, who sealed the whole area and caught him on the way to his final target practice, prevented him from fulfilling his dream. This case went unreported, as the papers were too busy covering the crime statistics in New York, that citadel of capitalist greed.

Kostia's reaction to my announcement that I was leaving was that of disbelief. 'Stop talking bollocks,' he advised, 'and suck in another glass.' Only documentary evidence in the shape of the exit visa convinced him I wasn't putting him on.

We had three weeks left before I stopped being a Russian. At the end of that time the two of us went for a farewell bash at *Peking*, then the only Chinese restaurant in Moscow. I thought it served the best food in our city, but luckily not many people shared that view. So we easily got a table in a cavernous, half-empty room with murals depicting Chinese communists firing Russian-made PPSh guns.

The waitress Tonia, a peroxide blonde shaped like a Steinway leg, knew us well. She respected Kostia's lean aristocratic posture, but had a few years earlier refused to go to bed with either or both of us because we were 'intel' wimps.

She came to the table, fully expecting our stock line 'Tonechka, make sure the rice is hot and the vodka is cold – not the other way around.' In that expectation she was disappointed, for the occasion was sad and we didn't feel like making glib jokes or indeed gorging ourselves.

'Never mind the food, Tonechka baby.' As I could never find the right tone of voice when talking to working-class girls, I usually tried to imitate theirs, unsuccessfully. That's probably why my earlier attempts on Tonia's virtue, along with many other similar attempts, had failed so miserably. 'Just bring us a bottle of vodka, a bottle of mineral water and some, you know, pickles. Okay, love?'

It wasn't okay, Tonia explained, not with the new regulations in place since yesterday. 'And what regulations might those be, flower?' Even as I spoke, my heart sank since I remembered that yet another anti-drunkenness drive had just been announced.

'No vodka without food, and even then no more than a hundred grams a snout,' explained Tonia impatiently. It was time for Kostia to put his aristocratic foot down and to show that the skill of dealing with help just might be genetically transmitted.

'Tonia,' he said in a sharp yet benevolent way. 'Food is no problem. You can bring us some shredded steak with mushrooms, and perhaps an order or two of wontons. But a hundred grams a snout is a joke I do not find in the least amusing. I'm saying goodbye to an old and dear friend, and you must find a way for me to do so properly.'

Tonia knew authority when she saw it. 'The regulations don't say nothing about wine,' she said, and Kostia reacted instantly. 'Right. So you can bring us two hundred grams of vodka and a bottle of Georgian dry white.'

The two beverages were consumed with a haste that belied the mournful seriousness of the situation, and it was time to talk to Tonia again. Kostia said he'd handle it.

'As you can tell, my dear,' he intoned with the haughty inflection that must have been a throw-back to Pushkin's time, 'my friend and I are perfectly sober and behaving in a reasonable, mature fashion...'

I couldn't wait any longer: 'Tonechka, love, we want more!'

Somehow, Tonia warmed up to that Dickensian plea but remained true to her duties while dropping a telling hint. 'I can't give you more. Not on this bill.'

With the mental sharpness honed at the best Moscow universities, we took the hint. 'Right,' we said in chorus. 'Let's settle this bill and start another. We'll have another two hundred, another bottle of white and one more order of dumplings.'

Tonia saw nothing wrong in that arrangement, which we subsequently repeated twice more, but skipping the wine. We were flush at my last pissup in Russia, and the evening went like a dream.

That was more than I could say about the farewell party at the airport two days later. The scene featured a silent girl wearing a stark white blouse and a face to match, Mama who was weeping so much she couldn't even say good-bye, and Papa whose face had suddenly acquired an uncharacteristic look of solemnity.

Mama was sobbing uncontrollably, I was holding her close, her tears mixing with mine, or maybe they were all hers, and I had just managed to hold mine in. Before the plane even took off I was desperately missing them all, and especially the little boy who at that time looked just like me and could already speak such beautiful Russian.

I was sure I'd never see any of them again, and was wondering whether their tangible suffering was worth my nebulous freedom. At that moment I was inclined to think it wasn't and cursed my unfeeling selfishness. But subsequent events have somewhat vindicated self-interest as an acceptable motive for our behaviour.

The little boy soon came to America with his mother, forgot his beautiful Russian and replaced it with intentionally demotic English. He then stopped being a child who disapproved of me and became a grown-up bent on proving that Oscar Wilde was wrong when saying that children eventually forgive their parents. His mother, my first wife, has become an internationally known professor of Russian at UCLA.

The white-faced girl joined me in the States and in due course we got a divorce after 11 years of happy but mutually unsatisfying marriage. (I could explain this seeming paradox, but if you are married you understand anyway, and if you're not you probably won't believe the explanation.)

And, to the dismay of my wife Penelope, about 25 years ago Papa began to come every year for stays ranging from a few weeks to three months, until he died at 92. Penelope didn't believe he came to visit his son. She maintained, not without *prima facie* evidence, that his sole purpose was to bug our friends with queries of how much money they made.

Only Mama didn't manage to give the lie to some of my macabre premonitions. She died without ever seeing her only son again. That happened merely a year before the post-glasnost government could have allowed her to come for a visit. Surrounded by the dingy concrete of Sheremetievo Airport that day, she must have sensed that the part of her life devoted to me – which is to say her life – was coming to an end.

'I'll write, Mama, I promise I'll write,' I kept repeating, aware of how grossly inadequate those words were, not finding better words, knowing there weren't any better words to find. 'I promise I'll write. It'll be okay, Mama. It'll be fine...'

It'll be fine, Mama. I'm only leaving for ever.

EPILOGUE
OR THE RIGHT TO EMIGRATION

1

'The wops ['*italiashki*'] are like our Gypsies,' declared Yefim, a burly, heavily tattooed thief from Odessa. 'They can't work or fight like us.'

I had been living in Rome for only a few weeks and hadn't formed my own opinion on the subject. Indeed I was amazed that Yefim had, what with his limited knowledge of the local mores and a weak frame of reference, at least as far as work was concerned.

Still, he may have been right for all I knew, even though I doubted it. Gypsies to me were the people who stole horses in Russian villages and sang lachrymose songs in Moscow restaurants. And Italians painted ceilings, wrote about the Inferno and sang Leoncavallo in opera houses. On second thoughts, Leoncavallo was lachrymose, too; so perhaps Yefim was on to something.

I had run into Yefim and his two flunkies in Rome where we and a few hundred other Russians lived while waiting for U.S. immigration papers to come through. The third wave of Russian emigration had just started, the first two having come in the wake of the 1917 revolution and the Second World War. That made us the first large group of ex-Russians brought up entirely under Soviet rule. Few if any of us had escaped the predictable effects of the future that worked.

The first batch of Roman, soon to be American, Russians included a few people like me – 'intel' pests annoying enough to throw out, not annoying enough to kill. The larger group consisted of common criminals, people whom the Soviets wanted to become someone else's headache (a stratagem refined by Castro). Back in Russia the two groups never mixed and typically weren't even aware of each other's existence. But in Rome the 'intels' and the thugs formed a close-knit community.

Rome was to us a limbo, harbouring wretched souls who had been jettisoned from the inferno but lacked the baptism of a U.S. visa to be admitted to paradise. The normal course of our lives was on hold, and so, it seemed, was our moral judgement.

So don't be surprised that I accepted Yefim's invitation to move with him, his girlfriend and two stooges into a three-bedroom flat in Viale Regina Marguerita, not too long a walk from, well, everything in Rome. The girlfriend's name was Inna. She played a bit role in my life before moving on to a lucrative career as a perfect Size 20 model with American makers of ready-to-wear dresses.

We lived on stipends generously provided by various refugee charities. Seventy thousand lire a month only amounted to about $115 in 1973, which explains the need for shared quarters. But what with a bottle of the cheapest brandy costing 800 lire, we had nothing to complain about. Each of us contributed 30,000 lire a month for rent and 10,000 or so for petrol (we had all chipped in to buy a $150 heap). The rest was spent on brandy occasionally accompanied by food.

Crumbling moral standards notwithstanding, I was ill at ease with my flatmates. They spoke in socially unacceptable accents, threw up right on the floor and never cleaned up. By contrast, I spoke a clipped Moscow Russian, a couple of other languages, and always made it to the loo in the nick of time. In addition to their hygienic habits, I was more than a little bothered by the boys' chequered pasts.

Yefim, for example, bragged that on his last day in Russia he had murdered his mistress, having been unable to think of any other way to ensure her lasting fidelity. Grisha, who had known Yefim all his life, validated the story, but added confidentially that Yefim only thought he was tough. In fact, after crossing some really tough men back in Odessa, he had been made to fellate two of them by way of punishment. Nonetheless, I was sufficiently impressed with Yefim's rigorous views on conjugal fidelity to steer clear of Inna and even refrain from casting furtive glances at her massive legs.

Grisha, at 50 or so the oldest of us all, lamented that his best days were behind him. That admission was as obviously true as it was superfluous in view of his stooping frame, red road-map face and grey hair.

'You should've known me when I was your age,' he once confided in me. 'I could carry a bucket of water on my dick and was the best stopper in Odessa.' I didn't ask for translation, having learned by that time that 'stopper' meant 'mugger' in their parlance. But I did ask him to be more specific about the first part of his claim. 'Did you have to tie it up in a knot?' Clearly, I didn't know what being a real man meant. The pugilist Mark completed the triumvirate. Having been discharged from the Soviet Merchant Marine for uncouthness, he had become a professional boxer. (Officially there were no professional athletes in Russia, but the good ones got paid unofficially.)

His face resembled a pensive paperweight and bore ample proof that in the ring, or during his subsequent career as Yefim's enforcer, he hadn't counted primarily on his defensive skills. Mark was a taciturn man who knew about 100 Russian words but frequently used just those 10 that appear only in the unabridged dictionaries.

The boys treated me as an oddity, but a useful one. I could speak English and French and taught them, at their request, some Italian words they needed to conduct meaningful discourse with the aboriginal population.

After each lesson they'd go out into the street and try their newly acquired vocabulary on any Italian male who wasn't quick enough to cross the street before they grabbed him: '*Brutto, cretino, stupido, porca Italiana, capito?*' The Italians always acknowledged understanding by nodding, on average, three times.

Having to learn so many foreign words wasn't easy for the boys. And they couldn't get their heads around the fact that different Italian words, even if they had phonetic similarities, could mean different things.

Shortly after we moved into the flat, the landlord's wife came to ask if we needed anything. She was a pleasant plump lady at the cusp of old age, when Italian women begin to allow themselves to go to pot.

Actually, there was one thing the boys needed: an extra key. It fell upon Yefim to communicate that request to the matron. 'Signora,' he said politely. '*Una chiavarte. Per favore.*' As the lady's face evinced terror, I quickly corrected my friend. 'You mean *chiave*, not *chiavarte*. *Chiave* means "key". *Chiavarte* means "fuck" '

Yefim had a short fuse. 'What the hell's the difference?' he growled and turned back to the woman. '*Chiave, chiavarte*, it's all the same shit! Give!!!' he shouted. The lady fled at a speed one wouldn't have expected from someone her age and weight.

Yefim had been right in one respect: Romans didn't fight. In the five months I spent there I saw only one altercation between the natives, and even that really was a pugilistic parody. The two combatants bent backwards, tapped each other a few times with the tips of their fingers and walked into a café together.

By contrast, you should have seen the faces of the passers-by who witnessed a fight between Mark and another Russian in front of *Pensione Lamarmara*. Mark kept ramming the other man's face into the *Pensione*'s wall, and blood was gradually transforming the stucco into a Kandinsky-style painting, not that Mark would have been able to identify the exact visual idiom. The Italians were viewing the scene, common where we came from, with expressions that suggested they had never seen anything like that before, hoped they'd never see it again, and didn't much care about that genre of art.

I would be insincere if I didn't admit that such scenes added an element of physical fear to my feelings about the boys. In fact, though the thought of looking for less disreputable accommodation had crossed my mind a couple of times, I had dismissed it as the boys wouldn't have understood. So, since beating them was out of the question, I joined them.

My contribution wasn't limited to linguistics. Drawing on the experience amassed during my innocent childhood and more sinful adolescence, I told the boys stories adapted from all kinds of books ('…and then Natasha blew Pierre Bezouhov like a suction pump…'). I also settled all conflicts with the landlord and spoke to the cops when the need arose. Actually, the need arose often because we were all bad, and frequently drunk, drivers.

We had purchased the moribund Volkswagen in Piazza Spagna, which featured the famous Steps and, in those days, an auto exchange an American would have taken for a junk yard. Considering the reasonable price of the vehicle, it was hardly surprising that it came with expired Dutch plates and no registration papers or insurance. None of us had a driving licence, but that was no problem since Italian cops could be fooled by any piece of paper in Russian: an old laundry receipt, a doctor's prescription and so forth.

What was a problem was our driving, which caused half a dozen accidents, mostly minor ones. Once Grisha went into the back of a tiny Fiat 500, in which, as we soon found out, an off-duty policeman was taking his pregnant wife to hospital.

The boys jumped out to chastise the 'Gypsy', whose occupation they hadn't guessed, for not having got his car out of the way in good time. The offender didn't join battle, choosing instead to stay in his locked car, speaking into a walkie-talkie.

As the boys were letting the air out of his tyres, rubber screeched all around us. A second later we were surrounded by futuristically blinking blue lights and a dozen of the offender's colleagues led by an officer.

'*Arabo*?' asked the officer, misled by the dark hair of my companions. That was a loaded question, as barely a week had elapsed since the PLO had had some fun with machine pistols at Fiumicino airport, mowing down 20 people. It was grovelling time.

'*Signor Coronel*,' I began, but before I could finish Yefim pushed me aside. '*Si*,' he confirmed with gusto, '*Terroristi Arabi! Memore Aeroporto Fiumicino? Terroristi Arabi, polizia Italiana, rat-tat-tat*,' and he mimicked the action of spraying bullets about him.

The cops took no chances. They levelled their Berettas at us, slapped handcuffs on our wrists and took us to a police station. Luckily, the officer on duty must have had prior experience dealing with Soviet refugees of conscience. Or else he simply was more perspicacious than the others.

'*Russi*?' he asked before we uttered a word. '*No, Signor*,' I lied. '*No Russi. Americani.*' That surprised the cop and he took a closer look. '*Russi*,' he reiterated with certainty.

I don't know what kind of deal the refugee charities had struck with the Italian authorities, but they always let us go, as they did on that and a few other occasions. Such as the time when Mark confused the brake and accelerator pedals and drove the car through a beautifully designed shop window. He couldn't even back out into the street because the Volkswagen stalled upon impact, dying right in the middle of the frantically gesticulating owners and patrons.

'*Porchi Italiani*,' Mark greeted the crowd as he got out. He then tried to translate for their benefit a popular Russian expression which, to his audience's consternation, came out as '*chiavarte tei Mame.*' Mark proceeded to minister to his motor and was so successful that he managed to drive away before the police arrived. He was intercepted 10 minutes later and, in another hour or so, let go.

If you're getting the impression that the boys learned nothing from me but a few broken Italian words, you're wrong. That's probably my fault; I haven't told you about some of the Moscow pranks I taught them. Such as the old shop-window trick (not the one I've just told you about; that one was inadvertent).

Sauntering down Via Veneto or some other smart street, we'd select a shop where the clerks sported Armani suits and the customers talked without using their hands. They wouldn't let us in, of course, what with our unkempt visages, disreputable clothes and cask-strength breaths. But thanks to the large windows, we didn't have to go in to make a nuisance of ourselves.

We'd flatten our bearded faces and unwashed hands against the glass and slide down, leaving murky trails on the shiny surface. Hilarious as it seemed to us, the customers usually didn't like that performance one bit. And the clerks, who liked it even less, probably wanted to run out and chase us away. However, they invariably suppressed that urge after one look at Mark.

Yefim was the only one of us who ever got his comeuppance, which improved his view of Italian masculinity. You see, the boys used the services of the young ladies who lined up in a dark alley behind Terme Caracalla. The girls wore risqué outfits of transparent halter tops, mini skirts with manifestly no knickers underneath, and high boots. They were less desirable than the Sophia Loren look-alikes in Via Veneto, but by charging 20 thousand lire a throw those ladies had priced themselves out of the boys' market.

The Terme Caracalla girls were cheap in more ways than one, and the boys often sought brief solace in their mercenary embrace. Yefim wasn't immune to their charms either, even though he was the only one of us who had a live-in receptacle for his affection. He often went as far as to express his contempt for me after yet another refusal to follow suit. 'Hey, I'll pay, eh?' he'd say. 'What's the matter, can't you get it up no more?'

In fact, at a hormonally active age of 25 my protracted celibacy was sheer torture. There was little I could do about it though, for the only Russian woman I had access to was Inna, and she was off-limits – even though something in her manner suggested she wasn't indifferent to the big-city boy who was marginally sleeker than her swain.

Italian women were inaccessible, for I looked like nothing on earth, didn't even have enough money to buy a girl a drink and, most important, didn't have enough Italian to chat a woman up. As I had found out, one didn't get far by winking at a girl, saying '*belissima*', '*molto bene*' and poking the index finger of one hand through the circle formed by the thumb and index finger of the other.

Unfortunately, however, the Terme Caracalla beauties offended both my olfactory sensitivity and fiscal prudence. Yefim had neither problem; the first because his own odour overpowered everybody else's, the second because he supplemented his income by prodigious shoplifting. That was yet another concession to his idea of masculinity I simply wouldn't make.

That evening he began courtship in his usual forthright manner. '*Puta*,' he yelled from the car window. '*Quanta costa?*' The question was superfluous since all the ladies there had the same rate, 5,000 lire, about $8.

Having quickly come to terms, the 'puta' entered the van and sat down next to Yefim on the bench front seat. The lady's first act was putting her left leg over the back of the seat, the pungent result of which indiscretion made me wince and roll down my window. Yefim wasn't similarly deterred, and the couple consummated their union with what appeared to me adequate ballistic proficiency if singular lack of finesse.

Everything would have ended beautifully had Yefim, in a Freudian act of post-coital aggression, not attempted to push the girl out of the van without paying. Her shrieks brought to the scene three of her financial managers who dragged Yefim out into the dust, kicked him for a few minutes, yanked his wallet out of his pocket, honestly took just the due amount and left. Mercifully, they hadn't noticed me cowering in the back seat.

All this gaiety came to an abrupt end when the U.S. Embassy informed the boys that their visas had been granted and they were to leave for New York in three days. That didn't leave them much time for the serious business left to attend to: some last-minute shoplifting, packing, shaving – and settling the lease.

Yefim, not having known or perhaps cared how long the Roman holiday would last, had signed a one-year lease. Though we had lived in the flat for only three months, the landlord, who looked like a baddie from an early Fellini film, demanded we pay at least half the rent for the outstanding nine months.

By way of counter-proposal, the boys offered to perpetrate acts of unspeakable ghastliness on his flat and indeed person. Their sudden eloquence and insistence on providing the minutest details of the forthcoming retribution were straining the halting French into which, my Italian not being up to the task, I was interpreting their remarks (*'Nous allons emmerder votre plafond'* was the surreal end of a broad spectrum of threats).

Finally, an equitable deal was struck. The landlord would drop his outrageous demands, the boys wouldn't molest his flat or his body. As a gesture of good faith, Yefim tore up his own copy of the lease, then the landlord's – with which the latter had parted somewhat reluctantly.

The next day I took the boys to the airport and saw them take off on an Alitalia flight. They hardly spoke to me on the way, sensing that our association was about to come to an end. They talked among themselves though, and I overheard some snippets of a conversation between Mark and Grisha. The subject was New York's 'blackarses'.

'They only think they are tough,' pronounced Mark. A discerning listener could detect a promise in his tone. 'Maybe they really are,' cautioned Grisha. 'We'll see about that.' Mark's inflection shifted from promise to a distinct longing.

Subsequent events showed that Grisha's common sense, born of a long life in which nothing had ever come easy, was closer to the truth than Mark's pugnacious optimism. Shortly after arriving in New York, Mark got a job as cab driver. He was judged to be amply qualified on the strength of his embryonic English, uncertain driving skills and complete ignorance of the geography of any of the five boroughs.

On his first day of employment, a black gentleman asked to be taken to Brooklyn and Mark inadvertently drove him to the Bronx instead. If you know those parts (or have read *The Bonfire of the Vanities*), you'll be aware that the Bronx is easier to drive into than out of, which Mark was to find out empirically.

Having spent an hour proving that the Möbius strip isn't the only possible representation of infinity, Mark realised they were going nowhere slowly. However, innate bashfulness prevented him from sharing that insight with his fare, who took another 15 minutes to come to the same realisation.

When he did come to it, he demanded that Mark stop the car. He then got out, banged the door and began to walk away without as much as attempting to pay the $17.50 on the meter. Mark, though remiss in his knowledge of some other basics of his new profession, knew for a fact that such an action was unfair. He jumped out of the car and, drawing on his scanty reserves of English, demanded an immediate restitution.

The negro explained, reasonably, that he didn't feel called upon to pay anything as he had been fraudulently taken in a direction diametrically opposite to the one he had specified. 'In that case,' snarled Mark, stretching his English past a breaking point, 'I'm going to kick your black ass $17.50's worth.' That he tried to do, but the victim refused to roll over and play dead. Instead he brandished a gun, mercifully only a .22, and put five rounds into Mark's barrel chest.

It's a tribute to the latter's vitality and ox-like strength that, after a month in intensive care and a prolonged convalescence afterwards, he pulled through. Unfortunately, the lesson Mark learned from the incident was as light on common sense as it was heavy on the negative emotions concerning people of objectionable nativity or race.

Barely a month after his discharge from hospital, another negro bumped into Mark on the N Line going from Manhattan to Brooklyn. By that time Mark's English had improved to a point where he could enunciate 'I'll kick your black ass' coherently enough to elicit a quick response. The gentleman stepped on Mark's foot and punched him on the jaw with a knuckleduster. My erstwhile flatmate ended up with a broken jaw, sprained ankle and a sneaky suspicion that maybe Grisha had been right after all.

At the time though, these and many similar tribulations were quite some time ahead, and all in all the boys were looking forward to seeing their motherland-to-be. My own feelings about their departure were mixed. On the positive side, once the novelty appeal had worn off, their company began to bother me, and I was glad to see the last of them. Also, Inna still had a few more weeks left in Rome, and something in her eyes suggested the unspoken promise that I was about to be cured of my protracted celibacy.

On the other hand, there was no way I could afford to rent my own flat. Thus I had to embark on a bothersome search of alternative accommodation and, ergo, new alliances.

My solution was to look up the few 'intels' I had known back in Moscow, reviving the friendships that had suffered considerably, though not irreparably, from the company I had been keeping.

The intels were broadly divided into several social classes, depending on the number of icons they had managed to get out of Russia. The initial allowance was two per person. Even though really valuable pieces were off limits, this could add up to a nice reinforcement of our stipends. So the very first batch of Russo-Roman intels, those who had left before mid-1973, were sitting pretty.

Then, by July, when I left, the Soviets had cut the allowance down to one icon, thus creating a lower middle class. I belonged to that group even though most of the proceeds I realised from the sale of my icon went towards the debt I had incurred scraping together the requisite 1,000 roubles to pay for the exit visa. Half of that amount went towards renouncing Soviet citizenship. This I had to pay even though, as I pointed out to the cashier, it was illogical to have to pay for giving something away.

The third category included the lumpen proletariat, those unfortunate souls who left a couple of months after I did, when the Soviets had slapped a total ban on the export of icons. These paupers had to make do with trying to flog Soviet cameras and tins of caviar in the 'round' fleamarket at Piramide.

Perched on the highest rung of the social ladder were intel aristocrats, the enterprising individuals who had found a way to smuggle out a number of icons well in excess of any official quota. At the very top of the upper class sat Pasha Varlamov, a capable artist and an underground icon dealer of some renown.

Pasha had pulled off the deal of a lifetime by painting some modern rubbish over several masterpieces. The fakes fooled the Art Ministry inspector (a donation to his favourite charity may have contributed to his temporary myopia), and upon reaching Rome Pasha had washed the top layer off and become rich.

But he wouldn't rest on his laurels. When I knew him he was cranking out endless canvases that were in high demand among exotica-seeking tourists. One American paid $1,000 for a painting Pasha had knocked off in a couple of hours. It showed a flaxen-haired beauty with a picture of Nicholas II dangling between her naked breasts, against the background of St Basil's. 'Gee,' the American said, 'Them Russkies are real spiritual.'

But Pasha wasn't the only nouveau. Quite a few other lovers of sacred arts had quickly exchanged their loads of St Nicholases, St Georges and assorted Virgins for small fortunes well into six figures U.S. That enabled them to start their political emigration without the penury one tends to associate with that process.

I knew three of those Croesuses well. Out of the kindness of their hearts they agreed to accept 30,000 lire a month for a room in what they by then had turned into a reasonable facsimile of a Moscow communal flat. They were all married, with three children among them, so my arrival brought the number of tenants in the Via Cavour flat up to 10. That was chickenfeed by the standards of 1/12 Ogarev Street, where I grew up, but enough to put a contemptuous smile on the landlord's face every time he came to collect rent.

One of the three men was Dr Danov, the eminent psychiatrist. He was depressed at the time, even though the good doctor would never have described his condition in such a clinically imprecise way. I know as much because he once chastised me for having misused 'depression' to mean 'lousy mood'.

Depression was a biochemical condition, he explained, a legitimate disease, and it was therefore treatable with drugs of which lithium sprang to Dr Danov's mind. And so only an ignoramus like me would use that word to describe what he was feeling at the time. It was a bad mood, pure and simple, and the only chemical compound with which it could be treated was C_2H_5OH *in vitro*. That, in case I was ignorant of organic chemistry as well, was ethyl alcohol in a glass.

In clinical practice, however, his particular type of lousy mood could only be cured by eliminating the underlying cause. In other words, by murdering that two-timing bitch, his wife. The lady in question was indeed acquiring a reputation in the Russian colony by conducting an affair with an unsavoury character.

Lyonia Belanov was a man of uncertain occupation, but his rugged appearance made him irresistible to most of the intels' wives, and certainly to Mrs Danov. In fact, this was his second such involvement. The previous husband was different from Dr Danov in that he was, according to his wife, impotent, understood her needs and obligingly went for long walks whenever Lyonia (or any other suitor) dropped by.

What impressed me about Belanov was that he had taken no time to learn some rudimentary Italian, so he could bark '*Pronto!*' at a garage assistant filling up his car. He also knew how to harass Soviet tourists, especially those who'd break away from their groups to sneak into *Valturno*, at the time the only strip joint in Rome.

Public displays of nudity were to most Soviets what the West was all about, and they were prepared to risk the wrath of the KGB minders who accompanied each group. When Lyonia espied them inside Valturno, his usual hangout, he'd approach them from behind and hiss in a Russian voice that bespoke authority, 'Back to your hotel immediately, we're going to have a talk!' As his panic-stricken victims fled, Lyonia would fire a parting shot: 'You can kiss your travel privileges good-bye, perverts!'

Taking a leaf out of Lyonia's book, I once played a neat prank on two Soviet tourists who sat next to me on an underground train. They had lost their group, which fact they lamented, realising that this could well mean they'd never again be allowed to travel abroad. The two Russians were blue-collar lads who must have been awarded the trip for having exceeded their production quotas. They were talking freely in front of me as by that time nothing in my appearance betrayed me as a Russian.

When the train stopped at my station, I got up and muttered out of the corner of my closed mouth, the way those things were always said in Soviet spy films, 'Follow me!' As the victims had been brought up on the same films, they did as they were told. We walked out into the street, with me leading the way.

I had a few errands to run that day and pounded the streets for hours. All that time the obliging Soviets were following me as if dragged by an invisible lead. Eventually I led them back to the same station and said in a solemn voice, 'Thank you, comrades, for having watched my back. When you return to the motherland, tell our people Number 23 is doing all right.' The poor Soviets promised they would, with equal gravity.

When I told that story to Belanov, he smiled with the pride of a teacher whose disciple had come of age. Humourous viciousness was one of Lyonia's most prominent qualities, but reticence wasn't, which is why stories of Mrs Danov's alleged ability to suck the chrome off a bumper were widely ciculating in the area around *Termini*.

According to Dr Danov, his wife had hoped he wouldn't find out about her shenanigans. That was an unrealistic expectation due to Lyonia's gregarious nature. So find out he had and he'd be damned if the bitch wouldn't live to regret her indiscretion, not that it was her first.

'I'll dump her the moment we land at JFK,' said the heir to the Russian psychiatric tradition. 'No trade, no skills, no nothing. The bitch will be selling her superannuated arse in the streets. If she finds any takers, that is.'

His professional insight into human nature led Dr Danov to believe that my fluent English could only have come courtesy of the KGB, which insight he saw fit to share with the U.S. Embassy. The subsequent extended vetting prolonged my stay in Rome by a month or so. But, if one had to be stuck somewhere, Rome wasn't the worst place. It was only made to appear so because of the company I had been thrust into.

Dr Danov, the serial cuckold cum snitch, you've already met. There were also the Sokolskies, the famous art historian, his corpulent wife and two children, a boy of 16 and a girl of five.

Then there was Misha Basov, the film critic, accompanied by his wife, a jittery brunette 10 years his senior, and her 15-year-old daughter from a previous marriage. Both the arts and the sciences were thus represented in the flat, and my expectations of an interesting time were as high as they soon turned out to be groundless.

All my new flatmates had foregone the humanities as a cognitive tool and begun to look upon life in purely arithmetic terms, constantly assessing the best ways of spending their newly acquired iconic wealth. Clothes provided the most obvious outlet.

Back in Russia, clobber was the most important status symbol. One was seen as a pariah in Moscow's smart circles if one didn't possess, as a minimum, a pair of jeans (60 roubles in the black market), a foreign leather or suede jacket (500) and a Seiko watch (250).

My fellow political émigrés were imbued with the social importance of sartorial elegance. Having heard somewhere that Italy was the best place for clothes, they began to stock up. The men bought a life's supply of tight, flared trousers with zips everywhere but on the front, loud silk shirts worn open to the navel, tailored jackets of shiny leather and slim suits with narrow waists and lapels that never quit.

I'd probably have followed suit, as it were, but was mercifully prevented from doing so by a chronic lack of funds. Not that I didn't think their broad Russian bodies looked risible clad in clothes designed for the streamlined physiques of young Italian proles. We all lost touch once we got to the States, but I wonder in what charity shop all that splendour ended up once the proud owners landed in places like Omaha, Nebraska. In those centres of genuine doubleknit-polyester fashion, most Italian clothes rival homosexuality for putative subversiveness.

The women looked marginally better in their slapper attire of tiny suede skirts, high boots and hugging blouses, even though the tight silk only served to emphasise the ziggurats of their flesh. Then again, in my sexually disadvantaged state no woman could have looked ridiculous for long. I was beginning to ogle even Mrs Danov with lust, wondering if Lyonia had been lying about her oral competence.

A small part of my friends' fortune was spent on touring Italy in their new $200 banger. That to them essentially meant shopping in Florence or Milan rather than merely in Rome. Out of concession to their intellectually overburdened pasts, they did pop into a few churches and museums. But there they looked not so much at the paintings as at the artifacts, wondering how much all those chalices could set one back.

Out of loneliness I once went on a trip with them ('What, you haven't done Assisi yet?'), and they demanded that I join their gushing chorus of delight over Giotto's frescoes. But I wasn't in the mood for tourist enthusiasms, so Giotto had to wait a few years for my gasps.

My flatmates were getting transparently, and justifiably, fed up with my gloomy countenance, irreverent remarks about artistic matters, and destitution that rendered mutual shopping trips impossible. In any case, our cohabitation came to an abrupt end over an issue as trivial as telephone bills, or rather our refusal to pay them.

The landlord had never thought this problem would arise because he had attached a lock to the dial of the only phone in the flat. This way we could receive incoming calls but couldn't make any outgoing ones – or at least so he had thought. But his peasant cunning was defeated by Russian ingenuity honed by advanced university degrees.

The combined efforts of V.I. Danov, M.D., and G.V. Sokolsky, PhD, brought to the problem an awesome combination of sequential thinking and artistic intuition, and the tiny nickel-plated lock didn't stand a chance. In a flash of lateral thought, the astute gentlemen loosened a couple of screws, removed the dial, lock and all, and learned how to make calls by rotating the dial base with a pair of pliers.

They were thus able to indulge their Moscow habit of spending hours on the phone, but this time the calls were all long-distance, going to places like California, Argentina, Russia, Australia and New Zealand. Since there were six of them, the phone was in constant use. The bill was to reach millions of lire in short order, what with the families trying to arrange job interviews in the States well in advance.

They also used the phone to settle accounts with old enemies in Russia by calling them in the middle of the night and, knowing that all foreign calls were recorded by you know whom, saying things like 'I don't have time to talk, so grab a pencil and write down: 22-45-96-81-124-975-73-01-63.' One has to be Russian to understand their victims' panic.

Having about half a million dollars in cash between them, my flatmates didn't have to resort to larcenous ways of making phone calls, but 'waste not, want not' was a principle they were rapidly learning. Judicious application of this principle would make them all comfortably well off within their first few years in America.

Actually, this wasn't the only time my 'intel' friends had applied lateral thinking – before the term was even invented – to the everday problems of life. For example, they got all their petrol free by solving the mystery of the petrol machine.

Those convenient contraptions adorned most Italian filling stations. You'd simply stick a banknote into a slot and receive the amount of fuel that denomination could buy. It didn't take my flatmates long to figure out that the machines operated on a photo element reacting to the pattern of the banknote design. Therefore it wouldn't be sensitive to the colour or weight of the paper.

Completing the theoretical part of the research, this discovery led to the experimental phase wherein Dr Danov, still muttering that his wife possessed every trait of a dog except fidelity, went to a local DIY Xerox outlet and got a stat of a 10,000-lire note. The three families watched intently as Dr Sokolsky then stuck the carefully trimmed stat into a petrol machine – and bingo! Out came the elixir of vehicular life.

Later we found out that, much in the manner of Newton and Leibnitz independently developing integral calculus at the same time, other political émigrés had made the same discovery. This explains how they could satisfy their cultural curiosity by travelling all over Italy at an affordable cost.

The three families got away with that larceny, and would have got away with the telephone trick as well had the bills been sent directly to the flat. Unfortunately, the landlord had arranged for them to arrive at his office. One fateful day he turned up at the flat, waving the phone bills with one hand, a copy of the lease with the other, and screaming such unfriendly Italian words as *polizia* and *porchi Russi*.

The situation was hairy to say the least, even though Messrs Danov, Basov and Sokolsky pinned the noisy capitalist down, removed the incriminating documents and destroyed them on the spot. The landlord departed bawling what could only be obscenities and promising to get copies of the evidence with which he would have us all put away. But not before he collected every penny due him and punitive damages on top of that.

He never got the chance, however, because the moment he banged the door the families packed up and beat their retreat, dragging me along as an innocent bystander. (I had tried to make one free phone call to Russia but hadn't got through, so my conscience was clear.) We loaded their communal van up to the gunwales. After that the men, leaving the ladies to look after the luggage, went back to make sure they hadn't left anything valuable behind. They hadn't, even though they didn't have a legitimate claim to some of the items.

Before we left for good, Basov cast one last glance at the flat and asked me in a matter-of-fact way, 'When was the last time you took a shit?'

The surreal question came with so much shock value that I answered automatically, 'At nine in the morning. Why?'

'Well, we're not going to leave without teaching that bastard a lesson,' explained Misha, whose erudite articles on Alain Resnais and Ingmar Bergman had earned him the respect of many a Moscow 'intel'.

He and Dr Sokolsky then proceeded to defecate on the floor. And

Dr Danov, who evidently remembered some physics as well, ripped the cord out of the standard lamp, plugged it into an outlet and taped the naked end to the metal doorknob. We then climbed out of the window, with my erstwhile flatmates laughing hysterically at the anticipated shock the despicable landlord was going to receive when he arrived to investigate the stench emanating from his flat.

In the unlikely event he called the police we decided to go our separate ways. The others used their iconographic wealth to rent some reasonable accommodations, while I had to ask someone else for shelter. The problem was solved quickly as by that time my cousin Alec had emigrated as well and was now sharing a flat with an elderly Leningrad lawyer and his young wife.

The lawyer had a contact with a CIA-sponsored publishing house whose function was to print anti-Soviet books and smuggle them into Russia. The Americans who ran the place had been impressed with the distinguished Russian gentleman of the bar. They had readily believed his assurances that he knew many Soviet visitors who could act as conduits of printed matter. On those pretences, the nobly grey-haired Mr Taskin received several crates of Russian books which he immediately flogged to fellow immigrants. That supplemented the proceeds he had realised from several nineteenth-century Virgins and one reasonable eighteenth-century St Nicholas.

Alec had a bedroom in their flat and agreed to let me have one of the two twin beds put side by side – on the understanding that I'd clean up after myself, share the cooking chores and in general, for once in my life, act like a normal human being. I said I would, because my residential crisis was then even more desperate than back in Moscow. There I had never had my own room but at least I had always had a roof over my head.

It soon transpired that Alec's idea of normal human behaviour didn't accommodate Inna who by that time had delivered on every unspoken promise her fluttering eyelashes had ever made. Until then, my crowded living arrangements had accounted for a lot of *al fresco* romance. But now that I was sharing quarters with my kin I didn't feel outdoor groping was any longer necessary.

Alec didn't see things quite the same way. On the very first evening we shared the bedroom, he categorically refused to go for a prolonged walk before dinner. 'I feel like taking a nap,' he maintained over my protests. Inna sat in the corner, demurely waiting for the outcome of the negotiations between the men and not looking as if she cared much one way or the other. 'This is my room,' said Alec and climbed into one of the beds. 'It's our room,' said I and lowered Inna on the other. Throughout the next hour or so Alec heroically pretended to be asleep, snoring demonstratively and never turning towards us.

As a post-scriptum, that affair came to a natural end when both Inna and I moved to the States. But not before I had got the fright of my life.

My first lodgings in New York were a tiny room in a residential welfare hotel at the corner of Broadway and 70th Street. The hotel bore most of the hallmarks of a Soviet communal building, what with its endless dark corridors meandering around numerous bends. The good difference was the presence of en-suite facilities; the bad difference was the crunchy carpet of cockroaches evenly covering every inch of the floor.

Back in Moscow I had never seen a cockroach; the bedbug had been the fashionable insect. Irrepressible Muscovites didn't mind bedbugs much and even cracked jokes about them, to the effect that they had one thing in common with capitalists in that both sucked the blood of the working classes.

New Yorkers, as I found later, do mind cockroaches but, with characteristic American pragmatism, appreciate the futility of any attempt to get rid of them once and for all. Not that any such attempt had ever been made at Embassy Hotel.

One of my first evenings in New York, I returned home after a stroll, and was zigzagging through the corridor to the bottle of vodka awaiting me in my infested room. Suddenly a dark silhouette stepped from around a corner and blocked my way. Having heard all the usual stories about crime in New York, I was scared. But then I identified the man as Yefim, and fear gave place to sheer panic.

Here was a man who took conjugal fidelity seriously enough to have killed his mistress prophylactically even before she was unfaithful to him. It didn't take much imagination to figure out what he'd do to the seducer of his current girlfriend. Much as I hate to write a cliché like 'my whole life flashed before my eyes', this is an accurate description of how I felt. Especially since Yefim didn't respond to my grovelling greeting of 'Hi, old man, how are you?'

Any hope that maybe he didn't know evaporated when Yefim didn't respond to my greeting, and instead hissed a rhetorical question, enunciating every word separately. 'Have. You. Shagged. Inna?'

What was I to say? The very fact that the question had been posed evinced prior knowledge, and denying the obvious could only make matters worse. Fighting Yefim was out of the question even if he didn't have a weapon on him, which was unlikely. Running was possible, but, like Joe Louis's opponent, I could run but I couldn't hide. Yefim knew where I lived and sooner or later he'd have me.

That narrowed the options and I muttered, 'Well... yes... in a manner... of speaking...,' also keeping my words separate, but producing a decidedly different effect.

Yefim rushed towards me, I rendered my soul to God and prepared to die. But his intentions weren't murderous. Yefim grabbed me in a bear hug, kissed me on the cheek and yelled, 'Great! You see, the bitch is pushing me to marry her, but now I'm gonna tell her no way – not if you've let Boot shag you. Thanks, mate, you saved my hide!'

'Glad to be of service,' I muttered with relief and invited my old friend in. We finished my bottle, then the one he fished out of the pocket of his leather jacket, talking about this and that, but mainly comparing intimate notes about his fiancée.

Yefim told me about the misfortunes that had befallen Mark. He also informed me that Grisha had attempted to ply his old 'stopping' trade in the streets of Brooklyn and had been deported back to Rome as a result. Then he walked out of my life into the free world bustling outside.

How the Future Worked

How the Future Worked

288